THE WEEKLY GROCERY SHOP

THE WEEKLY GROCERY SHOP

Nabula El Mourid
of Supermarket Swap

Hardie Grant
BOOKS

Introduction 7

Part 1: The Shop 10

Navigating the aisles 12
Understanding labelling 38
Setting up your kitchen for success 52

Part 2: The Cook 68

Using the meal plans 70
Warming & comforting 77
Light & fresh 165

Index 250
Thank you 255
About the author 255

Introduction

I can't quite believe I've written a book to help people navigate the grocery store. Only a few years ago, I felt totally overwhelmed in the aisles.

As a mum to a newborn and a toddler, I had the responsibility of feeding my family *multiple times every day*, and while it was a privilege to be able to do so, it didn't come with a manual. What it did come with was a lot of expectation. Every time I scrolled social media, I was inundated with perfection – beautiful home-made meals, abundant veggie gardens, sourdough starters resting on sunlit benches and children dressed in pristine white eating spaghetti bolognese. Meanwhile, I was overflowing with love for my children, but I was operating on four hours of sleep a night, I couldn't keep up with the dishes and my kitchen bench was never spotless.

I wanted to be more organised. I wanted to cook more. I wanted to be healthier. I wanted to save more. I wanted to wash my hair more. Looking back, I can see that it was the pressure of perfection that made me think I needed to be doing 'more'.

I remember taking my children to my favourite organic market in Adelaide. Determined to stock up on fresh produce to make a batch of baby purees, I'd planned to go to the butcher and grocery store afterwards. Before children, I had always shopped this way. But now, something about the packing required, the double pram, and having to stop to breastfeed and again to diffuse a toddler meltdown made me realise I had to shop smarter (and faster). *Times had changed.*

I am passionate about food; my Greek upbringing instilled the importance of delicious, nutritious goodness. My mother and yiayia were kitchen superstars, always (over)feeding the family, fuelled by so much love. While I inherited their love of food, I didn't want to be a slave to the process. Soon to be returning to a career I missed, I didn't have the luxury of leisurely cooking. I happily accepted that I was more of a get-the-food-on-the-table kind of girl (sorry, Yiayia!).

Feeding a family isn't a small task – it can take up a lot of our mental load. Plan meals, shop (be healthy! save money!), unpack groceries, store food, cook meals, clean up, repeat *forever*. Okay, dramatic, but it can feel like a full-time job. So, I decided to focus my attention on one place: the grocery store.

My toddler was having behavioural issues and people would tell me not to give him sugar – but he hardly ate any sugar. He mainly ate at home, and I didn't feed him any 'junk'. I started to research the effects of additives and preservatives on sensitive individuals, especially children. This meant many late nights reading research papers while the children were asleep. The more I learnt, the more I wanted to know. It was fascinating, but also concerning. I knew that artificial ingredients are loaded into 'junk' food, but I had never considered that they might be added into our 'everyday' foods too.

I was surprised when I went through my pantry and discovered the array of additives in products such as chicken stock (bouillon) cubes, sauces and spreads. To be honest, I had given up properly checking ingredient lists; they were so lengthy, and full of number codes and names I didn't recognise. That day, I became a mother on a mission. I decided to read the ingredient list on every item I purchased. My goal was to improve the quality of what we ate by only buying products that predominantly contained real, recognisable ingredients. I couldn't believe how much products varied, even those sitting next to each other on the shelf.

I was happy to discover that many healthier options were available at the grocery store. I didn't need to trek around or make everything from scratch; I just needed to swap what I was buying.

When the Covid-19 lockdown happened, I decided I would start to share my 'simple swaps' on social media, to help others who wanted to eat well and look after their health. I wasn't sure whether groceries were too uncool for social media, but it turned out that hundreds of thousands of other people also wanted to do better, in a manageable way. The support from the beautiful community that formed was unreal and has continued to drive me forwards.

With the help of a team of experts, I have combined everything I have learnt along the way into this two-part book. Part 2 contains many of my favourite recipes, set out in weekly meal plans to make your life easier. But this is more than a cookbook. Part 1 is a practical guide to help you understand nutrition, navigate the supermarket aisles, and feed your family delicious, real food without overspending or being chained to the kitchen. This is what I wish I'd had when I first became a mum: a life hack to reduce the sense of overwhelm and make both the grocery store and the kitchen less daunting.

Remember, perfect is boring. Real food is important, but it doesn't need to be overcomplicated. Do what works for you.

Because *you* are doing a great job.

Happy shopping and cooking!

Nabula

PART

Navigating the aisles

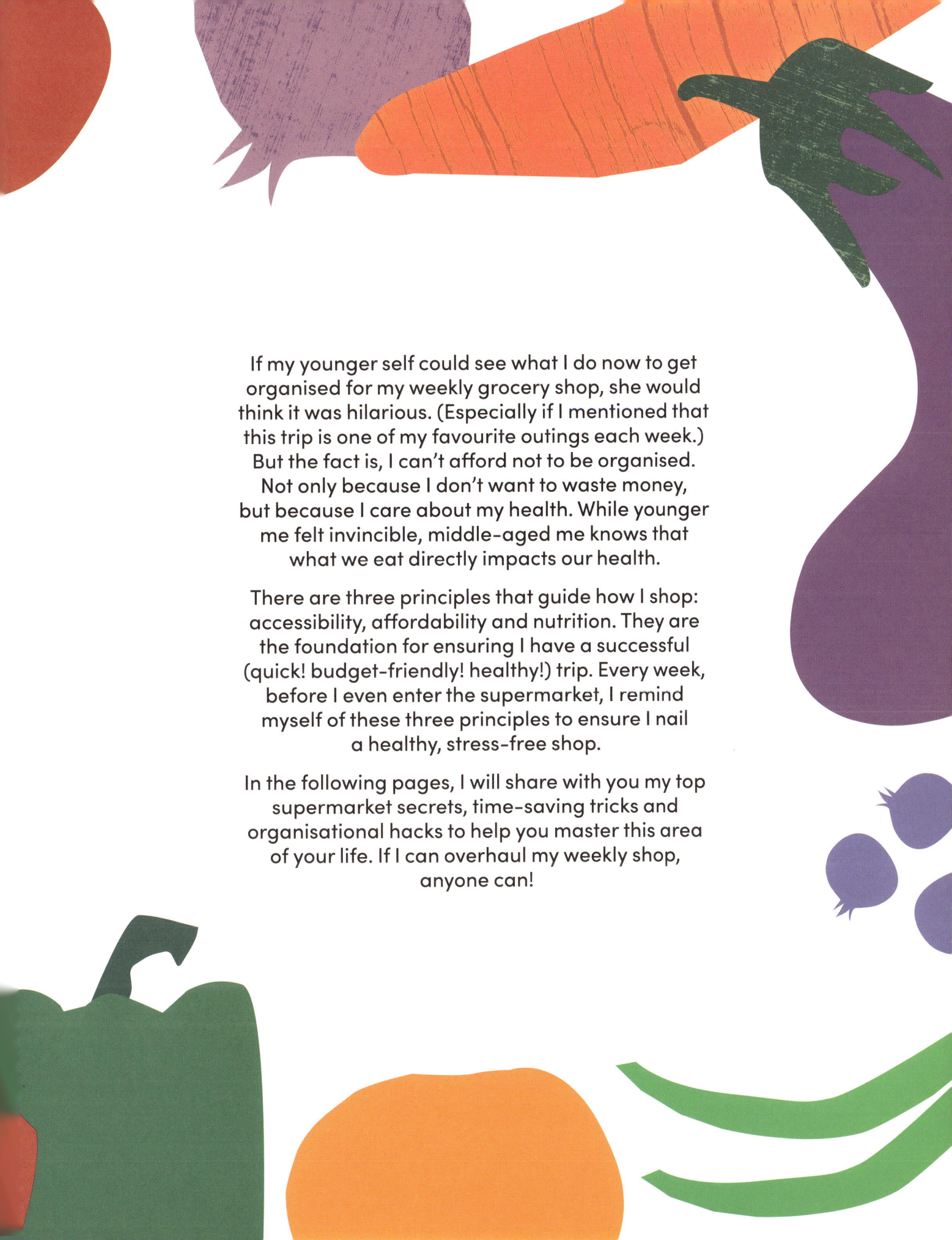

If my younger self could see what I do now to get organised for my weekly grocery shop, she would think it was hilarious. (Especially if I mentioned that this trip is one of my favourite outings each week.) But the fact is, I can't afford not to be organised. Not only because I don't want to waste money, but because I care about my health. While younger me felt invincible, middle-aged me knows that what we eat directly impacts our health.

There are three principles that guide how I shop: accessibility, affordability and nutrition. They are the foundation for ensuring I have a successful (quick! budget-friendly! healthy!) trip. Every week, before I even enter the supermarket, I remind myself of these three principles to ensure I nail a healthy, stress-free shop.

In the following pages, I will share with you my top supermarket secrets, time-saving tricks and organisational hacks to help you master this area of your life. If I can overhaul my weekly shop, anyone can!

Accessibility

Once upon a time, I had the luxury of visiting markets, butchers and bakeries, as well as my local grocery store. Then along came my children and my time evaporated into a bubble of love and chaos. Things had to change, especially the way I approached my weekly shop. If I had any chance of eating well, shopping had to be easy and accessible – a single, well-planned trip to the local supermarket each week. And with the grocery shop done, the markets became a family outing on Sundays, where we could relax and enjoy a leisurely croissant and coffee.

Affordability

Educating myself in the aisle and making some small changes to how I approached my shop meant that I could rely on the grocery store to provide nutritious, bang-for-buck weekly meals. We all want to eat well, but with the increased cost of living, and grocery price hikes in particular, we have to find ways to make a healthy shop affordable.

The belief that only the affluent can afford to eat well is false. I have found many ways to improve what we eat without increasing our spend – in fact, many of these techniques result in a reduced grocery bill. By following my tips, you'll be able to improve your diet and make more of your food budget.

Nutrition

Nutrition is about understanding what's in our food and how it affects our health. Nourishing your body with the right nutrients helps you become the best version of yourself by improving your physical and mental health. Sounds good, right? But where do you start? The world of nutrition can be confusing! This simple guide will give you the foundation you need to make informed choices at the supermarket.

The nutrients in our food can be divided into two broad categories: **micronutrients** ('micros') and **macronutrients** ('macros').

Micronutrients (vitamins and minerals) do not provide energy but are crucial for overall health. The body needs small amounts of each vitamin and mineral to function properly. Examples include iron, calcium, zinc, B vitamins and vitamins A, C, E and K. We need micros to prevent disease, support immunity, produce energy, regulate hormones and ensure healthy development, including blood and bone health and brain function. Our bodies cannot produce most micros, so we need to get them from our food.

Eating a balanced diet, including a variety of fruits, vegetables, whole grains, lean proteins and healthy fats, helps you to get all the micros you need.

Macronutrients (carbohydrates, protein and fat) are needed in larger amounts and provide your body with the energy it needs to function. There are three main types of macros in food: proteins, carbohydrates (including fibre) and fats.

NAVIGATING THE AISLES

Proteins

Proteins are essential to our health. When we eat proteins, we provide our body with the building blocks it needs to build and repair cells (muscles, organs, bones, skin, hair), produce essential enzymes and hormones, and maintain a healthy immune system. Proteins also help balance blood sugar levels and keep us feeling full after eating.

We can get high-quality proteins from both plant and animal sources.

Plant sources

nuts

seeds
(e.g. hemp, chia, pumpkin and sunflower seeds)

lentils

beans and peas
(e.g. kidney beans, black beans, pinto beans, chickpeas)

soy products
(e.g. tofu, tempeh, edamame, soy milk, soy yoghurt)

amaranth and quinoa

Animal sources

dairy products
(e.g. milk, yoghurt, cheese)

eggs

meat
(e.g. beef, chicken, pork, turkey)

fish and other seafood

Carbohydrates

Many people fear carbohydrates, but high-quality, nutritious carbohydrate foods are an important part of a healthy diet. They provide sustained energy, along with fibre, vitamins and minerals that support overall wellbeing.

During digestion, carbohydrates are broken down into glucose, which enters the bloodstream ('blood sugar') and is transported to the body's cells, tissues and organs for energy. Glucose can be used immediately or stored in the body for later use.

The glycaemic index (GI) is used to rank carbohydrate foods based on how quickly and how much they raise blood sugar levels after eating.

Lower GI foods

release glucose slowly over several hours, leading to more stable blood sugar levels and sustained energy.

Examples include

unprocessed or minimally processed whole grains, starchy vegetables, fruits, legumes (e.g. lentils, chickpeas, beans), milk and yoghurt.

Higher GI foods

are digested quickly, causing a rapid spike in blood sugar and fluctuating energy levels.

Examples include

white bread, chips, soft drinks, cookies, sweets, juices, ice cream, desserts and ultra-processed foods (UPFs*) such as cereals and snack foods.

*UPFs

Ultra-processed foods (UPFs) undergo extensive industrial processing and have substances added, changing their original form. Designed to be highly palatable, convenient, affordable and long-lasting, they are typically high in fat, sugar and salt, and low in vitamins and minerals. For more on UPFs, see page 40.

Fibre

Fibre is a type of carbohydrate that is not digested or absorbed by the body. Instead, it passes through the digestive system to the colon (large intestine), where it can be broken down by the gut microbiome (the bacteria and other organisms that live in your gut). Fibre is naturally found in plant foods such as vegetables, fruits, legumes, nuts, seeds and whole grains. A high-fibre meal is digested more slowly, helping you feel full for longer.

Fibre is a powerhouse nutrient for your health and an essential part of the diet. It promotes healthy and regular bowel movements, reduces inflammation, regulates blood sugar and cholesterol levels, and lowers the risk of many diseases, including cardiovascular disease, obesity, type 2 diabetes and certain cancers. A diet rich in fibre also supports gut health and boosts immunity by encouraging the growth of a healthy gut microbiome, which is crucial for overall wellbeing.

Plant foods contain a mix of different dietary fibres in variable amounts. These fibres can be classified into three groups:

Soluble fibre

absorbs water and slows down the passage of food through your digestive system, helping you feel full for longer.

Examples include

bananas, apples, oranges, pears, berries, oats, barley, legumes, okra, eggplants (aubergines), peas, corn, avocados, sweet potatoes, carrots, chia seeds and flax seeds.

Insoluble fibre

is the 'roughage' that adds bulk to the stool and draws water into the bowel, making stools soft and easier to pass.

Examples include

fruits and vegetables (particularly those with edible skin), whole grains (e.g. rye, quinoa, barley), legumes, nuts and seeds.

Resistant starch

feeds the good bacteria in your gut, promoting gut health.

Examples include

cooked and cooled potatoes, rice, quinoa and pasta, unripe bananas, legumes and oats.

Fats

Fats are an important part of a healthy diet and are essential to overall wellbeing. Additionally, they help in the absorption of fat-soluble vitamins such as A, D, E and K. There are three main types of naturally occurring fats in our diet: monounsaturated, saturated and polyunsaturated.

Monounsaturated fats

These are found in olive oil, avocados, avocado oil and some nuts. They have been shown to have anti-inflammatory properties and are good for heart health.

Saturated fats

These are mainly found in animal products (milk, cream, butter, cheese, meat), some plant oils (palm oil, coconut oil) and ultra-processed foods (UPFs). The World Health Organization recommends that no more than 10% of your daily energy intake should come from saturated fats.

Fats to avoid

In addition to the three naturally occurring fats essential to a healthy diet, there is a fourth type of dietary fat – trans-fatty acids – that is best avoided. 'Trans fats' are created when liquid vegetable oils are turned into solid fats during food processing. They are found mostly in UPFs and can potentially increase your risk of heart attack, stroke and type 2 diabetes.

Polyunsaturated fats

Our bodies can't make these fats on their own, so we need to get them from our food (they are found in both plant and animal foods). There are two types: omega-3 and omega-6 fatty acids. While both are necessary for good health, it's important to have more omega-3 than omega-6 fats in your diet. Modern Western diets often contain too much omega-6 (mostly from UPFs), which can lead to inflammation and other health issues.

Omega-3 fats are rich in docosahexaenoic acid (DHA) and eicosapentaenoic acid (EPA), essential fatty acids that the body cannot produce on its own. They are found in fish (especially oily fish like salmon, mackerel and sardines), walnuts, flaxseeds and chia seeds. Omega-3s help to reduce inflammation, support brain function and contribute to heart and skin health

Omega-6 fats are found in seed oils (such as sunflower, soybean, canola and corn oil) and UPFs. They are also found in nuts (walnuts, almonds and Brazil nuts) and seeds such as hemp and sunflower seeds.

Healthy cooking oils

Containing varying amounts of monounsaturated, polyunsaturated and saturated fats, oils differ in their nutritional value. The oils below are less processed and offer more nutritional benefits than others. Each has a different smoke point (the temperature at which it begins to break down and release harmful compounds). Choosing the right oil for your cooking method helps preserve both the flavour and nutritional benefits of the oil.

Oil	Pros	Cons	Smoke point	Uses
Extra-virgin olive oil	> High in antioxidants > Anti-inflammatory properties > Antibacterial properties > Rich in monounsaturated fat > Promotes heart health	> None*	190–210°C (375–410°F)	> Drizzling on cooked dishes > Frying > Roasting > Salad dressings > Sautéing
Avocado oil	> High in antioxidants > Promotes heart health > Rich in monounsaturated fat	> None	270°C (520°F)	> Frying > High-heat cooking > Roasting > Salad dressings
Flaxseed/linseed oil	> Anti-inflammatory properties > High in omega-3 fatty acids	> Low smoke point (should not be heated)	107°C (225°F)	> Drizzling on cooked dishes > Salad dressings > Smoothies > Avoid heating because of the low smoke point
Butter	> Source of vitamins	> Mostly saturated fat	150–175°C (300–345°F)	> Baking > Low- to medium-heat cooking > Sautéing > Topping
Coconut oil	> Antibacterial properties	> Mostly saturated fat	177°C (350°F)	> Baking > Medium-heat cooking > Sautéing > Stir-frying
Ghee (clarified butter)	> Source of vitamins	> Mostly saturated fat	250°C (480°F)	> Frying > High-heat cooking > Roasting

Seed oils

Seed oils (canola, corn, soybean, sunflower, safflower, rapeseed) are present in over 80% of products on the store shelf. Manufacturers use them because they are cost-effective and have a long shelf life. But the extraction method for seed oils involves high temperatures, solvents, bleaching and deodorisation, which removes the oil's nutrients and leaves behind chemical residues. Consuming large amounts of seed oils can lead to an imbalance of omega-6 fatty acids, and is associated with inflammation and poor health outcomes. A consumer shift away from seed oils has resulted in major brands releasing chips (crisps) and other products made with avocado oil instead.

Easing the overwhelm

When you are responsible for feeding people seven days a week, it can start to feel like a monotonous chore. Planning meals, writing shopping lists, grocery shopping, unpacking, cooking, tidying. Repeat. *Forever!* The food shop becomes another task on your weekly to-do list and it can add to your feeling of overwhelm, especially with the magnitude of choice in the aisle.

At the risk of using a modern-day buzzword, my tip is to make a meal plan before you shop. Allocating 30 minutes a week to planning your meals is a powerhouse tool to reduce your mental load. Forget what you see online – your plan doesn't need to be fancy or complicated – but *plan* is the key.

Why plan?

Save money

We've all been there – I'm just going to pop into the store on my way home to pick up a few items for dinner. Goodbye $80! Avoiding multiple trips to the store is a guaranteed way to help you stick to your weekly budget.

Reduce waste

If you check your pantry and fridge before you go shopping, you'll avoid buying what you already have. No one needs four bags of flour – unless you are a baker!

Achieve your targets

Ditch perfect. Meal plans fail when we aim too high. The truth is, I don't want to cook seven nights a week. Personally, I plan for five nights, and the other two are 'whatever nights' (leftovers or an easy meal, such as eggs or a toasted cheese sandwich). I find that by setting a realistic target, I stick to it. And, I avoid over-shopping and watching the food go to waste when the end-of-week fatigue kicks in.

Enjoy cooking

It's okay if you don't love to cook. But you do need to eat. Aim to reduce the amount of time you spend in the kitchen by planning meals that you can cook once and repurpose into two or three different meals. Or batch-prepare meals and freeze in portions. I love cooking, but when it became a daily responsibility (and my little people refused to eat what I made), it certainly lost its shine.

Save energy

With a meal plan, you can prepare dinner in the morning (when you might have time or when your energy levels are high), ready to be popped into the oven before dinnertime. Or better yet, invest in a slow cooker and simply serve at dinnertime. There is no better feeling than knowing that dinner is done, especially if you are in the phase of life that involves a witching hour.

Save time

By doing your weekly shop in a single trip, you'll save time. And that, my friend, is the most valuable thing of all. Enjoy the extra time in your week to make yourself a cup of tea instead. You deserve it.

Supermarket shopping guide

Imagine if the first time you entered the supermarket you were handed a guide to explain each section. From fresh produce to dairy and beyond, there is a lot that is not explained to consumers; we are left to our own devices when we enter through the large shiny doors. So, in the following pages, you'll find my supermarket shopping guide, to help you understand what to buy and when, how it will contribute to your health, and how it can save you money. You'll also find some of the secrets that supermarkets use to trick you into spending more than you need.

Which fruit and veggies to buy when

We seem to be able to buy almost all fruits and vegetables at any time of the year now. But depending on the time of year, these items are either in season or out of season.

In-season produce can be more nutritious, as it is harvested at its peak ripeness. It is also more sustainable as it is often grown locally. Eating what is in season is a great way to vary your family's diet (variety has a positive effect on gut health because different plants contain distinct prebiotics that feed different gut bacteria to create a diverse microbiome). It is an easy way to increase your daily vitamin intake and to try different produce while it is at its most affordable and delicious.

Out-of-season produce is often grown in greenhouses outside of its usual season or imported from other states or countries. The flavour is likely to be compromised because it has spent time in transit and storage, and it tends to be a lot more expensive.

Use the chart opposite to help you buy in-season produce at different times of year. (This chart is a guide only, as seasonality of produce depends on your location and each season's weather conditions. For more specific information, look at a guide for your local region.)

THE WEEKLY GROCERY SHOP

Spring

Avocados, grapefruits, honeydew melons, rockmelons, pineapples.

Artichokes, Asian greens, asparagus, beans, beetroot (beets), brussels sprouts, cabbages, fennel, leeks, parsnips, peas, radishes, rhubarb, silverbeet (Swiss chard), spinach, sweetcorn.

Summer

Apples, apricots, blackberries, blueberries, cherries, grapes, mangoes, nectarines, Valencia oranges, peaches, pineapples, plums, raspberries, rockmelons, watermelons.

Asparagus, beans, beetroot (beets), capsicums (bell peppers), carrots, celery, chillies, cucumbers, eggplants (aubergines), leeks, lettuce, rhubarb, snow peas (mangetout), spinach, spring onions (scallion), sweetcorn, tomatoes, turnips, zucchini (courgette).

ALL YEAR ROUND

Bananas
Beansprouts
Broccoli

Cauliflower
Lemons
Mushrooms

Autumn

Apples, avocados, figs, grapes, kiwifruit, nectarines, passionfruits, peaches, pears, persimmons, plums, quinces.

Asparagus, Asian greens, beans, beetroot (beets), capsicums (bell peppers), carrots, celery, cucumbers, eggplants (aubergines), lettuce, potatoes, pumpkins (winter squash), snow peas, spinach, spring onions, sweetcorn.

Winter

Avocados, grapefruits, kiwifruit, limes, mandarins, oranges.

Asian greens, brussels sprouts, cabbages, capsicums (bell peppers), carrots, celery, cucumbers, eggplants (aubergines), fennel, kale, leeks, parsnips, potatoes, silverbeet, spinach, turnips.

Eggs, meat and dairy

When buying eggs and meat, you'll often see references to how the protein was sourced. Here, I explain what each label means to help you make the best choice based on your budget. Dairy is also an important part of your diet, but how do you make a good choice when you are presented with so many options? See below for some fail-safe tips to help you choose wisely.

Caged hens

Caged hens, used for egg production, are kept in large sheds in confined cages. In most cases, the cages restrict the hens' ability to behave as they naturally would (nesting, foraging and perching). While eggs from caged hens are usually the most affordable, animal welfare organisations recommend choosing cage-free when possible.

Free-range

Free-range is a term often used on egg and chicken labels to refer to farming methods where animals have some level of access to the outdoors. What qualifies as 'free-range' varies by country.

In Australia, free-range egg farming density standards require a maximum of 10,000 hens per hectare of land and the birds must have access to the outdoors for at least 8 hours per day.

Grass-fed meat

Grass-fed meat comes from animals whose diet consists primarily of grass and forage rather than grains or other feed. Grass-fed animals are usually raised in a more natural environment, resulting in meat that has a lower total fat content and a more distinct flavour.

Organic meat

Organic meat and eggs come from animals that are not given antibiotics or growth hormones and are fed with organic feed free from pesticides, synthetic fertilisers or genetically modified organisms (GMOs).

These animals must have outdoor access and more space than conventionally farmed animals, though the exact requirements vary.

Pasture-raised animals

Pasture-raised animals typically graze in open fields or paddocks, where they can carry out natural behaviours. Their diets tend to be more varied, which research suggests can result in meat, eggs and dairy products having potentially higher nutritional value than those from animals raised in confined spaces.

Wild-caught or sustainably fished seafood

Wild-caught or sustainably fished seafood is a good option, as it is sourced from its natural environment rather than a fish farm, where fish are often overcrowded and fed synthetic grain. Frozen fish is an economical option, as it's cost-effective and nutrient-dense (it's often frozen within 24 hours of being caught).

Butter

Butter should contain only two ingredients: milk and cream (and sometimes salt).

Cheese

Buy cheese in block form and grate it yourself (use a food processor to save your arm) for better value and to avoid additives like anti-caking agent used in pre-grated cheese. Store it in the freezer for later if you buy in bulk.

Cream

Avoid artificial thickeners and stabilisers that are added to cream for texture and longevity. Look for a pure cream that has real ingredients and whip it to the consistency you require.

Milk

Choose a full-fat (whole) milk, as it has a higher nutrient value, including omega-3.

Yoghurt

Organic full-fat natural or Greek-style yoghurt is the best in terms of ingredients. You can jazz it up with fruit, honey or crushed nuts. Avoid flavoured yoghurts unless they are flavoured with real ingredients. Avoid artificial flavours and added sugar.

Pantry staples

A well-stocked pantry is pure joy. It is the heart of your kitchen, containing the foundation of most meals (plus it's home to snacks!). Ensuring your staples are the most nutritious yet cost-effective options is a key building block to improving the quality of your diet.

Bread

There are many preservative-free options. The key is to freeze whatever you don't need immediately so it is readily available and fresh when defrosted.

Cereal

Look for a cereal that contains whole grains. Rolled (porridge) oats, muesli or granola offer a more nutrient-dense option. Be careful of excess added sugar and additives, especially in cereals marketed to children.

Chips (crisps)

The best chips are the plain, salted type and preferably cooked with avocado or olive oil rather than a seed oil.

Crackers

Opt for a plain or sea salt variety to avoid the additives.

Dried fruit

Most dried fruit is treated with sulphites (a naturally occurring chemical compound) to keep it soft, preserve its original colour and prolong its shelf life. Some people may have a particular sensitivity to sulphites (see page 46); if this is you, choose organic or sulphite-free dried fruit.

Flour

Choose organic where possible and wholemeal (whole-wheat) for an extra nutrient boost.

Legumes

Organic tinned legumes are great for a convenient option, but buying loose or packaged dry legumes will save you money.

Nuts

Buying nuts loose rather than packaged can be more cost-effective. But either way, check the ingredients to ensure your nuts are, simply, nuts (with perhaps a little salt). Flavoured nuts often contain artificial ingredients. While nuts are high in healthy fats, the key is moderation.

Olive oil

Choose an extra-virgin olive oil as this is the oil that comes from the first press of the olives and is the purest and highest quality.

Pasta

Switch regular white pasta to a spelt, wholegrain or pulse (buckwheat or chickpea) option. These are generally higher in protein, fibre, vitamins and minerals.

Rice

Buy organic where possible and opt for brown or basmati rice, which are lower GI and higher in fibre than white rice, making them more nutritious alternatives.

Salt

Choose a good quality sea salt or pink Himalayan salt as they are less processed and often contain extra trace minerals that may enhance flavour.

Sauces

Store-bought sauces often contain artificial colours, flavours and excess added sugar. See pages 72–73 for easy recipes for healthy, home-made sauces and pastes.

Stock (bouillon)

Traditional stocks tend to be very high in sodium and loaded with artificial additives. Choose an organic stock or an option with recognisable ingredients. Or, if you have the time, make your own, such as the Chicken bone broth on page 139.

Tuna

Choose a plain tuna in spring water or olive oil. Check the label and stick to those with recognisable ingredients rather than artificial flavours.

Vinegar

White vinegar contains naturally occurring sulphites. For those sensitive to sulphites, apple cider vinegar is a good choice, as it has lower sulphite levels as well as other health benefits.

Fruits and vegetables

How many times have you stood in front of the produce section and wondered which is the best avocado or which watermelon to choose? Your produce selection has a significant impact on how long your purchases will last. Here is the inside word on what to look for when selecting fruits and vegetables.

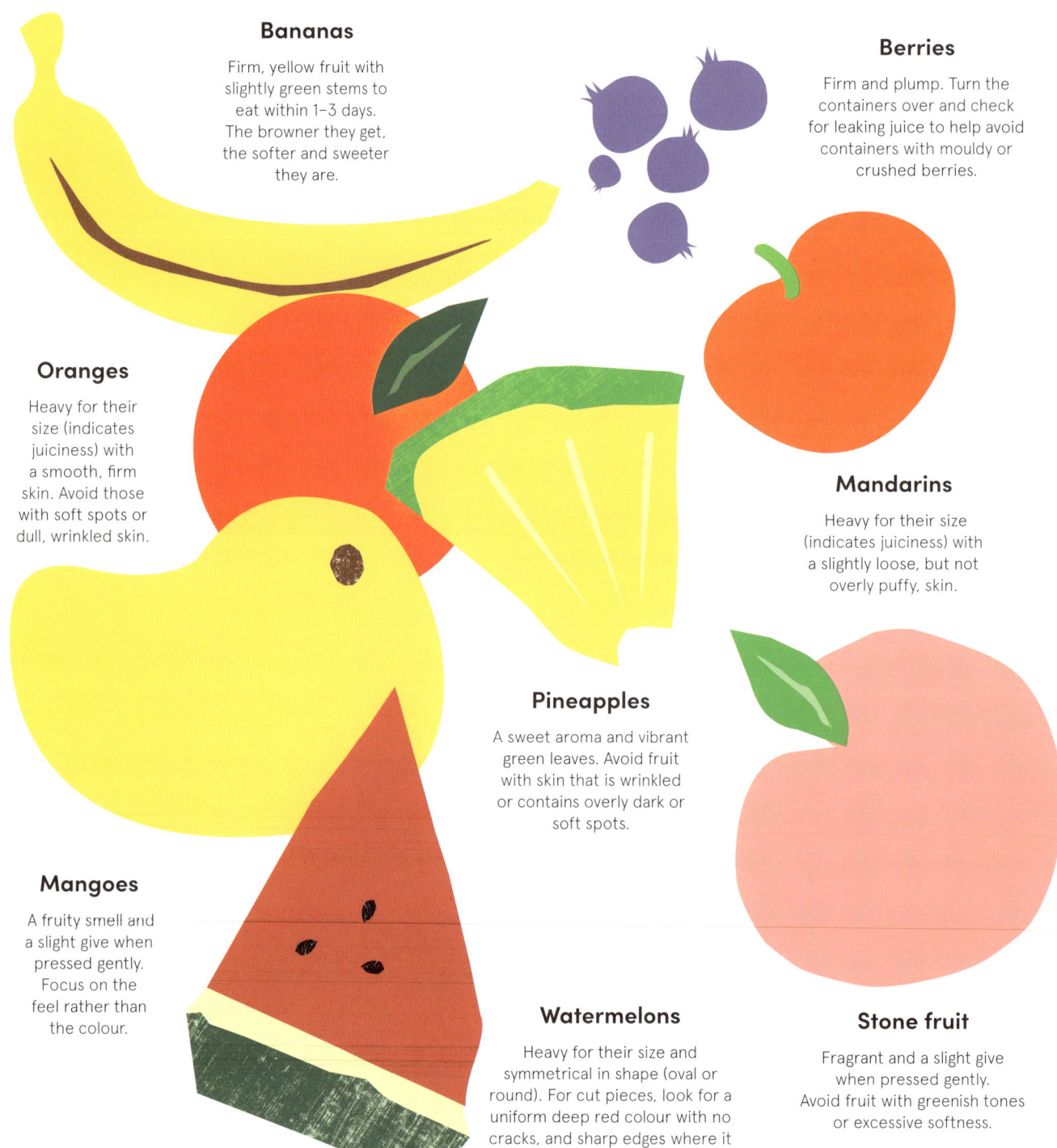

Bananas
Firm, yellow fruit with slightly green stems to eat within 1–3 days. The browner they get, the softer and sweeter they are.

Berries
Firm and plump. Turn the containers over and check for leaking juice to help avoid containers with mouldy or crushed berries.

Oranges
Heavy for their size (indicates juiciness) with a smooth, firm skin. Avoid those with soft spots or dull, wrinkled skin.

Mandarins
Heavy for their size (indicates juiciness) with a slightly loose, but not overly puffy, skin.

Pineapples
A sweet aroma and vibrant green leaves. Avoid fruit with skin that is wrinkled or contains overly dark or soft spots.

Mangoes
A fruity smell and a slight give when pressed gently. Focus on the feel rather than the colour.

Watermelons
Heavy for their size and symmetrical in shape (oval or round). For cut pieces, look for a uniform deep red colour with no cracks, and sharp edges where it has been cut.

Stone fruit
Fragrant and a slight give when pressed gently. Avoid fruit with greenish tones or excessive softness.

Garlic
Firm to the touch with tight, unbroken skin. Avoid bulbs with soft spots or those that show signs of sprouting.

Broccoli
Tight, firm florets that are dark green or purplish. Avoid heads that have yellow or orange spotting.

Corn
Heavy for its size (indicates a juicier cob). Gently squeeze the corn from top to bottom to ensure even firmness. The husk should be bright green and tightly wrapped around the cob. Choose cobs with silk of a pale colour (avoid those with sticky black, dark brown or matted silk).

Avocados
For immediate use, select avocados that are turning from bright green to dark green and that give to gentle pressure without feeling mushy.

Herbs
Bright in colour and free from wilting or yellowing. The leaves should be aromatic and firm, not slimy or dry.

Bok choy (pak choy)
Firm, white stalks and crisp, dark green leaves. Avoid yellowing leaves or signs of wilting.

Onions
Firm and dry with no soft spots or sprouting. The skin should be papery and free from any strong smell.

Potatoes
Firm and smooth with no green spots, cuts or sprouts.

NAVIGATING THE AISLES

Five ways to keep costs down

Everyone wants to save money on their grocery shop, but recent hikes in global grocery prices have made it a necessity. It's my mission to ensure that everyone, regardless of personal budget, can have access to good quality food. It's about shopping smart. These simple cost-saving tips will help you save money without compromising on quality. You may need to adjust your approach to shopping, but by using these five strategies, you'll get the best value.

① Check the unit price

Every price tag on the shelf contains two prices: the promoted price (often large and in bold) and a smaller price (in fine print) that lists the cost per unit (100 g or 100 ml). We are measuring the nutrition of a product per 100 g, so it makes sense to measure the price in the same way. This means that when you compare prices, you are comparing apples with apples. Otherwise, you're likely to find yourself instinctively drawn to the 'cheaper' price, but you may be receiving less. Here are two examples:

Cheese slices

$11
500 g (1 lb 2 oz) per 30 slices
$2.20 per 100 g (3½ oz)

$7.50
250 g (9 oz) per 15 slices
$3 per 100 g (3½ oz)

For an extra $3.50, you receive double the quantity. In this instance, instead of purchasing a small packet per week, purchase the larger one every fortnight and you will save $4.

Rolled oats

$4.50
500 g (1 lb 2 oz)
$0.90 per 100 g (3½ oz)

$5
1 kg (2 lb 3 oz)
$0.50 per 100 g (3½ oz)

The price may appear to be lower in the first option, but when you compare the unit cost (per 100 g), you will notice it is nearly double the price. For an extra $0.50, you receive DOUBLE the quantity. By comparing the unit cost, you can see which item truly costs less.

NAVIGATING THE AISLES

② Buy in bulk

Identical products can vary dramatically in price* depending on the total (net) weight. I may be a verified grocery geek, but I was excited by how much you could save on your annual grocery bill by making this simple swap. We are accustomed to planning our weekly shop based on a weekly budget, so we tend to choose the lowest-price option to try to keep the bill down at the checkout. But, as we discovered above, the lowest price tag doesn't always equal the best value for money.

By buying some items in bulk, you may initially feel like you are spending more, but in essence, you are paying a lot less for exactly the same product. Over the course of a year, this strategy could save you hundreds of dollars.

Consider these examples:

Greek-style yoghurt

2 kg (4 lb 6 oz): $12.60
($0.63 per 100 g/3½ oz)

1 kg (2 lb 3 oz): $8.30
($0.83 per 100 g/3½ oz)

170 g (6 oz): $2.40
($1.41 per 100 g/3½ oz)

For Greek-style yoghurt, the 2 kg option is less than half the price of the 170 g option. If you like smaller serves, or would like to send yoghurt to school, purchase a set of reusable silicone ziplock pouches. They are not expensive and allow you to buy in bulk and portion as you choose, instead of paying double for the brand to portion for you.

Raw sugar

2 kg (4 lb 6 oz): $3.20
($0.16 per 100 g/3½ oz)

1 kg (2 lb 3 oz): $3.20
($0.32 per 100 g/3½ oz)

500 g (1 lb 2 oz): $2
($0.40 per 100 g/3½ oz)

Sugar is a non-perishable item so there is no reason not to buy in bulk. As you can see here, the savings are substantial.

* Prices in this book are given in Australian dollars ($A), but the prices themselves are not significant; rather, I want you to look at the comparative prices between product options.

③ Buy loose, not pre-packaged

What a difference this makes. The cost per kilogram drops significantly when you buy loose produce or pantry staples. Not only is this a cost saver, but it is better for the environment as less packaging is required. Consider these three items:

Cayenne chilli

Loose

$30 per kg
(2 lb 3 oz)

Packaged

$76 per kg
(2 lb 3 oz)

Green beans

Loose

$6.90 per kg
(2 lb 3 oz)

Packaged

$15.59 per kg
(2 lb 3 oz)

Mushrooms

Loose

$12.50 per kg
(2 lb 3 oz)

Packaged

$20 per kg
(2 lb 3 oz)

④ Plan before you go

Earlier, I mentioned the importance of embracing meal planning for several key reasons (hello, saving money and time!). If you want to save, you simply need to know what you are going to eat for the week before you go to the grocery store. Cruising the aisles, thinking maybe I'll make this or that, is an easy way to over-shop and overspend, along with the added 'quick' trips to the store during the week because you forgot to buy an ingredient (which inevitably results in extra, unnecessary purchases). Oh, and plan to eat before you do your weekly shop so that you're not hungry when you're making your buying decisions.

⑤ Check the specials

Once you have embraced these four ways to save in store, the weekly specials become a bonus! They are another reason to move your mindset from weekly spending to monthly, because if one of your essentials is reduced, it's worth stocking up. While it may increase your weekly spend slightly, your return on investment over the next month will be high. These days, it's easy to browse specials and compare prices online – or use an app to organise your weekly shop and track specials.

Supermarket secrets

Supermarkets are a billion-dollar industry. Their goal, of course, is to maximise profits year on year. While it has been positive to see an increase in the healthier options available to consumers, supermarket ploys to increase your spend are still visible in every aisle. The tactics below will help you see through their secrets.

Look beyond eye level

The arrangement and positioning of products is a calculated strategy that plays on the fact that we are busy and racing through the aisle. Often, the most expensive options are placed at eye level so that we see them immediately. It pays to compare eye-level products with those on the top and bottom shelves, as this is where you may find some well-priced, healthy alternatives.

Stay focused

We've all been there: you need to dash into the store to buy a loaf of bread and a carton of milk. These are possibly the top-sellers in store, but where are they located? At the back. Why? Because the supermarket is banking on you being enticed to buy non-essentials as well. Stay focused!

Consider the home brand

A secret I love. The home brand version is often better quality than the premium brand. It has a cheaper price point and sometimes contains zero artificial ingredients. It pays to compare.

Don't be fooled by ridiculous specials

I'm a fan of specials, but only if they are of high value. When considering a special, ask yourself whether it will actually reduce your grocery bill. Supermarket tactics, such as multi-buys, trick customers into buying more of a product than they need. If one packet of steak is $8 and two packets are $15, is it worth buying double the quantity (and likely wasting some, unless you freeze it) to save $1?

Avoid the treats

You've made it through the weekly shop only to reach the checkout where the treats, strategically placed at children's eye level, threaten to incite a toddler meltdown. There goes a few extra dollars. Instead, before you reach the checkout, let the kids have a snack from your trolley so they are already entertained, or offer them a helpful task: 'Why don't you help put the bags in the trolley?' or 'Would you like to give the money to the cashier?' The key is to keep them distracted from the shiny treats!

Simple swaps

Making these simple swaps in my weekly grocery shop has had
a positive impact on the quality of what we eat.

Product	Swap to	Why?
Artificially flavoured crackers or chips (crisps)	Crackers or chips flavoured with sea salt	While it may take a moment for your tastebuds to adjust, you will avoid a lot of artificial ingredients.
Caged eggs	Free-range, organic or pasture-raised eggs	They have a higher nutritional value than those from animals raised in confined spaces. Good ethical practice does not support caged farming.
Flavoured yoghurt	Natural or Greek-style yoghurt	It is less likely to contain added sugar or additives and is a good source of fat and protein.
Low-fat dairy	Full-fat dairy	According to the Heart Foundation, the general population should choose unflavoured, full-fat milk, yoghurt and cheese. Children benefit from full-fat sources of dairy and the fat from dairy should not be restricted.
Margarine	Butter	100% butter contains only two simple ingredients (milk and cream) and is a good source of fat-soluble vitamins.
Processed or deli meats	Nitrate-free smallgoods	The World Health Organization has stated that the nitrates or nitrites added to cured meat to preserve it can have a negative impact on human health.
Refined cereal	Wholegrain cereal	It is higher in fibre, vitamins and minerals, and will provide a slower, steadier release of energy.
Refined seed oils (vegetable, soybean, sunflower, canola, palm oils)	Extra-virgin olive oil or avocado oil, or small amounts of ghee, coconut oil or grass-fed tallow	The fats in these oils are made up of healthier monounsaturated fatty acids.
White bread	Wholegrain and wholemeal (whole-wheat) bread	Whole grains provide fibre, vitamins, minerals and other nutrients.
White pasta	Spelt/buckwheat/ wholegrain or pulse pastas	These pastas increase overall fibre intake and contain vitamins and minerals, such as iron and zinc.

Understanding labelling

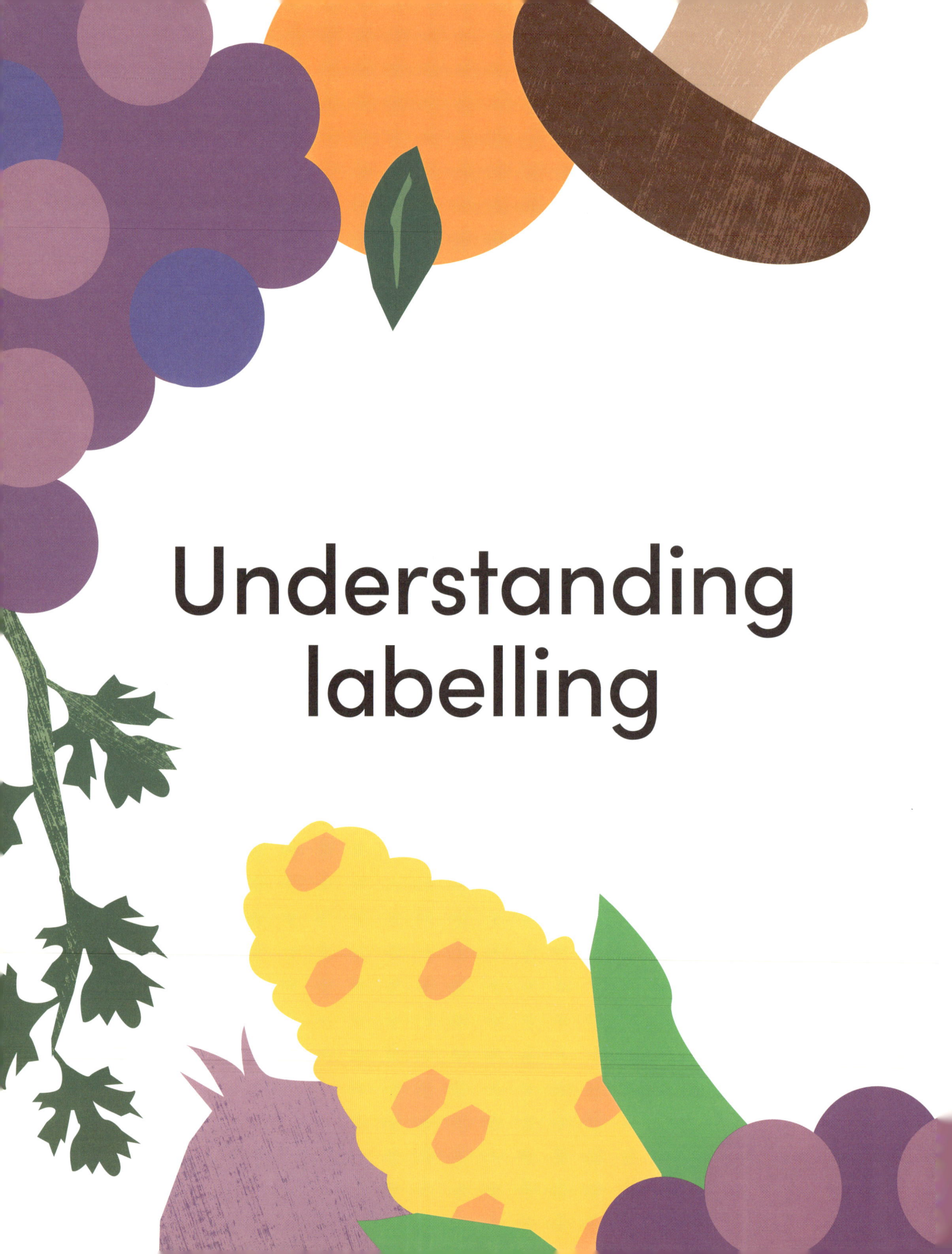

In the 1960s, the grocery shopping experience differed greatly from today, with stores stocking a total of around 400 products to choose from. Fast-forward to today and we are confronted with an overwhelming selection of more than 50,000 products every time we step into a store. Shelves are now dominated by highly processed, packaged convenience foods designed for a long shelf life and quick preparation.

This shift towards packaged foods over the past 60 years can be largely attributed to changes in global food production and distribution. Advances in agricultural practices and food processing techniques, as well as the integration of biotechnology and food additives, has enabled large-scale food companies to produce vast quantities of packaged food that can be distributed globally. With modern lifestyles leaving less time for home cooking, there's been a growing consumer demand for quick and affordable packaged food options. Responding to this trend, food companies have filled supermarket shelves with thousands of highly processed, budget-friendly packaged foods, using clever marketing techniques to make them highly desirable to consumers, including children.

It can be hard to see through all of the clutter.

Processed foods

In one social media post, I compared a packet of sweet potato crisps found in the health-food aisle with a packet in the regular chip aisle. The post went viral, with over 10 million views. Why? Because the packet in the regular aisle contained simple, better quality ingredients AND it cost less.

Just because a product is featured on the shelf in the health-food aisle doesn't mean it is better for you. The key is to treat every product individually and only trust what you read on the ingredient list or nutrition information panel (more on this shortly). Ignore any fancy claims on the packaging and the positioning of the item in the store.

The goal of this book is to arm you with enough knowledge to make your own informed decisions and not to succumb to the store or manufacturer tactics.

Ultra-processed foods

Ultra-processed foods (UPFs) undergo extensive industrial processing and have substances added, changing their original form. Designed to be highly palatable, convenient, affordable and long-lasting, they are typically high in fat, sugar and salt, and low in vitamins and minerals. UPFs have become a dietary staple, with many of us getting more than half of our energy needs this way.

UPFs often claim health benefits such as 'source of protein' or 'high in fibre', which can mislead consumers into believing they are healthy choices. In fact, evidence suggests that consuming these products can negatively impact our health.

There are two ways to easily reduce your consumption of UPFs. First, swap a store-bought product for a home-made version. Second, look at the ingredient list on the packet and choose the option that contains only simple, recognisable ingredients.

Why should we reduce our consumption of ultra-processed foods?

- Eating more UPFs leaves less room for nutritious foods.
- There is evidence linking a high UPF intake to health issues like obesity, type 2 diabetes, heart disease and others.
- UPFs often contain lots of saturated fat, salt, sugar and additives.
- UPFs have a big environmental footprint, contributing to greenhouse gases, biodiversity loss and waste.

Four degrees of food processing

It's helpful to understand the different levels of food processing. The Nova food classification system, which was developed by researchers at the University of São Paulo in Brazil in 2009, sorts foods into four categories based on how much they are processed.

Unprocessed or minimally processed foods	Processed culinary ingredients	Processed foods	Ultra-processed foods (UPFs)
These are mostly whole foods with little to no processing. **Examples include** eggs, fish, fruits, meat, milk, nuts, seeds, spices and vegetables.	These are products used to season and cook foods (they are generally not consumed on their own). They are usually extracted from nature through processes like grinding or refining. **Examples include** butter, honey, oils, salt and sugar.	These are made by adding processed culinary ingredients (like salt, sugar or oil) to unprocessed or minimally processed foods to preserve them or make them tastier. **Examples include** cheese, freshly made bread, jam, legumes, pickles and tinned vegetables.	These are defined as industrial formulations of ingredients made up almost entirely of substances extracted from foods (oils, fats, sugar, starch, proteins) derived from food constituents (hydrogenated fats and modified starches) or synthesised in laboratories (e.g. food additives). They tend to include ingredients that are not typically used in home cooking and have a long shelf life. **Examples include** instant soups, mass-produced bread, packaged snacks and reconstituted meat products.

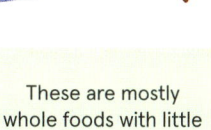

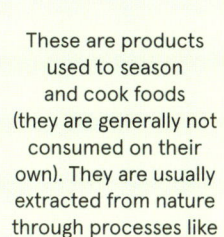

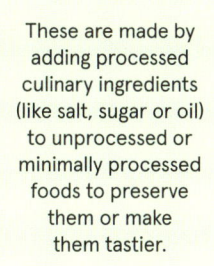

UNDERSTANDING LABELLING

Nutrition information panel

This quick lesson on the nutrition information panel will provide you with years of clarity in the aisle and help you avoid being taken in by health claims on food packaging. Legally required on any packaged food item, the panel tells you what nutrients and other ingredients are in the product. It is sorted in two ways: serving size (let's be real – this may not be the same as the serving size you consume) and per 100 g (useful when comparing products so that you can compare like with like). It is then broken down by key macronutrients to tell you how many grams of each are in the product.

What is in a nutrition information panel?

Energy The total number of kilojoules/calories released by the body when the food is consumed and digested.

Protein The sum of protein content listed as grams of protein present.

Fat, total The sum of the food's saturated fats, polyunsaturated fats, monounsaturated fats and trans fats.

Saturated fat Aim for the lowest per 100 g when comparing products, or choose foods with less than 3 g per 100 g (except for butter, cheese, nuts, coconut and seeds, which are naturally higher in fat). The amount of saturated fat in the food must be listed separately. (There is no requirement in Australia for manufacturers to declare trans fats on nutrition labels.)

Carbohydrates Total carbohydrates, including starches, sugars and fibre.

Sugars Includes the naturally occurring forms of sugar found in some fruit, and lactose in milk and dairy products, as well as 'added' sugar. Choose foods with less than 15 g per 100 g (for quick reference, 4 g = 1 teaspoon).

Fibre Choose foods with 3 g or more per serve. Aim for 25–30 g fibre per day. (Not all nutrition information panels include fibre.)

Nutrition information		
Servings per package: 1		
Serving size: 35 g		
	Per serve	Per 100 g
Energy		
Protein		
Fat, total		
– Saturated fat		
Carbohydrates		
– Sugars		
Fibre		
Sodium		

Sodium The amount of salt the food contains. Less than 120 mg per 100 g is best, especially for children. But food with less than 400 mg per 100 g is acceptable for food purchased in the aisle. Be aware that some foods (such as cheese, sauerkraut and soy sauce) are higher in sodium.

THE WEEKLY GROCERY SHOP

Ingredient list

If you're confused by ingredient lists, you're not the only one. On top of mystifying names and codes, there are often multiple names for the same ingredient. My simple tip? Look for lists with recognisable ingredients that you would have at home in your pantry.

The ingredient list not only describes what is in the food but also the percentage of each ingredient in descending order. If an ingredient appears at the start of the list, then the food contains more of this than other ingredients further down the list. Food additives must be identified in the ingredient list, usually by the additive name and/or number code.

Remember, if an undesirable ingredient, such as sugar, vegetable oil or salt, is at the top of the ingredient list, it means the product contains a high quantity of this ingredient and you may want to swap the item for a better option.

① Breadcrumbs

Wheat flour, salt, sugar, yeast.

② Breadcrumbs

Wheat flour, wholemeal (whole-wheat) flour, mixed whole grains (kibbled rye, kibbled wheat, kibbled purple wheat, rolled (porridge) oats, kibbled corn, kibbled barley, brown rice, buckwheat, triticale, millet), wheat gluten, seeds (linseed, pepitas ((pumpkin seeds)), canola seeds, poppy seeds, red quinoa, sunflower seeds, sesame seeds), vinegar, iodised salt, vegetable oil, fine ground meal, kibbled soy, bakers yeast, rye flour, wheat fibre, wholemeal rye flour, soy flour, oat fibre, corn starch, emulsifiers (481, 472e, 471), oat bran, soy fibre, vegetable gums (412, 466, 415), dextrose, sugar, malted wheat flakes, cultured whey, wheat bran, soy flour, barley malt flour, wheat malt flour, milk minerals, fish oil, minerals (ferric pyrophosphate, zinc sulphate), vitamins (vitamin e, niacinamide, thiamine, pyridoxine, folic acid, thiamine), fish gelatine, soybean oil.

Consider the ingredient lists on two different options for breadcrumbs.

Option 1 shows that the lengthy list of ingredients (and additives) in option 2 is simply unnecessary. The goal is to choose a product that contains only simple, real and recognisable ingredients.

Let's compare the ingredient lists for two oat bars.

In option 1, three of the four top ingredients are best eaten in moderation, and there are three forms of added sugar.

In contrast, option 2 uses organic honey and coconut (less processed) for sweetness and texture, and contains less sugar and no added salt or oil.

And, option 2 COSTS LESS!

① Oat bar
$2.74 per 100 g (3½ oz)

Wholegrain rolled (porridge) oats (60%), sugar, vegetable oils, honey (3%), salt, molasses, emulsifier (lecithin), raising agent (sodium bicarbonate).

② Oat bar
$2.60 per 100 g (3½ oz)

Organic rolled (porridge) oats, organic wholemeal wheat flour, organically produced honey, organic coconut, salt-free butter (cream and water), banana (10%), natural banana flavour, baking soda.

Other names for sugar

There are more than 60 names for added sugar, including agave, brown sugar, cane sugar, corn syrup, dextrose, fructose, fruit juice, glucose, golden syrup, honey, maltodextrin, maltose, raw (demerara) sugar, rice malt syrup and sucrose.

Manufacturers also add fruit concentrate for sweetness. It's made by removing most of the water from fruit through heat, evaporation and extraction. During this process, nutrients such as vitamin C, B vitamins and fibre are lost from the fruit, leaving the concentrate with little or no nutritional benefit. In ingredient lists, you'll often see 'fruit juice concentrate'; don't be fooled, it's just one more name for sugar.

Additives

Have you ever wondered why store-bought bread can last a week on your kitchen bench without going mouldy? Or why your home-made mac 'n' cheese never tastes quite like the ones you can buy in a box? Welcome to the (somewhat confusing) world of food additives!

Food additives are substances added to food to keep it fresh for longer or to alter its colour, flavour or texture. They can be derived from plants, animals or minerals, or they can be chemically synthesised in laboratories ('synthetic additives').

You won't typically find food additives in home kitchens because they are primarily used by companies for large-scale processing and production. Over time, thousands of additives have been developed to meet the demands of large-scale industrial food production. Additives are the most prevalent group of ingredients found in today's packaged foods and beverages.

The additives listed in the following cheat sheet are the main groups to avoid in your weekly shop. (Note that as new research is published, the advice may change.)

Flavour/natural flavour

One of the most confusing names you will see on an ingredient list is 'flavours'. Flavours are manufactured in a laboratory to replicate a 'real' flavour and often contain more than 50 chemical ingredients. Consumers will never know exactly what the flavour contains as it is the intellectual property (IP) of the brand.

You may spot a strawberry *flavoured* yoghurt, or a maple *flavoured* syrup, but don't be fooled – these products don't contain any strawberry or maple. Yes, that's right, a 'flavour' has simply been added to replicate the real deal.

Labels might say 'flavour', 'natural flavour', or 'artificial flavour' – the terms are used interchangeably. These flavours (aka mystery ingredients) are very commonly used in UPFs such as biscuits, drinks and cereals, as they are a cheap alternative. Flavours used in certified organic products are the exception – they're made from organic materials and must meet strict criteria.

In most cases, it's easy to avoid flavours by either making recipes at home or switching to products made only with real and recognisable ingredients. Instead of buying a breakfast cereal that contains flavours, why not try the Home-made granola recipe on page 189 – no artificial flavours there!

Maintaining perspective

We should aim to reduce our consumption of additives where possible to avoid the potential side effects associated with exceeding the Acceptable Daily Intake (ADI). This can easily occur when you are unknowingly consuming additives multiple times a day. The goal is not to avoid additives completely (this is impossible in modern society), but to be aware of what you are consuming so that you can make informed decisions in the aisle.

Additive cheat sheet

These are the main groups of additives to be aware of in your weekly shop.*

Additive group	What is it?	Found in
Artificial food colours	> Synthetic petroleum-based dyes used to change or enhance the colour of a food.	Breakfast cereals, chewing gum, condiments, confectionery, cordials, flavoured milk, ice cream, sauces, snack foods, soft drinks.
Artificial sweeteners	> Synthetic chemicals added to foods to provide an intense sweet flavour without the addition of sugar. Also referred to as 'non-nutritive sweeteners'.	Products labelled 'sugar-free', 'low sugar' and 'diet', such as chewing gum, confectionery, cordial, flavoured yoghurt, soft drinks, sweet desserts.
Benzoates	> Can occur naturally in some food or be used as a synthetic food additive. > Used to prevent the growth of mould, yeast and bacteria in food. Also used to extend the shelf life by preserving colour, flavour and texture.	Carbonated drinks, condiments, fruit juice, jam, margarine, mayonnaise, sauces, soft drinks, tomato paste (concentrated puree), vegetable juice.
BHA/BHT/TBHQ	> Synthetic petroleum-based preservatives used to prevent fats in food from going rancid.	Biscuits (cookies), bread, cakes, cereal, chewing gum, condiments, margarine, pastries, processed nuts, sauces, seasonings, snack foods, stock (bouillon) cubes and powders, vegetable oils, wraps.
Flavour enhancers	> Synthetic additives used to intensify the savoury taste of a food, enhancing its taste and appeal to consumers.	Condiments, instant noodles, fast food, flavoured snack foods (e.g. chips/crisps, crackers), marinades, processed meat, ready-made soups, stock (bouillon) cubes and powders, sauces, seasonings.
Nitrates and nitrites	> Used to prevent the growth of mould, yeast and bacteria in food. > Also used to enhance flavour and colour.	Pickled vegetables, processed meats (e.g. ham, bacon, sausages, hot dogs, corned beef), smoked or cured fish, some cheeses.
Propionates	> Used to prevent the growth of mould, yeast and bacteria in food.	Bread, breakfast cereals, cakes, cheese, noodles, pasta, pastries, pizza dough, processed meat, tortillas.
Sorbates	> Used to prevent the growth of mould, yeast and bacteria in food.	Baked products (e.g. biscuits, cakes), bread, cheese, chicken nuggets, dried fruit, dried meats, ice cream, juices, margarine, soft drinks, yoghurt.
Sulphites	> Can occur naturally in some food or be used as a synthetic food additive. > Used to prevent the growth of mould, yeast and bacteria in food. > Also used to preserve colour.	Beer, cider, cordial, dried fruit, frozen potato products (e.g. frozen French fries), fruit juice, grapes, hamburger patties, salad dressings, sausages, soft drink, vegetable juice, wine.

THE WEEKLY GROCERY SHOP

* As new research is published, advice may change.
** Potential side effects: sensitivity to food additives varies; reported effects are based on research findings and may not be experienced by all individuals.
*** Based on Food Standards Australia New Zealand (FSANZ), 2024. Other countries may vary in their standards.

Potential side effects **	What to look out for ***
> Hyperactivity and behavioural problems in children, especially those with ADHD. > If sensitive, may cause headaches, migraines, asthma, hives, rashes and rhinitis.	**Additive numbers:** 102, 104, 110, 122, 123, 124, 127, 129, 132, 133, 142, 143, 151, 155. **Additive names:** Tartrazine (102), quinoline yellow (104), sunset yellow FCF (110), azorubine/carmoisine (122), amaranth (123), ponceau 4R (124), erythrosine (127), allura red AC (129), indigotine (132), brilliant blue FCF (133), green S (142), fast green FCF (143), brilliant black BN/PN (151), brown HT (155).
> Some research suggests higher intakes are associated with higher rates of obesity, type 2 diabetes, impaired glucose tolerance, hypertension, cardiovascular disease and possibly cancer, although more robust studies are needed to investigate this further. > The World Health Organization recommends against the use of artificial sweeteners for weight control due to potential health risks associated with their use.	**Additive numbers:** 950–952, 954–955, 961–962, 969. **Additive names:** Acesulphame potassium (950), aspartame (951), cyclamates (952), saccharin (954), sucralose (955), neotame (961), aspartame-acesulphame salt (962), advantame (969).
> Hyperactivity and behavioural problems in children, especially those with ADHD. > If sensitive, may cause shortness of breath, wheeze, cough, rash, hives, itching, nausea, vomiting and abdominal pain.	**Additive numbers:** 210–218. **Additive names:** Benzoic acid (210), sodium benzoate (211), potassium benzoate (212), calcium benzoate (213), propylparaben/propyl-p-hydroxy-benzoate (216), methylparaben/methyl-p-hydroxy-benzoate (218).
> Sensitivity reactions (hives, eczema, rashes, dermatitis). > Suspected carcinogen. > Suspected endocrine hormone disruptor.	**Additive numbers:** 319–321. **Additive names:** Tert-butylhydroquinone (TBHQ) (319), butylated hydroxyanisole (BHA) (320), butylated hydroxytoluene (BHT) (321).
> If sensitive, may cause difficulty breathing in asthmatics, hives, rhinitis, gastrointestinal discomfort, headache, migraine, nausea, heart palpitations, numbness and tingling, drowsiness or weakness. > Some evidence suggests certain flavour enhancers increase appetite (by making food more appealing), which may lead to overeating and obesity.	**Additive numbers:** 620–635 or listed as 'flavour enhancer'. **Additive names:** 'Flavour enhancer', L-glutamic acid (620), monosodium L-glutamate (MSG) (621), monopotassium L-glutamate (622), calcium glutamate (623), monoammonium L-glutamate (624), magnesium glutamate (625), disodium-5'-guanylate (627), disodium-5'-inosinate (631), disodium-5'-ribonucleotides (635).
> Consumption of processed meat containing nitrates/nitrites has been linked to a higher risk of stomach and bowel cancer. > The World Health Organization recommends avoiding nitrates/nitrites in processed meats to reduce cancer risk. > Recurrent respiratory tract infections. > If sensitive, may cause headaches, migraines, hives, itching or anaphylaxis.	**Additive numbers:** 249–252. **Additive names:** Potassium nitrite (249), sodium nitrite (250), sodium nitrate (251), potassium nitrate (252).
> Irritability, restlessness, poor attention and sleep issues in children. > Linked to insulin resistance and weight gain in humans although more research is needed.	**Additive numbers:** 280–283. **Additive names:** Propionic acid (280), sodium propionate (281), calcium propionate (282), potassium propionate (283).
> If sensitive, may cause headaches, asthma, rhinitis, hives and skin irritation. > May affect how some types of white blood cells work, but more research is needed to understand exactly how this affects human health.	**Additive numbers:** 200–203. **Additive names:** Sorbic acid (200), sodium sorbate (201), potassium sorbate (202), calcium sorbate (203).
> Can worsen asthmatic symptoms (wheeze, difficulty breathing, cough) in people with asthma. > If sensitive, may cause rashes, hives, swelling, abdominal pain, nausea, diarrhoea, anaphylaxis (can occur even when consumed in low doses).	**Additive numbers:** 220–228. **Additive names:** Sulphur dioxide (220), sodium sulphite (221), sodium bisulphite (222), sodium metabisulphite (223), potassium metabisulphite (224), potassium sulphite (225), potassium bisulphite (228).

Decoding labels

The *only* information you can trust on a packaged product is the information listed on the back (the nutrition information panel and ingredient list). Many brands try to lure you to buy with positive health claims on the front. While these claims may sound enticing, they are often used to distract you from the product's less desirable aspects.

Many companies also attempt to trick eco-conscious consumers by 'greenwashing' – i.e. making their products seem more environmentally friendly, sustainable or ethical than they actually are. They are quick to highlight the positive aspects of the product, but often the negatives outweigh the positives.

Once you can see past these deceptive techniques, you will find yourself armed with grocery store superpowers.

Food labelling laws

At the risk of sounding nerdy, I'd like to take a moment to shine a light on food labelling laws. I am often asked why labels are not more transparent about what a product contains. In Australia, the US and the UK, laws require food manufacturers to provide details on a product's packaging about its ingredients, nutrition and potential allergens. However, each country has its own independent food regulation authority, so what is mandatory on labels varies between countries. For example, the EU has tighter regulations surrounding the use of artificial food colours. Products that contain certain artificial colours must contain a warning on the front: 'May have an adverse effect on activity and attention in children.'

We need to keep pushing for greater transparency in food labelling so that, as consumers, we can make our own informed choices about what we eat.

Percentage labelling

Use the percentages on ingredient lists to check that you're buying what you think you're buying. Does your falafel contain 30% chickpea or 70% chickpea?

Often, manufacturers will skimp on the key ingredient and bulk up the product with cheaper ingredients and/or additives.

Consider this ingredient list on a spinach wrap.

Wheat flour (62%) (thiamine, folic acid), water, vegetable oil, mineral salts (450, 500), iodised salt, sugar, spinach & herb seasoning (0.9%), colours (102, 133), emulsifier (471), vegetable gums (412, 466), acidity regulator (297), preservatives (282, 200).

Do you really want a spinach wrap that contains no spinach at all?

Farming practices

The origin of your fruits and vegetables can make a difference to both their quality and their environmental impact. The three main types of farming practice are conventional, organic and genetically modified (GMO).

Conventional

Conventionally farmed produce uses manufactured fertilisers and pesticides to help farmers grow more and keep prices lower. Just be mindful that this may result in some chemical residues left on your fruits and veggies, so make sure you wash them thoroughly (see tips on page 61).

If organic produce isn't within your budget, focus on buying produce listed in the 'Clean Fifteen' (see page 51).

Organic

Grown without synthetic chemicals, organic produce is farmed using natural fertilisers, such as compost. While organic is often more expensive than conventionally farmed produce, choosing in-season organic produce can make it more attainable.

If your budget will stretch to some organic produce but you can't afford to buy all organic, save your organic purchases for items that appear in the 'Dirty Dozen' list (see page 51), as these carry the highest levels of pesticides in conventionally farmed produce. It's less important for items in the 'Clean Fifteen' list to be organic, as the produce in this group contains relatively low levels of pesticide residues.

GMO

Genetically modified organisms (GMOs) can help increase crop yields, reduce the need for chemical sprays and improve nutritional value, but there is ongoing debate about the potential health and environmental risks of GMO crops. Some countries require GMO foods to be labelled, making them easier to avoid if desired.

Place of origin

In some countries, the origin of every product on the shelf is required to appear on the label. Food miles are important to many people who would like to support local suppliers and manufacturers.

Items in our grocery store can travel from down the road, interstate or even overseas. Some fresh produce travels thousands of kilometres from the other side of the world, packed and refrigerated so that it still looks fresh and appetising when it arrives in our stores. But not only has this produce lost some nutritional value and quality in transit, its long journey has had a significant impact on the environment and our carbon footprint.

In addition, food laws vary from country to country, so buying local means you are getting products that are regulated in a way you understand.

Marketing buzzwords to watch out for

Claim	Reality
Baked not fried	'Baked' does not always equate to healthier. A baked item can still be high in additives or fats, or contain other unhealthy ingredients.
Earth-friendly	This claim can be vague and is often unregulated. It might refer to only one aspect of the product, such as the packaging.
Good for gut health	It may be high in fibre or contain added probiotics or prebiotics, but the product as a whole could still be high in sugar or artificial ingredients that are not beneficial for overall health.
High in fibre	Cereals often make this claim and, while it may be true, there is also a lot that they don't promote, such as high levels of sugar, sodium or additives. Check the overall nutritional content.
Low-calorie/low-fat	Many snack bars and pre-made meals use this claim, but they often have lengthy ingredient lists containing multiple additives to enhance taste and keep the calorific or fat content low.
Natural	This term is not regulated in many countries and can be misleading. It doesn't necessarily mean that the product is made only from natural ingredients or is healthy.
No artificial colours	This is a claim often used on products marketed to children, such as cordial or biscuits. These products are still nutrient-void and can contain flavour enhancers and excess sugar.
No artificial preservatives	Even if a product does not contain preservatives, it may contain multiple concerning additives.
No MSG	Although this may imply a healthier option, the product might still have a high sodium content or include other artificial flavour enhancers.
No sugar or sugar-free	This is a popular claim on muesli (granola) bars. While the product may not contain added sugar, it could contain artificial sweeteners or other forms of sugar, such as fructose or maltodextrin.
Organic	While organic products are generally better in terms of pesticide and additive use, they can still be high in sugar, salt or fat.
Plant-based	Plant-based doesn't automatically mean that the product is high in nutrients or free from unhealthy additives. Some plant-based products can also be highly processed.
🌿	Symbols like green leaves or planet Earth are often used to imply that a product is healthy or environmentally friendly without providing any real information about its nutrition or production.

Dirty Dozen and Clean Fifteen

Every year, US-based non-profit organisation the Environmental Working Group identifies the twelve conventionally farmed fruits and vegetables with the most pesticides – the 'Dirty Dozen'. The same organisation researches the produce that contains the lowest levels of pesticide residues – the 'Clean Fifteen'. Here is the Dirty Dozen and Clean Fifteen for 2024.

2024 Dirty Dozen

1. Strawberries
2. Spinach
3. Kale, collard and mustard greens
4. Grapes
5. Peaches
6. Pears
7. Nectarines
8. Apples
9. Capsicums (bell peppers) and chillies
10. Cherries
11. Blueberries
12. Green beans

2024 Clean Fifteen

1. Avocados
2. Sweetcorn
3. Pineapples
4. Onions
5. Papayas
6. Frozen peas
7. Asparagus
8. Honeydew melons
9. Kiwifruit
10. Cabbages
11. Mushrooms
12. Mangoes
13. Sweet potatoes
14. Watermelons
15. Carrots

Setting up your kitchen for success

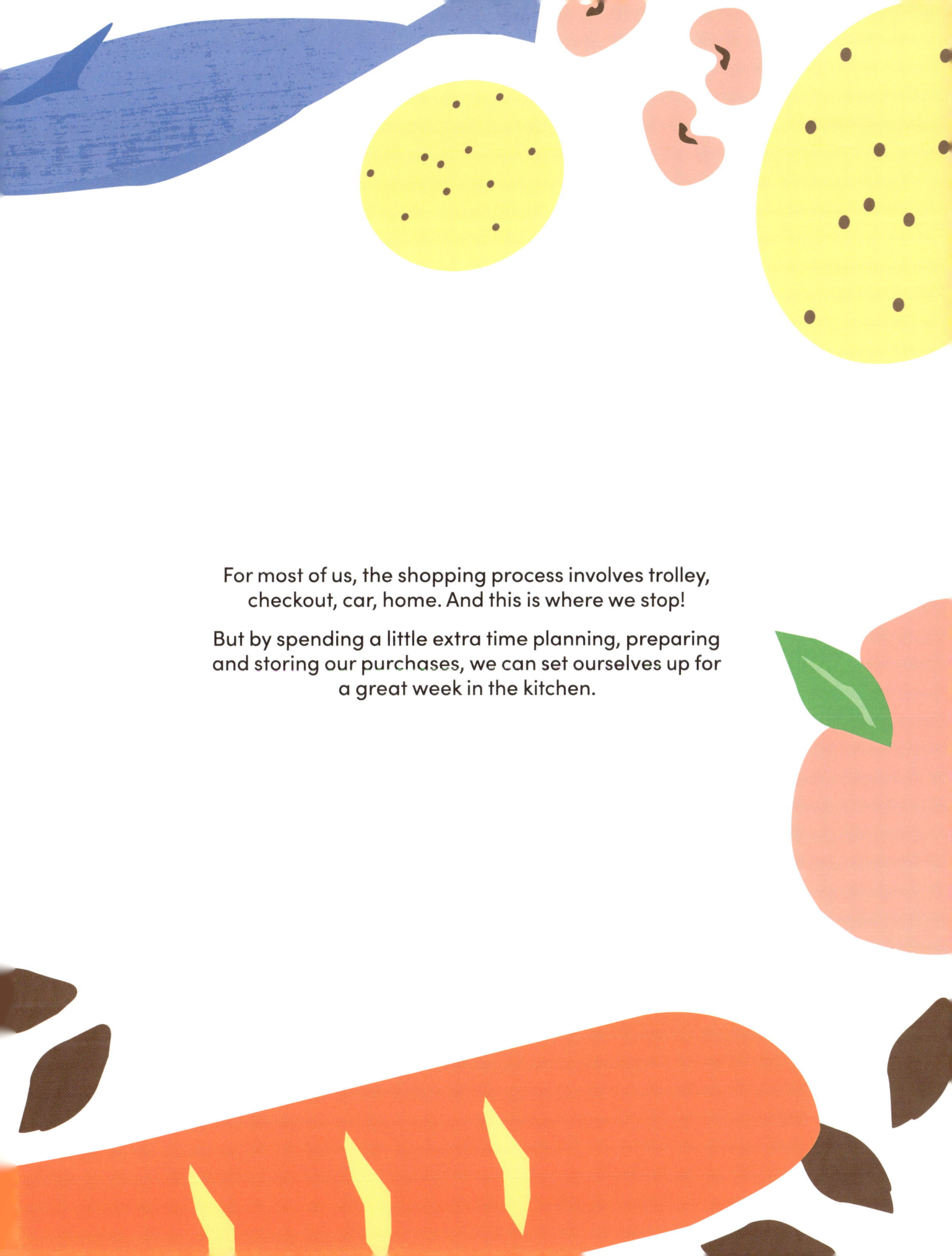

For most of us, the shopping process involves trolley, checkout, car, home. And this is where we stop!

But by spending a little extra time planning, preparing and storing our purchases, we can set ourselves up for a great week in the kitchen.

Storing fresh produce

By the time you get your groceries home, the last thing you want to do is unpack them. It's just another job – fact. But if you take an extra moment to put away your groceries carefully, you'll increase their longevity and appeal. How many times have you discovered a mouldy cucumber at the bottom of your fridge or gone to eat a cracker and found it stale because it has not been stored properly? You have worked so hard to save money at the checkout; don't throw it away when you get home.

These simple steps will help you transform your kitchen into a place of calm, order and possibly even joy.

An organised pantry

It's not the size that matters, it's the way you use it. Whether you have a small cupboard or a large walk-in pantry, the way you manage your food storage will impact how you feel about making food. If you can clearly see what is on offer when you open your pantry or cupboard, you will be more inspired to cook.

Invest in a good set of airtight storage containers to ensure that dried goods, from noodles to flour, last longer in your pantry. And a few pantry accessories can be an organisation game changer. Try a three-tier shelf to display your tinned goods or a clear spinning turntable to prevent items from getting lost at the back of the cupboard.

A clean fridge

Okay, so you may be thinking, 'Now I have to clean too?' But trust me, cleaning out your fridge is key to getting ready for a new week. Your fridge door is likely to be opened more than 50 times a week, so consider what joy it will prompt if every time you open it, you are presented with a tidy, organised space.

10 minutes to a clean fridge

- ☐ Check the use-by dates of the items in the fridge and discard anything that needs to go.
- ☐ Remove all remaining fresh produce and place it in a bowl on your bench.
- ☐ Fill a medium bowl with warm water and add a couple of drops of essential oil (I love lemon). If you don't have any essential oil, a few drops of fresh lemon juice also works well. I avoid chemical-based cleaners in the fridge as they leave a strong smell and residue.
- ☐ Dip a microfibre cloth or tea towel (dish towel) into the warm water and use it to wipe down the fridge shelves, produce drawers and door shelves. Don't forget to wipe the seals, as they tend to capture a lot of crumbs. I use a toothbrush to get into the groove and I am always slightly shocked by how much food gets trapped.
- ☐ Place the items back in the fridge. I put the remaining fresh produce directly back into the fridge in the bowl from the bench, to keep it separate from the produce I've just bought and to ensure that I use it up first.

Fridge storage

For years, I placed my fresh produce straight into the fridge produce drawer, mostly in the little plastic bag the store provided. However, if you want your produce to last, it's crucial to store it correctly. The best news is that this can be done in no time.

It's worth investing in some simple fridge-storage accessories:

Glass storage containers keep food fresh for longer and make it easy to see what's in the fridge.

Clear trays/drawers are very versatile, helping you to group foods together in an easily accessible, organised manner. I use mine for storing a range of cheese, yoghurt pouches and even whole apples.

Reusable ziplock bags/pouches (often silicone) are a compact way to store freshly prepped veggies or baked goods.

A lazy Susan turntable allows you to see smaller items such as condiments and ensures that nothing gets lost at the back of the fridge. I often find myself standing in front of the fridge and spinning my lazy Susan, admiring my selection of mayonnaises, pesto, sauces and dips!

SETTING UP YOUR KITCHEN FOR SUCCESS

Produce	Fridge storage method
Apples, pears, stone fruit, citrus	Can be left at room temperature but will last longer and ripen more slowly if refrigerated. Store in cloth produce bags in the produce drawer, away from vegetables if possible.
Avocados	Store at room temperature but, once cut, rub the cut surface with lemon juice (to stop it from going brown), cover with beeswax wrap and store in the fridge for up to 2 days.
Berries	Be gentle! Rinse and lay on a tea towel (dish towel) to dry – pat gently but be careful not to bruise your berries. Store in a container lined with paper towel in the middle of the fridge to avoid frostbite and overcrowding.
Broccoli, bok choy, brussels sprouts, green beans, asparagus	Store whole in a cloth produce bag or wrap in a tea towel.
Cabbage, cauliflower	Store whole in the fridge until ready to prep. Once cut, store in airtight containers or reusable ziplock bags.
Grapes	Wash and store in a cloth produce bag or bowl (for easy snacking).
Herbs (soft-stemmed)	Fresh, leafy herbs such as parsley and coriander should be released from any rubber bands or ties. Trim the bottom centimetre from the stems. Place the herbs upright in a small jar or glass half-filled with water (to submerge just the stem, not the leaves), then store in the fridge. (The exception is basil, which should be stored uncovered on the bench or windowsill.) If your herbs came wrapped in plastic, you can place the bag back on top of the herbs for extra longevity. If this method takes up too much space in your fridge, wrap your herbs in damp paper towels before refrigerating them in reusable ziplock bags.
Herbs (woody-stemmed)	Woody-stemmed herbs like rosemary, sage, oregano and thyme can be kept wrapped in damp paper towel or stored in an airtight container.
Leafy greens	Lightly sprinkle some water on a tea towel, wrap your leafy greens up in the slightly damp towel and place them in the produce drawer. They will stay crisp for double the time!
Lettuce	For whole heads of lettuce, remove the stalk and trim any outside leaves before wrapping in paper towel or a tea towel. For lettuce leaves, prepare by cutting them with a sharp knife to avoid bruising. Gently wash the leaves and use a salad spinner to dry (or pat dry with a tea towel). Once completely dry, store in an airtight container, with a paper towel at the bottom to absorb any moisture. Be careful not to overfill the container so there is enough airflow around the leaves.
Mushrooms	Store in a brown paper bag to enable them to breathe. Do not seal in an airtight container or plastic bag as they will sweat and degrade quickly.
Cut pumpkin (winter squash)	Store in an airtight container or reusable ziplock bag.

Out-of-fridge storage

Some fresh produce should not be stored in the fridge. The following items should be kept in mesh storage bags or trays (to allow them to breathe) in a cool, dark place:

- garlic
- onions
- potatoes
- whole pumpkin (winter squash)

Healthy snack storage

I have never met a person who doesn't appreciate a snack. But the quality of your snack matters. Practise a little self-love by preparing a few snacks at the beginning of the week – it's a great way to sneak a few extra nutrients into your diet while also satisfying those snack cravings.

Apples	Add freshly sliced apples to an airtight container with a cup of water and ½ teaspoon of salt to reduce browning. Store in the fridge.
Baked goods	You can freeze large batches of sweet or savoury muffins/slices to use in lunchboxes. Just make sure your baked goods are completely cool before transferring to airtight containers or reusable ziplock bags and storing in the freezer. Transfer the frozen snack from the freezer to the lunchbox in the morning and it will be defrosted by recess time.
Protein/bliss balls	Store in the fridge in an airtight container for up to 2 weeks (if they last that long!), or freeze for up to 3 months. Thaw overnight in the fridge or add straight to the lunchbox for same-day defrosting.
Veggie sticks	Store sticks of carrot, celery and cucumber in the fridge in jars or airtight containers filled with ½ cup of water to keep crisp (change the water every couple of days). Or wrap in moist paper towel in airtight containers or reusable ziplock bags.

Freezing food

Understanding the correct way to freeze food will save you time and money, and result in better tasting meals.

Temperature

Ensure your freezer is running at around −18°C (0°F).

Environmentally friendly freezing

Use airtight containers that are freezer-safe or reusable ziplock bags. Consider glass or stainless steel airtight containers, beeswax wraps, cellulose bags, parchment paper or, for bread products, fabric bags.

Safety

It is important to understand food safety; not only does it prevent food poisoning, but it also helps maintain the nutrient quality of your food.

- Only freeze food once (raw food that has been cooked can be refrozen, but some quality may be lost in the process).
- To avoid bacteria growth, defrost overnight in the fridge (not on the bench at room temperature).
- Cool hot food in the fridge before placing it in the freezer.

Prep

Use the freezer as a meal-prep tool. You will be filled with joy (no exaggeration!) when you are organised and have already prepped the majority of dinner.

- Prepare veggies by chopping, grating and dicing before freezing.
- Ensure that you divide prepped veggies into portions so they are ready to use.
- Remove meat from packaging and put it into airtight containers to avoid freezer burn (dehydration that occurs when frozen food is exposed to air).
- Leave space for liquids to expand when freezing.
- Label and date freezer packs to stay organised. (I find liquid-chalk markers best – they wipe off easily with a damp cloth, ready for next time.)

Freezer storage times

Food	Freezer storage
Bread	Up to 8 months
Butter	Up to 3 months
Cakes and biscuits (cookies)	Up to 4 months
Chicken, whole	Up to 12 months
Chicken breast and pieces	Up to 6 months
Cooked meats and meals	Up to 3 months
Cooked stock/broth	Up to 6 months
Fish and seafood	Up to 2 months
Fruits and vegetables	Up to 6 months
Milk	Up to 6 weeks
Pork	Up to 3 months
Processed meats (bacon, sausages, minced/ground)	Up to 3 months
Raw red meats (unprocessed)	Up to 6 months
Soup	Up to 6 months

Freeze your herbs

Avoid wastage by blending soft herbs such as basil, parsley and coriander with a little oil and freezing in ice cube trays, then transfer them to labelled containers to store in the freezer. Tough, hardier herbs such as rosemary can be wrapped in damp paper towel and stored in the freezer in reusable ziplock bags.

Prepping

I get it. Meal prep is just another job on your to-do list. The last thing you want to do after planning meals and shopping for groceries is prep. But trust me when I say that one 'hour of power' will save you three hours during the week. I'm not sure of the science behind it, but I think it's because not only does it reduce the amount of time you physically spend in the kitchen during your busy week, it also eliminates the constant thought of 'I have to make dinner' or 'What can I snack on?'. When your prep is sorted, it's a magical feeling.

Don't aim to do your meal prep the moment you get home from the supermarket – that's too ambitious and can feel overwhelming. Instead, shop one day and do your hour of prepping the next. (It's amazing what you can do when you are re-energised!)

Once a week (I do this on a Sunday), allocate an hour of power. As this practice becomes a habit, you will be surprised how much it reduces stress in the kitchen during the week. You might even find meal prep and cooking becomes enjoyable!

Here are my suggested prep steps for your weekly hour of power.

THE WEEKLY GROCERY SHOP

① Wash your produce

You need to wash your produce, not because a stinky hand may have touched it in the store (several hands will have touched it, guaranteed), but to remove excess dirt, bacteria and pesticides.

For years, I would wash an apple every time I went to eat one or put it in the lunchbox. It might seem like a small thing, but by washing all your apples for the week at once, you reduce your weekly tasks and reduce overwhelm.

Follow these simple steps to wash your produce:

- Clean your kitchen sink with a natural cleaner – bicarbonate of soda (baking soda) is great as it is a gentle abrasive, cutting through grime.
- Fill the sink with water and 125 ml (4 fl oz/½ cup) white vinegar for every litre (34 fl oz/ 4 cups) of water.
- Place all the fresh produce into the sink (except for the leafy greens; these are best washed in their own sink 'bath').
- For hardier produce, use a soft scrubbing brush to clean.
- Let all the produce soak for 15 minutes while you do other tasks.
- Place a tea towel (dish towel) on the bench and drain the sink.
- Put all the produce onto the towel to dry completely before storing.

Once you've washed your produce, follow the guide on page 56 to store it correctly and maintain freshness for longer.

② Get a head start on meals

During my weekly hour of power, along with washing and storing my produce, I spend some time getting ahead for weeknight dinners. Don't let social media convince you that you need to do it all, or that things need to be perfect. The goal is to do something that's achievable. Something is better than nothing.

Put on your favourite music and make this a positive, enjoyable task that you do for yourself and your family. No matter how small, it will save you time during the week (and make you feel like you're winning at life!).

During my hour of power, I alternate between prepping veggies (see pages 62–63), batch-cooking (see page 64) and some of the following tasks:

- boiling eggs
- cutting up fruit such as watermelon (do it now or you never will)
- decanting crackers into an airtight jar
- filling a small bowl with nuts for a quick grab-and-go bite
- grating a block of cheese and storing it in an airtight container.

③ Prep your veggies

We're all aiming to increase our veggie intake. When your veggies are prepped and waiting, they're guaranteed to make it into your dinner. Aim to chop, dice or grate as many items as you can during your hour of power using the tips on these pages. Store them in separate, appropriately sized airtight containers in the fridge.

Vegetables

Broccoli and cauliflower
Cut into small florets, and peel and slice the stems.

Cabbage
Shred cabbage for coleslaw or stir-fry.

Capsicums (bell peppers)
Core and slice into thin strips.

Carrots
Peel and julienne or slice on a diagonal. Store in an airtight container with ¼ cup of water to keep them crisp.

Green beans, snow peas (mangetout) or sugar-snap peas
Trim the ends and store whole in an airtight container.

Mushrooms
Wipe clean and slice. Store in a paper bag to prevent sweating and excess moisture.

Zucchini (courgette)
Slice into half-moons or julienne. Store in an airtight container lined with a damp paper towel.

THE WEEKLY GROCERY SHOP

Hints for storing prepped veggies

- Keep all vegetables and aromatics stored separately to maintain freshness and prevent flavours from mingling. Replace any paper towel you have used if it becomes too wet.
- For best results, store containers in the produce drawer of your fridge.
- If any prepped vegetables start to wilt, refresh them in a bowl of iced water for a few minutes before draining and using them.

Aromatics

Chillies
Slice or chop, depending on your preferred level of heat.

Garlic
To save time by peeling garlic in bulk, separate cloves from the bulb and place in a container with a lid. Shake vigorously for 30 seconds – the peels should fall off. Store peeled cloves in the fridge for up to a week or freeze in an airtight container or reusable ziplock bag for up to 6 months.

Ginger
Peel and julienne or finely mince.

Shallots
Peel and finely slice.

Spring onions (scallions)
Finely slice green and white tips. Store green and white parts in separate airtight containers for easy use when cooking.

Herbs

Chives
Pre-cut and store in a small jar with a lid for easy sprinkling.

Coriander (cilantro)
Wash, dry completely and chop the leaves. Line the airtight container with a dry paper towel.

SETTING UP YOUR KITCHEN FOR SUCCESS

④ Batch-cook

If you don't love cooking, you are about to fall head over heels in love with batch-cooking. Cook once and serve up to four times! The concept is to make a large 'batch' of something and then store it in portions so that you have other meals pre-made. And now that you know how to best use your freezer (see page 58), batch-cooking will be a breeze. Is there any better feeling than knowing dinner is already made?

Surprise, surprise, I like to keep it simple when batch-cooking. I either make a sauce that can be repurposed as a base for multiple different meals or prep proteins to cook up quickly on the day. If you made one batch of something every fortnight, you could potentially have eight meals in your freezer ready to go for the month. Maybe I am peak middle age, but the concept of not having to cook a meal from scratch every night is deeply exciting.

For batch-cooking, I highly recommend investing in a slow cooker, I have tried several and the one I found best was quite inexpensive, especially considering the amount of time it saves me. I particularly love it for preparing meat and soup.

You'll find some easy batch-cooking meal ideas on page 66.

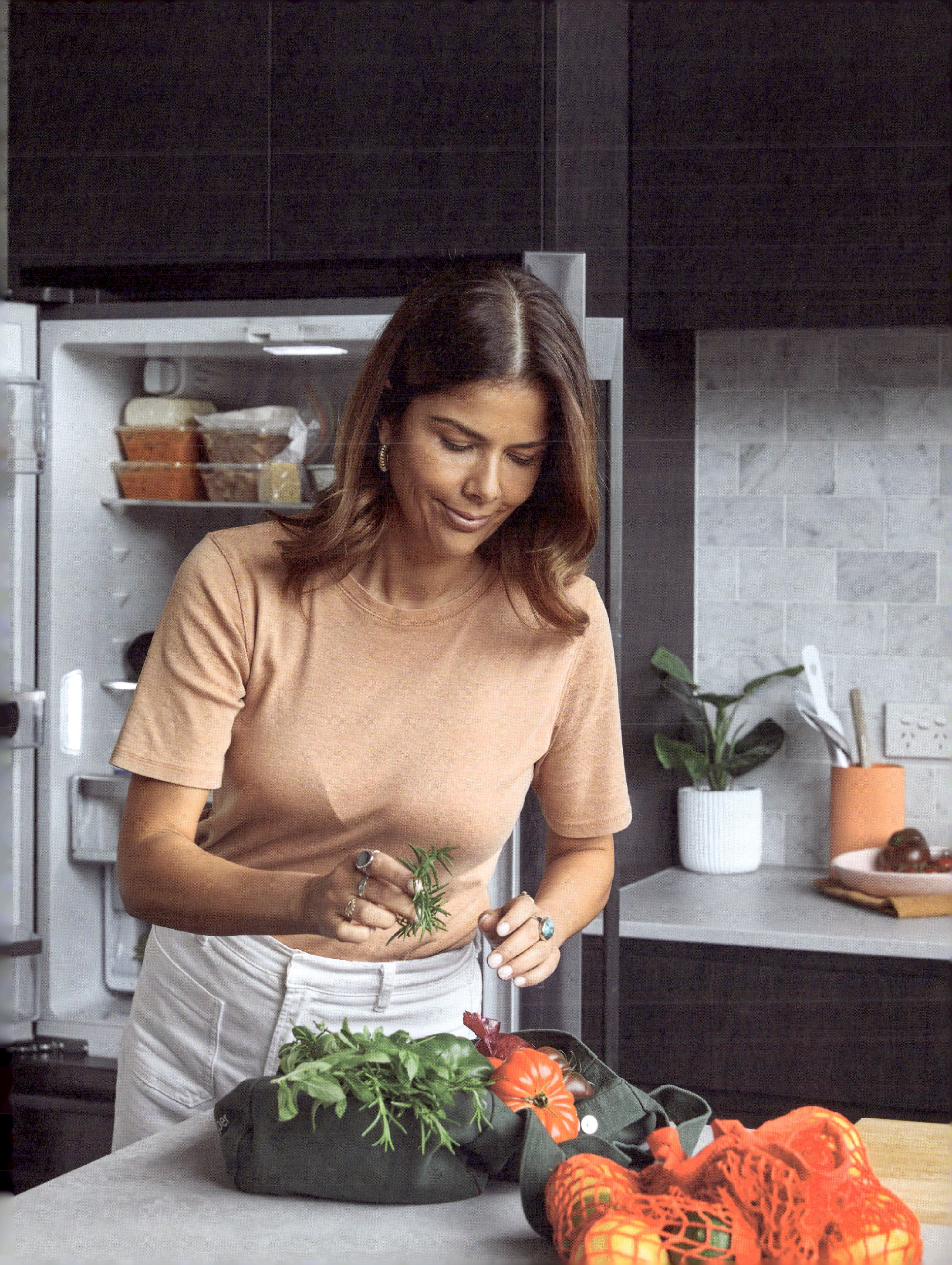

Easy batch-cooking meal ideas

Home-made passata

Later in the book you'll find a rich, delish Home-made tomato passata recipe (page 110). I make this at least once a month, but I multiply the quantities by four and freeze the other portions for future use. We'll enjoy a hearty penne ragu one night, and I might use a frozen batch of sauce as a base for a slow-cooked spicy Mexican dish or for oven-baked meatballs another night. You'll also find a recipe for Rose sauce (page 224) made with fresh tomatoes – it's perfect for the warmer months, adding a summery, light touch to your pasta meals.

Bolognese sauce

This rich meat sauce is a family favourite across the globe and a batch-cook hero. It can be repurposed into several different meals, from a classic spaghetti bolognese to lasagne, chilli con carne, nachos, tacos or loaded baked potatoes. If you are trying to eat better and cook more, start with a big batch of my Veggie-loaded bolognese sauce (page 108); it will serve you multiple times across the month and is one of the easiest recipes to make.

Curry sauce

Whether it's a red, green, massaman, dal or satay sauce, I often cook a curry packed with veggies on a Sunday. Perfect for freezing in portions, a curry is ideal for those emergency nights when you are tempted to succumb to takeaway. Instead, all you need to do is quickly defrost a delish, nutritious meal from your freezer. Curry in a hurry brings joy to my heart. You'll find my home-made Curry paste recipe (page 73) endlessly versatile.

Minced (ground) meat

Minced meat is a versatile protein that is ideal for batch-cooking. I always buy mince in bulk (2–3 kg/5–7 lb), as I know I will prep it all at once during my hour of power. Since I became a mum and kitchen CEO, I've been using my Seasoned beef mince recipe (page 169) as one prep that can result in three different meals: meatballs, burgers and koftas.

① **Meatballs**

Once I have made the mixture, I roll the balls in two sizes: a medium size, which I can place in a roasting tray with Home-made passata (page 110), and at least 24 mini meatballs, which I can place straight onto an oven tray to cook and have on hand for easy snacks or lunchboxes.

② **Burgers**

With the same mixture, I make a batch of 12 burger patties. I freeze these in a glass storage container, adding baking paper between the layers to ensure that they don't stick together.

③ **Koftas**

When it's time to make the Beef koftas (page 184), I might add some additional spices and fresh herbs to the mixture (or not) before shaping it into koftas on wooden skewers. I freeze the koftas in a glass storage container, ready to defrost and cook on the barbecue.

Slow-cooked meat

From a whole roast chicken to a 2 kg (4 lb 6 oz) beef brisket, cooking a large piece of protein low and slow results in incredible tenderness. This is a great place to start if you are new to batch-cooking, as being able to cook a large quantity with minimum preparation or intervention is a cooking revolution. Protein freezes extremely well, so it is simply a matter of defrosting portions and reheating another night.

Schnitzel

A crowd favourite! Batch-prepping schnitzels ahead of time and freezing them is a midweek life saver. All of the fiddly work is done; all you have to do is defrost and lightly fry them. On busy weeknights, you will be so grateful you introduced an hour of power to your schedule.

Soup

Cooking up a big batch of soup – whether it's nurturing chicken noodle, moreish creamy cauliflower or wholesome veggie minestrone – will make you feel like Martha Stewart. Soup freezes well, it locks in all of the nutrients and is perfect for when someone isn't well. It's also a nourishing meal to have on hand for an easy lunch or dinner, or if you want a meal with zero prep. Unlike most of the other batch meals we have discussed, soup requires absolutely no effort on the day; all you need to do is heat it up. Sign me up for zero-effort meals, thank you very much.

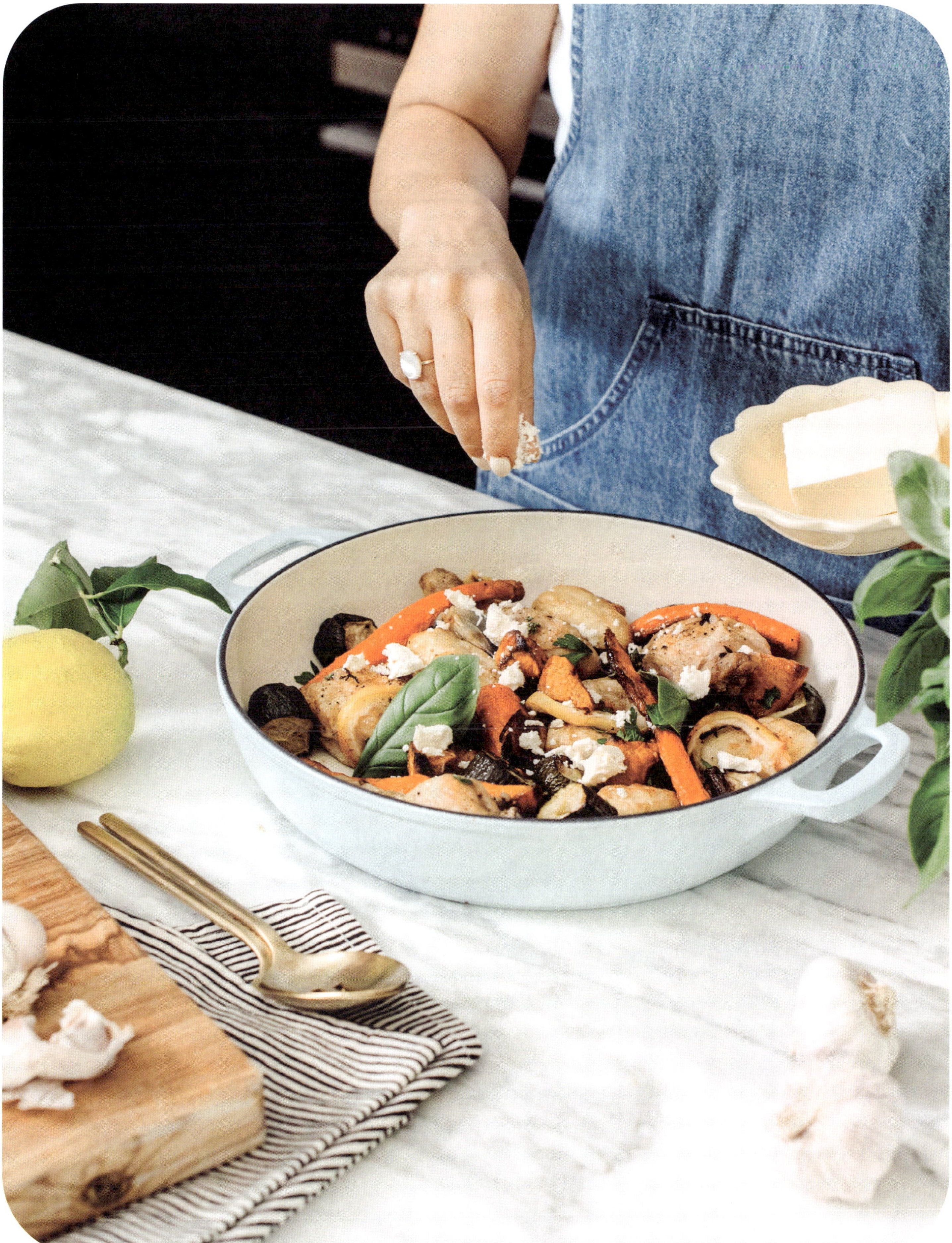

PART

The Cook

2

Using the meal plans

Part 1 of this book has given you the ingredients (tips) for a better weekly shop; Part 2 will give you the method (plan) for an easy week in the kitchen.

I have created six weekly meal plans for you, divided into two seasons: 'warming and comforting' plans for the cooler months, and 'light and fresh' for when the weather is warmer. Each meal plan includes seven dinners as well as a couple of easy breakfast recipes, a snack and a sweet (dessert). The shopping list at the beginning of each weekly plan has all the ingredients you need for that week's dinners, so that you can do your weekly shop in a single trip to the grocery store. The only ingredients not on this list are the staples that most of us already have in our pantries (see page 75); alternative ingredients mentioned in the dinner recipe 'hints'; and the ingredients used in the breakfast, snack and sweet recipes, as you might like to pick and choose which of these items you cook.

At the start of each week are some 'power prep' tasks. As we discussed in Part 1, by allocating an 'hour of power' at the start of each week to meal prep, you will drastically reduce the time you spend in the kitchen. For example, in the 'warming and comforting' Week 1 menu (page 78), you'll cook Beef brisket in your power prep, enabling you to produce two different meals very quickly during the following week: Beef brisket with vegetable gratin for one night and Nachos for another.

These meal plans are based on the notion of working smarter, not harder. In each plan, you'll find one dish repurposed into a new meal the next night, tips on how to tweak recipes based on your dietary preferences, and ways to freeze batches of leftovers so that some nights you won't need to cook at all!

We begin with some easy recipes for sauces and pastes – delicious, healthy alternatives to the store-bought versions, which tend to be loaded with artificial colours and flavours as well as sugar.

Healthy, home-made sauces and pastes

Stir-fry sauce

By pre-preparing this quick and easy sauce, you can have stir-fries on the table in minutes.

Makes 125 ml (4 fl oz/½ cup)

3 tablespoons soy sauce

2 tablespoons oyster sauce

1 tablespoon rice vinegar

1 tablespoon white (granulated) sugar or honey

Whisk all the ingredients together in a small bowl.

Store in a jar in the fridge for up to 1 week or freeze for up to 3 months. Shake well before using.

Garlic-ginger paste

Add depth to your stir-fries with this flavourful paste.

Makes 125 ml (4 fl oz/½ cup)

1 garlic bulb, cloves chopped

10 cm (4 in) piece of fresh ginger, peeled and chopped

4 spring onions (scallions), chopped

125 ml (4 fl oz/½ cup) avocado oil

Use a food processor to blend everything together. Heat the mixture in a small saucepan over low–medium heat for 10 minutes, until aromatic. Allow to cool.

Store in a jar in the fridge for up to 1 week or freeze for up to 3 months. Stir before using.

Black bean sauce

This versatile sauce is packed with umami and aromatic flavours and can also be used as a marinade.

Makes 125 ml (4 fl oz/½ cup)

2 tablespoons avocado oil

2 garlic cloves, minced

5 cm (2 in) piece of fresh ginger, peeled and minced

2 tablespoons fermented black beans (douchi), rinsed and mashed

2 tablespoons soy sauce or tamari

1 teaspoon white (granulated) sugar or honey

1 teaspoon rice vinegar

½ teaspoon chilli flakes (optional)

Heat the oil in a small saucepan over medium heat. Sauté the garlic and ginger for 30 seconds, or until fragrant. Add the mashed black beans, soy sauce, sugar, vinegar, 1 tablespoon of water and the chilli flakes (if using). Simmer for 3–4 minutes, until everything is well combined and the sauce is slightly thickened.

Allow the sauce to cool completely before transferring to a jar.

Store in the fridge for up to 2 weeks or freeze in portions for up to 3 months. When you're ready to use the sauce, bring it to room temperature if refrigerated (or thaw it in the fridge overnight if frozen), before gently reheating it in a saucepan and adding it to your stir-fry.

Curry paste

This gives a great flavour to so many dishes, including Butter chicken (page 80) and Tomato coconut dal (page 141). To save time, make extra and freeze it in portions.

Makes 500–600 ml (17–20½ fl oz/2–2⅓ cups)

3 tablespoons coriander seeds

3 tablespoons cumin seeds

1 tablespoon mustard seeds

1 tablespoon ground turmeric

1 tablespoon paprika

1½ teaspoons ground cinnamon

1½ teaspoons ground cloves

125 ml (4 fl oz/½ cup) avocado oil

3 large onions, finely chopped

12 garlic cloves, finely chopped

3 tablespoons finely chopped fresh ginger

½ teaspoon sea salt

125 g (4½ oz/½ cup) tomato paste (concentrated puree)

Toast the coriander, cumin and mustard seeds in a dry frying pan over medium heat until fragrant, about 3 minutes. Remove from the heat and allow to cool slightly.

Grind the toasted spices to a fine powder using a spice grinder or mortar and pestle, then mix with the turmeric, paprika, cinnamon and cloves in a small bowl.

Heat the oil in a large saucepan over medium heat. Add the onion and sauté until soft and golden, about 8 minutes. Add the garlic and ginger and cook for another 3 minutes. Add the ground spice mixture and salt to the pan and stir well to combine. Cook for 2 minutes, until fragrant. Stir in the tomato paste and cook for another 3 minutes, ensuring the spices and aromatics are well blended. Allow the paste to cool.

Store in an airtight container in the fridge for up to 1 week or freeze in portions for up to 3 months.

Hoisin sauce

Deliciously sweet and tangy, hoisin sauce is the perfect condiment for Asian dishes, both hot and cold. Try it in Hoisin meatloaf with potato gratin (page 154).

Makes 125 ml (4 fl oz/½ cup)

3 tablespoons soy sauce

30 g (1 oz) smooth peanut butter

2 teaspoons honey

1½ teaspoons rice vinegar

½ teaspoon avocado oil

1 garlic clove, minced

Whisk the ingredients together in a small bowl.

Store in a jar in the fridge for up to 5 days or freeze for up to 1 month. Whisk the sauce again before using. If using from frozen, allow the sauce to thaw in the fridge overnight, then whisk it to restore the smooth consistency. If the sauce is too thick, add a small splash of water to loosen it to the desired consistency.

Hints The ingredients for these sauces and pastes are not included in the weekly shopping lists. When buying what you need to make them, choose preservative- and sugar-free ingredients.

Always use a clean spoon when scooping out sauce or paste to prolong its shelf life and avoid contamination.

For a richer flavour for the Curry paste, add 1 tablespoon of coconut milk to the paste when making curries, or for a spicier paste, add chilli powder or chopped fresh chillies. For a smoother texture, blend the paste with a little water.

Notes

The recipes in this book use 250 ml (8½ fl oz) cup measurements and 20 ml (¾ fl oz) tablespoons.

In the US, a cup is 8 fl oz (240 ml), so American cooks should be generous in their cup measurements; in the UK, a cup is 9½ fl oz (284 ml), so British cooks should be scant with their cup measurements.

In the US, self-raising (rising) flour may not be readily available, but can be easily made at home by adding 2 teaspoons of baking powder for each 150 g (6 oz/1 cup) plain (all-purpose) flour.

The oven temperatures given are for fan-forced ovens. If using a conventional oven, increase the temperature by 35°C (95°F).

The recipes are labelled with the following symbols:

- (GF) gluten-free
- (NF) nut-free
- (DF) dairy-free
- (V) vegetarian
- (VG) vegan

However, please be aware that if you're using store-bought ingredients such as sauces and stocks, you will need to check the ingredient lists for the presence of gluten, nuts and dairy.

Pantry staples

These ingredients are used in the recipes but not included on the weekly shopping lists. By setting yourself up with a well-stocked pantry, you'll be ready for anything!

Herbs & spices

- black pepper
- cayenne pepper
- chilli flakes
- coriander seeds
- cumin seeds
- dried basil
- dried bay leaves
- dried chives
- dried dill
- dried oregano
- dried rosemary
- dried thyme
- garam masala
- garlic powder
- ground cardamom
- ground cinnamon
- ground cloves
- ground coriander
- ground cumin
- ground ginger
- ground nutmeg
- ground turmeric
- mustard powder
- mustard seeds
- nutritional yeast
- onion powder
- paprika
- sea salt
- sesame seeds
- smoked paprika
- sumac
- sichuan peppercorns
- taco seasoning
- white pepper
- white vinegar powder

Baking

- baking powder
- bicarbonate of soda (baking soda)
- cornflour (cornstarch)
- instant yeast
- plain (all-purpose) flour
- self-raising (rising) flour – see page 9
- semolina
- vanilla extract
- wholemeal (whole-wheat) flour

Condiments, sauces & stocks

- barbecue sauce
- beef stock
- beef stock (bouillon) powder
- black bean sauce
- chicken stock
- chicken stock (bouillon) powder
- chilli sauce
- chipotle paste
- Dijon mustard
- fish sauce
- sambal oelek
- soy sauce
- sriracha
- tamari sauce
- tomato sauce (ketchup)
- vegetable stock
- vegetable stock (bouillon) powder
- Worcestershire sauce

Dressings, oils & vinegars

- avocado oil
- apple-cider vinegar
- balsamic vinegar
- coconut oil
- extra-virgin olive oil
- light olive oil
- olive-oil spray
- red-wine vinegar
- rice vinegar
- vegetable oil
- white-wine vinegar

Other

- capers
- gherkins (pickles)
- honey
- pure maple syrup

Hint Additives, preservatives and added sugar are present in some pantry items, so be sure to check the labels.

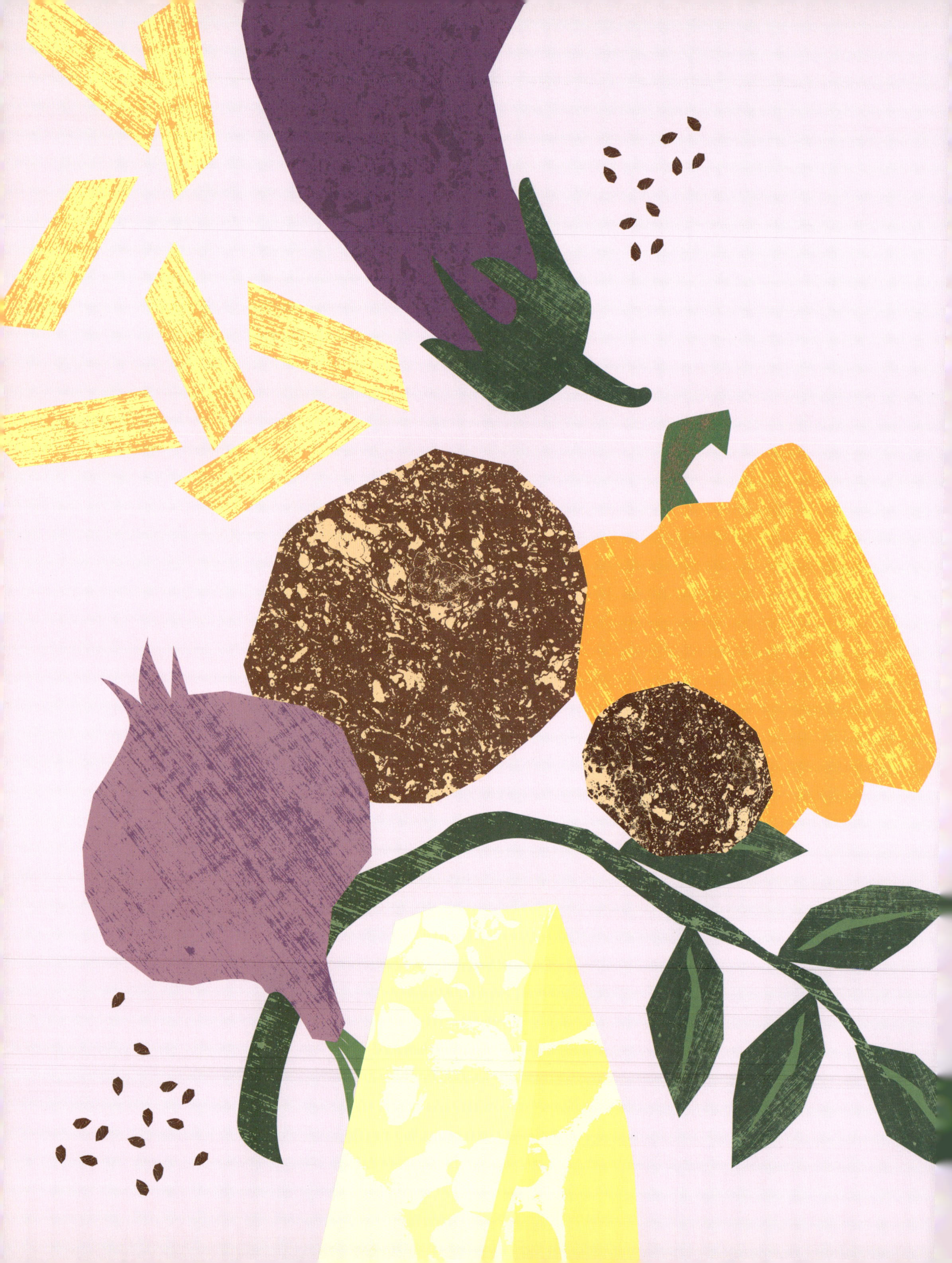

Warming & comforting

When it's cold outside, nothing is more comforting than the aroma of a wholesome meal drifting through your home. I enjoy spending more time in the kitchen during the cooler months, when pasta, noodles, pies and roasts all come into their own. These sorts of dishes lend themselves to batch-cooking, so you can prepare at least part of your meal ahead of time.

See page 74 for a key to the dietary symbols used on the recipes.

Week 1 menu

Power prep

Butter chicken
Pizza bases
Vegetable sauce
Beef brisket

Dinners

Butter chicken with flavoured rice and raita
Pizzas:
Butter chicken pizzas or Vegetable pizzas
Beef brisket with vegetable gratin
Nachos
Roasted tomato, kale and sausage penne
Baked chicken parmigiana with cauli-potato mash
Vegetable satay noodles

Breakfasts

One-pan wonder
Choc, oat and raspberry muffins

Snack

Cauliflower cheese bites

Sweet

Tahini maple caramel and choc coconut banana splits

Week 1 shopping list

Fruit & vegetables

- [ ] 2 avocados
- [ ] 1 bunch basil
- [ ] 2 broccoli heads
- [ ] 3 large + 1 medium red capsicums (bell peppers)
- [ ] 2 carrots
- [ ] 1 small cauliflower head
- [ ] 2 long green chillies
- [ ] 1 bunch coriander (cilantro)
- [ ] 1 Lebanese (short) cucumber
- [ ] 1 bunch dill
- [ ] 3 large handfuls spinach leaves
- [ ] 3 garlic bulbs
- [ ] 5 cm (2 in) piece of fresh ginger
- [ ] 1 bunch kale
- [ ] 2 lemons
- [ ] 3 limes
- [ ] 1 bunch mint
- [ ] 6 large onions
- [ ] 1 small + 3 medium red onions
- [ ] 1.4 kg (3 lb 1 oz) potatoes
- [ ] 500 g (1 lb 2 oz) pumpkin (winter squash)
- [ ] 1 bunch spring onions (scallions)
- [ ] 150 g (5½ oz) sugar-snap peas
- [ ] 1 kg (2 lb 3 oz) ripe tomatoes
- [ ] 100 g (3½ oz) cherry tomatoes + 500 g (1 lb 2 oz) cherry tomatoes on the vine
- [ ] 2 zucchini (courgettes)

Meat & poultry

- [ ] 1 × 2 kg (4 lb 6 oz) beef brisket
- [ ] 2 × large boneless chicken breasts
- [ ] 1.5 kg (3 lb 5 oz) boneless chicken thighs
- [ ] 6 pork sausages

Pantry & baking

- [ ] 30 g (1 oz) slivered almonds or sultanas
- [ ] 400 g (14 oz) tinned black beans
- [ ] 90 g (3 oz) Japanese breadcrumbs
- [ ] 400 g (14 oz) tinned chickpeas
- [ ] 125 ml (4 fl oz) coconut milk
- [ ] 230 g (8 oz) corn chips
- [ ] 400 g (14 oz) tinned corn kernels
- [ ] 1 kg (2 lb 3 oz) strong flour
- [ ] 200 g (7 oz) tinned lentils
- [ ] 60 g (2 oz) mayonnaise
- [ ] 400 g (14 oz) rice noodles
- [ ] 60 g (2 oz) smooth peanut butter
- [ ] handful of roasted peanuts
- [ ] 100 g (3½ oz) penne (or other pasta)
- [ ] 200 g (7 oz) basmati rice
- [ ] 100 g (3½ oz) soft brown sugar
- [ ] 1 tablespoon white (granulated) sugar
- [ ] 2 tablespoons taco seasoning
- [ ] 800 g (1 lb 12 oz) tinned crushed tomatoes
- [ ] 550 g (1 lb 3 oz) tomato paste

Fridge

- [ ] 60 g (2 oz) salted butter
- [ ] 250 g (9 oz) cheddar (more if you like)
- [ ] 250 g (9 oz) smoked cheddar
- [ ] 700 ml (23½ fl oz) whipping cream
- [ ] 40 g (1½ oz) ghee
- [ ] 100 g (3½ oz) goat's cheese (optional)
- [ ] 350 g (12½ oz) mozzarella
- [ ] 50 g (1¾ oz) parmesan
- [ ] 200 ml (7 fl oz) sour cream
- [ ] 200 g (7 oz) firm tofu
- [ ] 125 g (4½ oz) coconut yoghurt
- [ ] 200 g (7 oz) plain yoghurt

Butter chicken

Prep 15 minutes
Cook 50 minutes
Makes 2 meals for 4 people

1.5 kg (3 lb 5 oz) boneless chicken thighs, cut into bite-sized pieces

125 g (4½ oz/½ cup) plain yoghurt

3 tablespoons garam masala

40 g (1½ oz) ghee or salted butter

250 ml (8½ fl oz/1 cup) Curry paste (page 73)

500 g (1 lb 2 oz/2 cups) tomato paste (concentrated puree)

375 ml (12½ fl oz/1½ cups) whipping cream

2 large handfuls spinach leaves

sea salt

GF NF

This recipe makes enough for Butter chicken with flavoured rice and raita (page 84) and Butter chicken pizzas (page 86), but future-you will thank you if you make double and freeze some for another time.

First, marinate the chicken pieces by combining with the yoghurt and garam masala in a large bowl. Cover and allow to marinate in the fridge for at least 30 minutes (or up to 4 hours for deeper flavour).

Heat the ghee in a large saucepan over medium heat. Add the marinated chicken pieces, in batches, and cook until browned on all sides, about 5–7 minutes. Remove the chicken and set aside.

In the same pan, add the curry paste and cook for 2–3 minutes, until it becomes fragrant. Add the tomato paste and cook for another 5 minutes, allowing the flavours to meld.

Return the browned chicken to the pan. Stir in the cream, season with salt and simmer over low heat for 15–20 minutes, until the chicken is cooked through and the sauce thickens.

In the last 5 minutes of cooking, stir in the spinach until just wilted or warmed through.

If not using straight away, allow the butter chicken to cool, then transfer it to an airtight container and store it in the fridge for up to 4 days or freeze for up to 3 months.

Hints To avoid the chicken drying out, be careful not to overcook it when browning.

For a dairy-free version, replace yoghurt with plain coconut yoghurt, cream with coconut cream and butter with coconut oil.

Pizza bases

Prep 2 hours 30 minutes (including rising time and freezing time)
Cook 8–10 minutes
Makes 8 pizzas

| 1 kg (2 lb 3 oz) strong flour |
| 14 g (½ oz) instant yeast |
| 1 tablespoon sea salt |
| 700 ml (23½ fl oz) lukewarm water |
| 60 ml (2 fl oz/¼ cup) extra-virgin olive oil, plus extra for greasing |

This home-made pizza dough is simple to make and perfect for creating delicious, crispy pizzas (pages 86–87). Mastering your own pizza from scratch is an essential life skill; both your wallet and your tastebuds will be grateful.

Combine the strong flour, yeast and salt in a large mixing bowl. Make a well in the centre and pour in the lukewarm water and olive oil. Stir until a shaggy dough forms.

Turn the dough out onto a lightly floured surface and knead for about 10 minutes, until smooth and elastic. The dough should bounce back when you press it with your finger.

Grease a large bowl with the extra olive oil, place the dough inside and cover it with a damp tea towel (dish towel). Leave it in a warm place to rise for 1–2 hours, or until doubled in size.

Once risen, punch down the dough to release the air. Divide the dough into eight equal portions.

On a lightly floured surface, roll each portion into a thin circle or oval, about 30 cm (12 in) in diameter.

To freeze, place each rolled-out pizza base on baking paper and layer with more baking paper between each base. Wrap the entire stack tightly in plastic wrap, put them in an airtight container and freeze.

When ready to use, remove the desired number of pizza bases from the freezer and allow them to thaw in the fridge overnight or on the bench for a few hours.

Preheat the oven to 270°C (520°F), or as high as it will go, and bake your pizza with your choice of toppings for 8–10 minutes, or until golden and crispy.

Store the ready-rolled pizza bases in the fridge for up to 3 days or freeze for up to 3 months.

Hints Sprinkle the pizza trays with semolina before adding the bases to help prevent sticking.

If you have frozen your pizza bases and you prefer a chewier crust, let the thawed pizza bases rest at room temperature for 30 minutes before baking.

This dough can also be used for making calzones or focaccia.

(NF) (DF) (V) (VG)

WARMING & COMFORTING

Vegetable Sauce

Prep 30 minutes
Cook 60 minutes
Makes 1 litre (34 fl oz/4 cups)

1 kg (2 lb 3 oz) ripe tomatoes, quartered

2 large red capsicums (bell peppers), seeded and roughly chopped

500 g (1 lb 2 oz) pumpkin (winter squash), peeled, seeded and cut into small cubes

2 zucchini (courgettes), sliced into rounds

1 large onion, quartered

1 garlic bulb, unpeeled and cut in half horizontally

200 g (7 oz) cauliflower, broken into small florets

60 ml (2 fl oz/¼ cup) extra-virgin olive oil

125–250 ml (4–8½ fl oz/½–1 cup) vegetable stock or 400 g (14 oz) tinned crushed tomatoes, for thinning (optional)

sea salt

(GF) (NF) (DF) (V) (VG)

If you want to work smarter, not harder in the kitchen, this superstar sauce is for you. Not only is it nutrient-packed, it is highly versatile. Use it as a base for soups, stews or pastas. Use it for Butter chicken pizzas or Vegetable pizzas (pages 86–87). Or use it for Baked chicken parmigiana with cauli-potato mash (page 95).

Preheat the oven to 170°C (340°F) and line a large baking tray with baking paper.

Place the tomato, capsicum, pumpkin, zucchini, onion, garlic and cauliflower on the baking tray and drizzle generously with the olive oil and season with salt.

Toss the vegetables to ensure they are evenly coated with the oil and salt, then spread them out in a single layer on the tray.

Roast the vegetables, turning them halfway through cooking, for 45–60 minutes, or until they are tender, caramelised and juicy.

Remove the tray from the oven and allow the vegetables to cool slightly.

Squeeze the garlic from its skins and transfer the roasted vegetables to a food processor. Puree until smooth, adding vegetable stock or crushed tomatoes as needed to achieve the desired consistency. For a thicker sauce, suitable for pizza, add less liquid or none at all.

Taste and adjust the seasoning if necessary.

Use the sauce immediately, or let it cool completely before refrigerating or freezing. To freeze, spoon the sauce into ice cube trays and freeze until solid. Once frozen, transfer the cubes to a reusable ziplock bag for easy storage and defrosting as needed.

Store in the fridge for up to 1 week or freeze for up to 3 months.

Hints For a richer flavour, add 1 tablespoon of balsamic vinegar or 1 teaspoon of smoked paprika before blending.

For a quick bolognese, simply brown some minced (ground) beef and stir the sauce through.

For extra depth, roast with a handful of fresh herbs like thyme or rosemary, or stir in some basil leaves just before blending.

Beef brisket

Prep 10 minutes
Cook 8 hours
Makes 2 meals for 4 people

20 g (¾ oz) smoked paprika

2 tablespoons ground cumin

2 tablespoons garlic powder

2 tablespoons onion powder

80 g (2¾ oz/⅓ cup) soft brown sugar

2 teaspoons black pepper

2 teaspoons sea salt

1 × 2 kg (4 lb 6 oz) beef brisket

2 long green chillies, cut lengthways

250 ml (8½ fl oz/1 cup) barbecue sauce

125 ml (4 fl oz/½ cup) Worcestershire sauce

250 ml (8½ fl oz/1 cup) beef stock

This set-and-forget smoky and tender beef brisket is perfect for Beef brisket with vegetable gratin (page 88) and Nachos (page 90). Freeze any leftovers for your next Mexican night or grab-and-go dinner.

Combine the smoked paprika, cumin, garlic powder, onion powder, brown sugar, black pepper and salt in a bowl. Rub the spice mix all over the brisket.

Place the green chilli in the slow cooker, then put the seasoned brisket on top. Pour in the barbecue sauce, Worcestershire sauce and beef stock. Cover and cook on low for 8 hours, or until the brisket is tender. Alternatively, the brisket can be cooked in a covered roasting tin in the oven at 150°C (300°F) for 6–8 hours (make sure to check on it occasionally and add a few tablespoons of water if it's drying out).

Shred the brisket with a fork or slice it against the grain.

Store cooled leftover brisket in a container in the fridge for up to 1 week or freeze for up to 3 months.

(GF) (NF) (DF)

Butter chicken with flavoured rice and raita

GF NF

Prep 20 minutes
Cook 20 minutes
Serves 4

½ × quantity Butter chicken (page 80), hot
sea salt
spinach leaves, to serve (optional)

Flavoured rice

200 g (7 oz/1 cup) basmati rice
20 g (¾ oz) salted butter
1 tablespoon chopped dill
30 g (1 oz/¼ cup) slivered almonds or sultanas (golden raisins)

Raita

125 g (4½ oz/½ cup) coconut yoghurt
1 small garlic clove, minced
½ Lebanese (short) cucumber, grated and left to drain
1 tablespoon chopped dill
2 teaspoons lemon zest

There is no need for a store-bought paste with this easy, flavour-packed recipe that's sure to be a hit in your household. And since you've power-prepped the chicken, this truly is a 'curry in a hurry'.

For the flavoured rice, rinse the rice under cold water until the water runs clear.

In a large pot, bring 500 ml (17 fl oz/2 cups) of water to a boil, add the rice and season with salt. Reduce the heat to low, cover and cook for 12–15 minutes, until the rice is tender and the water is absorbed.

Once the rice is cooked, fluff it with a fork and stir in the butter, dill and slivered almonds or sultanas.

For the raita, combine the coconut yoghurt, garlic, drained cucumber, dill and lemon zest in a bowl. Mix well until combined.

Serve the butter chicken with the flavoured rice and top with a big dollop of raita. Scatter with some spinach leaves (if using).

THE WEEKLY GROCERY SHOP

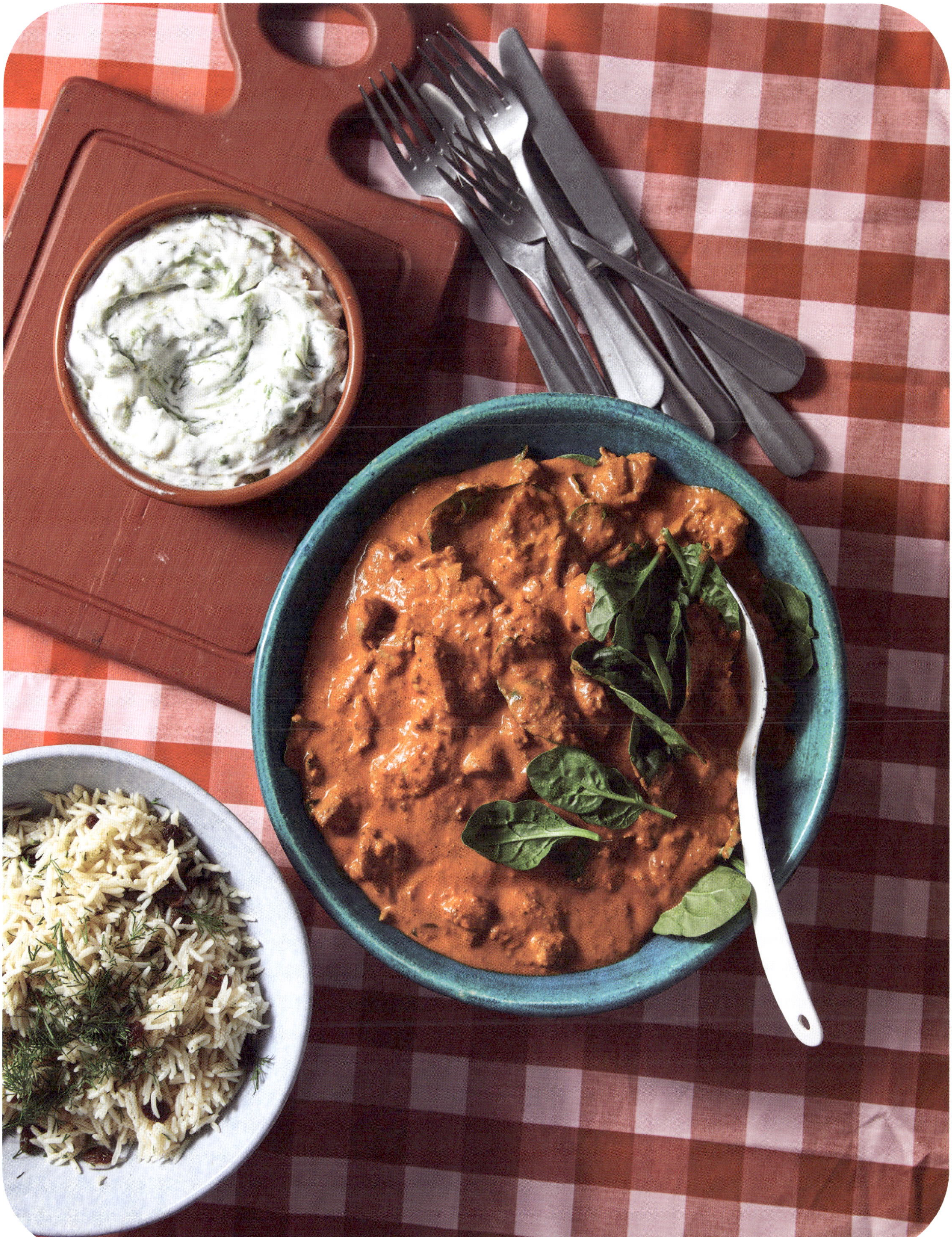

Pizzas

NF

Cook once, serve twice! Use your leftover Butter chicken by adding it to your DIY pizza base, then drizzle it with a creamy yoghurt sauce for melt-in-your-mouth Butter chicken pizzas. Or if you're after something lighter, try the Vegetable pizzas instead.

Butter chicken pizzas

Prep 15 minutes
Cook 15 minutes
Serves 4

1 × quantity Pizza bases (page 81)
250 ml (8½ fl oz/1 cup) Vegetable sauce (page 82)
200 g (7 oz) mozzarella, grated
1 small red onion, thinly sliced
350 g (12½ oz/2 cups) Butter chicken (page 80), finely chopped
chilli flakes, to serve
1 lemon, cut in half, to serve
coriander (cilantro) leaves, chopped, to serve (optional)

Yoghurt sauce

15 g (½ oz/¼ cup) mint leaves
15 g (½ oz/¼ cup) coriander stalks, chopped
60 g (2 oz/¼ cup) plain yoghurt, plus extra to fold through
sea salt

Preheat the oven to 220°C (430°F). If your pizza bases are frozen, lay them on baking trays and allow them to thaw slightly while preparing the other ingredients.

Spread each base with an even layer of the vegetable sauce. Add mozzarella to each pizza, then scatter the red onion over the cheese. Add the butter chicken pieces.

Bake the pizzas for 12–15 minutes, or until the edges are golden and the cheese is bubbling and slightly browned.

While the pizzas are baking, prepare the yoghurt sauce. Place the mint, coriander stalks and 60 g yoghurt in a food processor and blend until smooth and liquefied. Season with salt. Pour the mixture into a bowl and fold 1–2 tablespoons of extra yoghurt through the sauce to thicken it to your desired consistency.

Once the pizzas are ready, remove them from the oven. Drizzle each pizza with the yoghurt sauce, add chilli flakes and squeeze a bit of lemon juice over the top. Scatter with a handful of chopped coriander leaves (if using) and serve immediately.

Hints If you prefer a spicier kick, add some finely chopped fresh chilli along with the chilli flakes.

Make sure to blend the yoghurt sauce only briefly before folding in more yoghurt, as it can become too thin if over-blended.

You can prepare the pizzas ahead of time, then cover and refrigerate them until you're ready to bake and serve.

Vegetable pizzas

NF V

Prep 10 minutes
Cook 15 minutes
Serves 4

1 × quantity Pizza bases (page 81)
¼ broccoli head, thinly sliced
1 teaspoon extra-virgin olive oil
1 tablespoon lemon juice
½ teaspoon salt
125 ml (4 fl oz/½ cup) Vegetable sauce (page 82)
200 g (7 oz) mozzarella, grated
2 tablespoons onion jam or relish
goat's cheese, to serve

Preheat the oven to 220°C (430°F). If your pizza bases are frozen, lay them on baking trays and allow them to thaw slightly while preparing the other ingredients.

Toss the broccoli with the olive oil, lemon juice and salt in a small bowl.

Spread each base with an even layer of the Vegetable sauce. Add mozzarella to each pizza, along with the broccoli. Dollop the onion jam or relish on top.

Bake the pizzas for 12–15 minutes, or until the edges are golden and the cheese is bubbling and slightly browned.

Remove from the oven and top with a scattering of goat's cheese. Serve immediately.

Note If you plan to cook Vegetable pizzas, you will need to add these ingredients to the weekly shopping list on page 79. Only the ingredients for Butter chicken pizzas are on the list.

Hints Onion jam or relish can be found at the supermarket. It's likely to contain a high percentage of sugar, but you only use a small amount.

For a bit more texture, add some sliced cherry tomatoes along with the mozzarella.

This pizza is also delicious with a drizzle of extra-virgin olive oil just before serving.

WARMING & COMFORTING

Beef brisket with vegetable gratin

GF NF

Prep 20 minutes
Cook 1 hour
Serves 4

800 g (1 lb 12 oz) potatoes, peeled and quartered

400 g (14 oz) tinned corn kernels

1 large head of broccoli, cut into small florets

4 garlic cloves, minced

1 large onion, sliced

250 g (9 oz) smoked or plain cheddar, grated

1 tablespoon extra-virgin olive oil, plus extra for greasing

300 ml (10 fl oz) whipping cream

500 g (1 lb 2 oz) Beef brisket (page 83), sliced

sea salt and freshly ground black pepper

This rich and delicious main is perfect for sharing; the tender brisket complements the creamy, vegetable-packed gratin, making it a comforting family meal.

Preheat the oven to 180°C (360°F). Grease a casserole dish with the extra olive oil.

Place the potato in a large saucepan of salted water, bring to a boil and cook until just tender, about 10–12 minutes. Drain well.

Combine the cooked potato, corn kernels and broccoli florets in a large mixing bowl. Add the garlic, onion and three-quarters of the grated cheddar. Toss everything together with the olive oil, ensuring the vegetables are well coated. Season with salt and pepper, to taste.

Transfer the vegetable mixture to the casserole dish. Pour the cream on top, cover with baking paper and bake for 30–35 minutes, or until the vegetables are soft. Remove the baking paper, sprinkle the remaining cheddar on top. Increase the heat to 220°C (430°F) and bake for an additional 10–15 minutes, or until the top is golden and bubbly.

To reheat the brisket (if previously prepped), place the sliced pieces in a baking tray and cover with baking paper. Warm in the oven at 160°C (320°F) for 20–25 minutes, or until heated through. Alternatively, microwave on a medium setting in short intervals until warmed.

Serve the beef brisket alongside the vegetable gratin, allowing everyone to help themselves.

Hint The vegetable gratin can be made ahead of time and stored in the fridge for up to 3 days in an airtight container. Reheat in the oven at 180°C (360°F) until warmed through and bubbly for an easy side dish on the day of serving.

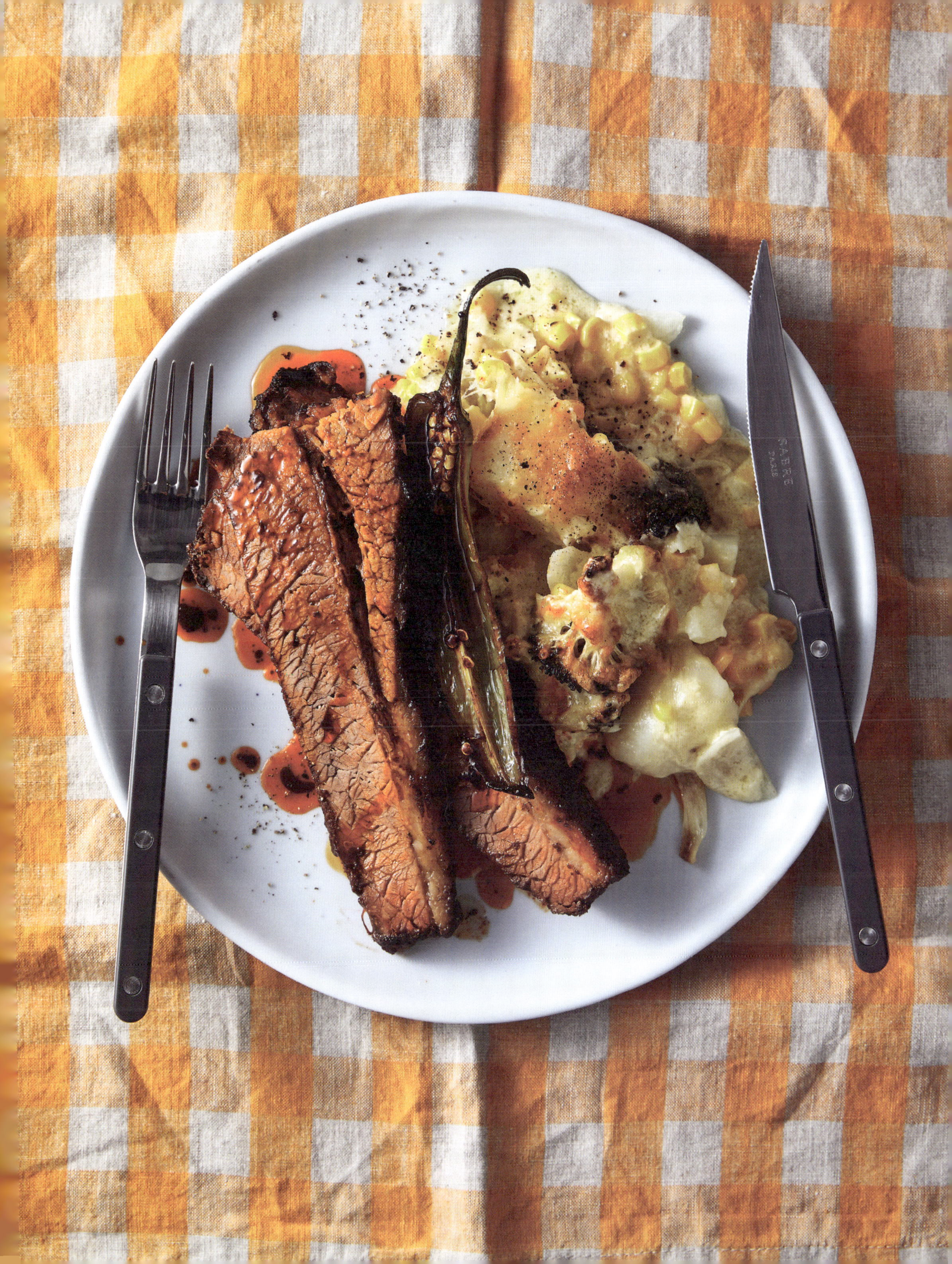

Nachos

GF NF

Prep 25 minutes
Cook 15 minutes
Serves 4

1 red capsicum (bell pepper), finely diced

1 red onion, finely diced

2 tablespoons taco seasoning

800 g (1 lb 12 oz) tinned crushed tomatoes

1 tablespoon tomato paste (concentrated puree)

400 g (14 oz) tinned black beans, drained and rinsed

500 g (1 lb 2 oz) Beef brisket (page 83), shredded

250 g (9 oz) cheddar, grated

230 g (8 oz) corn chips

olive-oil spray

chipotle paste, to serve (optional)

sour cream, to serve

Guacamole

2 avocados, roughly mashed

1 spring onion (scallion), finely chopped

100 g (3½ oz) cherry tomatoes, finely chopped

juice of 1 lime

sea salt

Up your nacho game with this gourmet, flavour-packed version. Quick to make, thanks to the cook-once-serve-twice beef brisket, this dish really comes into its own when you have a crowd to feed. Make it when avocados are in plentiful supply.

Preheat the oven to 180°C (360°F). Lightly spray a baking tray with olive-oil spray and set aside.

Heat a large saucepan over medium heat. Add the capsicum and red onion and sauté until softened, about 5 minutes. Stir in the taco seasoning, tomatoes, tomato paste and black beans. Add the shredded brisket and cook, stirring occasionally, until the mixture is thickened and heated through, about 10 minutes.

Scatter the baking tray with a handful of the grated cheese. Dollop half of the brisket sauce evenly over the cheese. Stand the corn chips upright, filling the gaps around the brisket sauce. Continue layering by dolloping the remaining brisket sauce and sprinkling cheese between the chips and sauce. Top the nachos with a final layer of grated cheese, ensuring it's evenly spread across the top, and lightly spray with olive-oil spray. Bake until the cheese is melted and bubbling, about 10–15 minutes.

While the nachos are baking, prepare the guacamole by combining the avocado, spring onion, cherry tomatoes, lime juice and salt, to taste.

If desired, mix the chipotle paste with sour cream for a smoky, spiced addition. Otherwise, serve the sour cream plain alongside the nachos.

Serve the nachos hot from the oven, topped with the guacamole and a side of sour cream.

Hints To make this dish ahead, prepare the brisket sauce and store it in the fridge in an airtight container for up to 1 week. Assemble and bake when ready to serve.

For extra crunch, grill (broil) the nachos for the last 2 minutes to crisp up the top layer of cheese.

Substitute corn chips with baked sweet potato slices for a twist on traditional nachos.

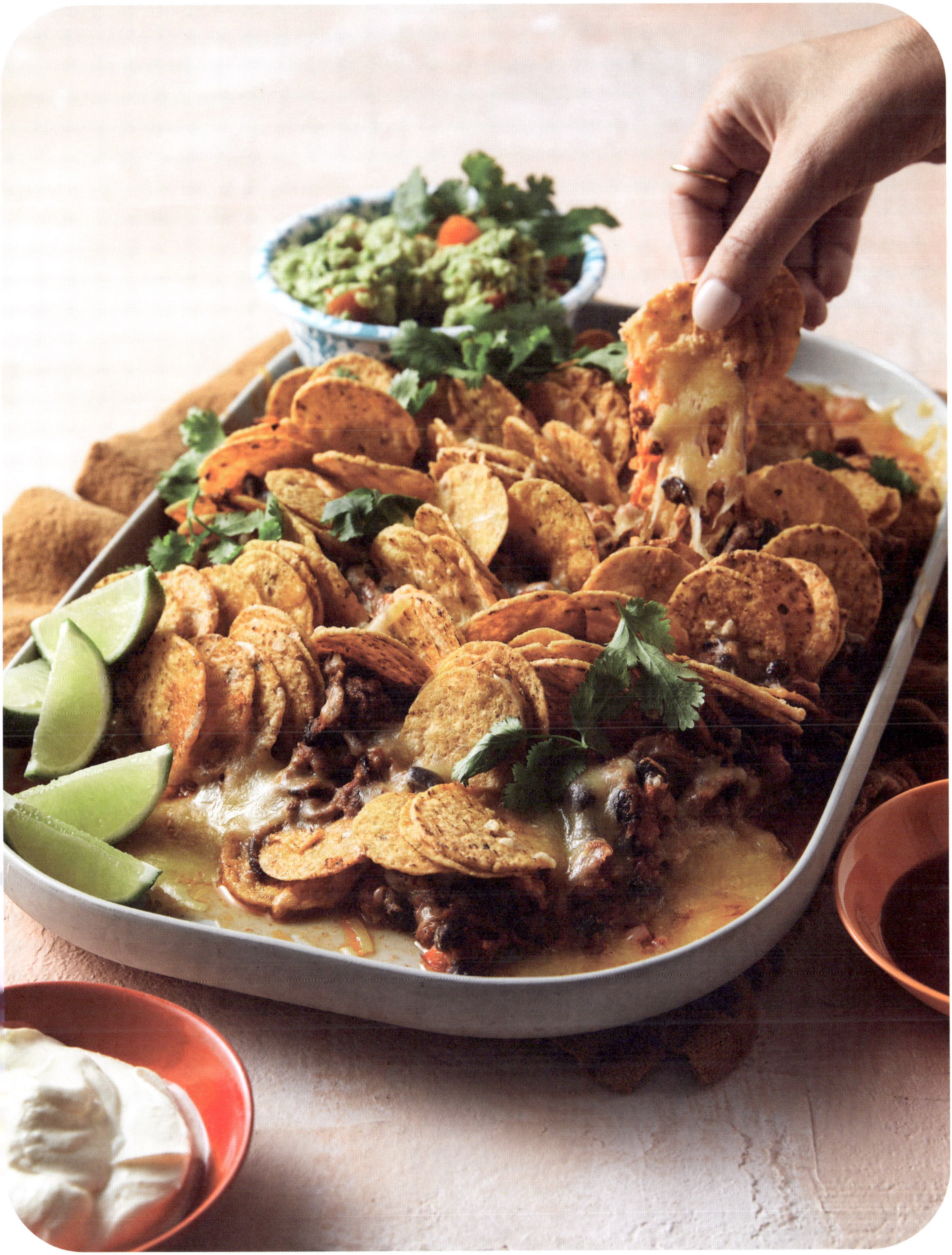

Roasted tomato, kale and sausage penne

NF

Prep 45 minutes
Cook 30 minutes
Serves 4

2 red onions, cut into wedges
4 garlic cloves, smashed
500 g (1 lb 2 oz) cherry tomatoes on the vine
6 pork sausages, casings removed and meat broken into pieces
½ bunch kale, stalks removed, leaves roughly chopped and massaged with extra-virgin olive oil
2 tablespoons extra-virgin olive oil, plus 1 tablespoon more
1 teaspoon paprika
1 teaspoon dried rosemary
400 g (14 oz) tinned chickpeas, drained
200 g (7 oz) tinned lentils, drained
2 tablespoons red-wine vinegar
50 g (1¾ oz) parmesan, grated, plus extra to serve
100 g (3½ oz) penne (or other pasta of your choice)
sea salt

The ultimate comfort food, this hearty pasta bake brings together vibrant vegetables, wholesome pulses and juicy pork sausages. Perfect for busy weeknights, it's both nutritious and nourishing.

Preheat the oven to 200°C (390°F).

In a large baking tray, combine the red onion, garlic and cherry tomatoes. Add the sausage pieces and kale to the tray. Drizzle with 2 tablespoons of olive oil, then sprinkle with paprika and dried rosemary. Add the chickpeas and lentils, and mix everything together. Season with salt, mix well and bake for 25–30 minutes, or until the sausage is cooked and the vegetables are beginning to crisp.

Meanwhile, cook the penne in a large saucepan of salted boiling water, according to the packet instructions, until al dente. Drain, reserving 60 ml (2 fl oz/¼ cup) of the pasta cooking water.

Remove the tray from the oven and, if you like, remove and set aside a handful of cherry tomatoes to serve on top. Drizzle with the red-wine vinegar and the remaining olive oil. Sprinkle generously with grated parmesan, then add the cooked penne and reserved pasta water to the tray, using a wooden spoon to scrape up any sticky bits from the bottom of the tray. Mix well.

Serve with the set-aside cherry tomatoes and extra parmesan on top.

Hints You can swap out the pork sausages for any sausages you prefer, including chicken or beef.

If you want extra crispiness, place the tray under the grill (broiler) for 2–3 minutes before serving.

The sausages and leftovers can be stored in the fridge and reheated in the oven or eaten cold as a pasta salad the next day.

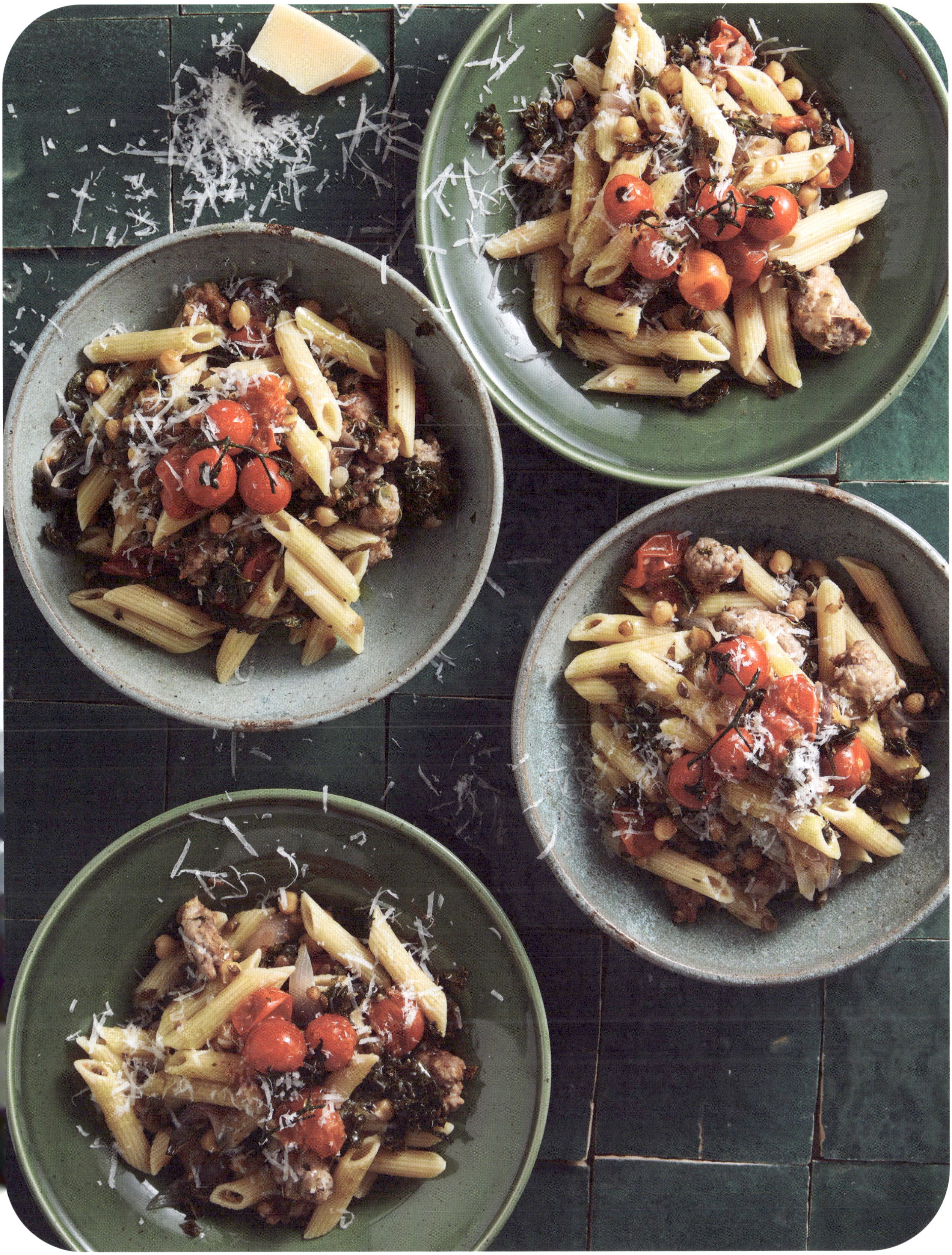

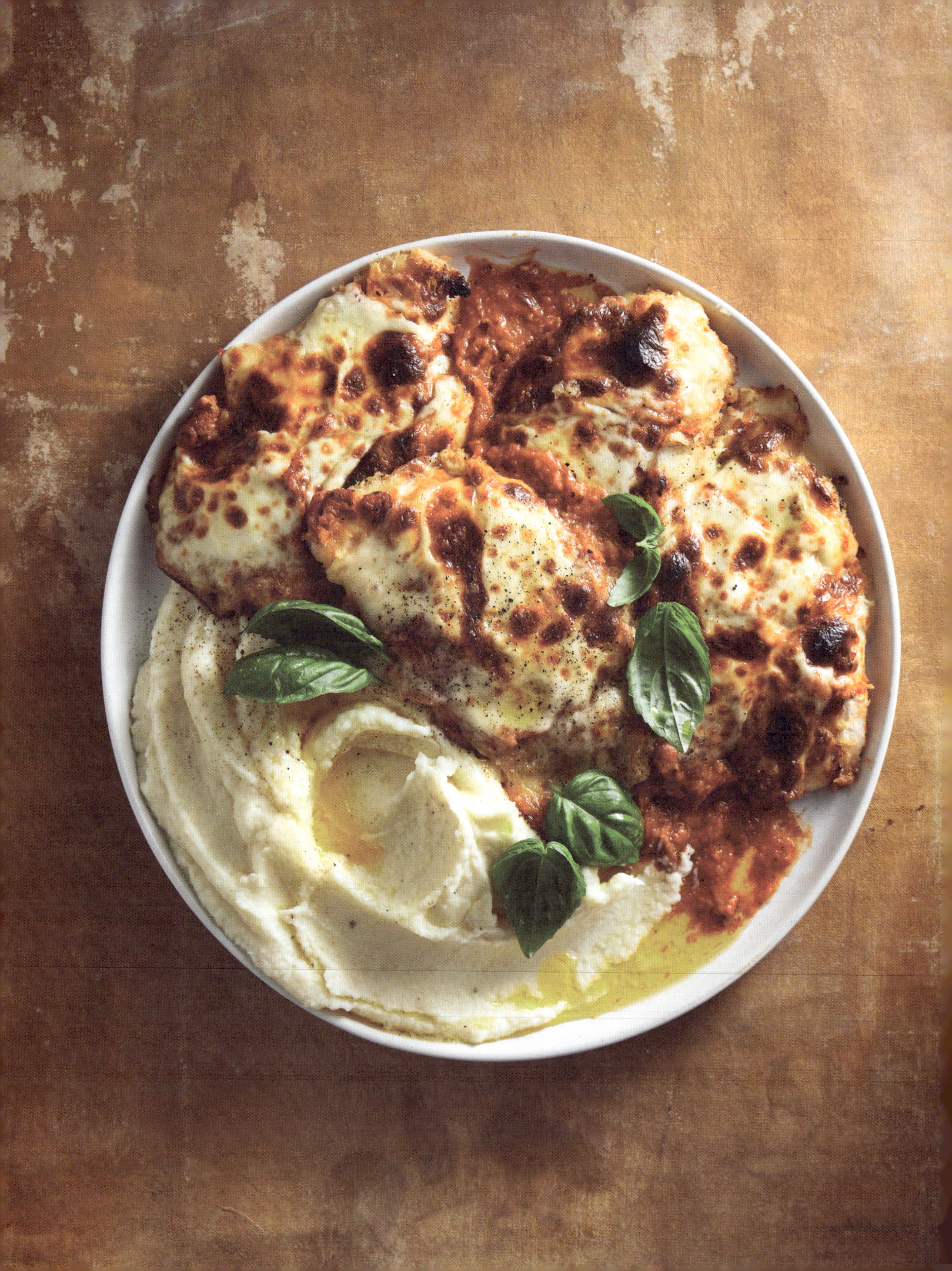

Baked chicken parmigiana with cauli-potato mash

Prep 45 minutes
Cook 30 minutes
Serves 4

90 g (3 oz) Japanese breadcrumbs

1 tablespoon dried oregano

1 teaspoon garlic powder

1 teaspoon onion powder

1 teaspoon chicken stock (bouillon) powder

2 × large boneless chicken breasts, cut in half horizontally and pounded thin

60 g (2 oz/¼ cup) mayonnaise

2 tablespoons extra-virgin olive oil

2 garlic cloves, crushed

½ bunch kale, stalks removed, leaves roughly chopped

sea salt

250 ml (8½ fl oz/1 cup) Vegetable sauce (page 82)

150 g (5½ oz) mozzarella, sliced

basil leaves, to serve

Cauli-potato mash

1 small head of cauliflower, cut into florets

2 large potatoes, peeled and chopped

40 g (1½ oz) salted butter

A cult classic with a twist, this chicken parmi is oven-baked for extra tenderness (and less time spent at your stove), then served with a double-veg mash.

Preheat the oven to 200°C (390°F) and line a baking tray with baking paper. Place a wire rack on top of the tray and brush it with olive oil.

Combine the breadcrumbs, oregano, garlic, onion and chicken stock powders in a bowl.

Brush each side of the chicken with mayonnaise, then coat with the seasoned breadcrumbs. Place the crumbed chicken on the wire rack.

Bake for 15–20 minutes, or until the chicken is golden and cooked through, turning once during cooking.

While the chicken is baking, prepare the cauli-potato mash. Boil the cauliflower and potato in salted water until tender, about 15 minutes. Drain, then mash with butter, adding salt to taste. Set aside.

Heat the olive oil in a saucepan over medium heat. Add the garlic and sauté for 30 seconds, until fragrant, then add the kale and cook for 3–5 minutes, until wilted. Season with salt and set aside.

Once the chicken is cooked, remove it from the oven and discard the wire rack. Place the chicken back on the tray. Ladle 60 ml (2 fl oz/¼ cup) of Vegetable sauce onto each schnitzel, spreading it evenly. Top with mozzarella slices, ensuring the cheese covers the chicken.

Switch the oven to the grill (broil) setting and place the chicken under the grill. Grill for 3–5 minutes, until the cheese is melted and bubbly, being careful not to burn the edges.

Serve the parmigiana with cauli-potato mash, sautéed kale (not pictured) and a scattering of basil leaves.

Hints Make sure the chicken is pounded uniformly to ensure even cooking.

Japanese breadcrumbs give a lighter, crispier texture than regular breadcrumbs.

Keep a close eye on the chicken while grilling the cheese to prevent it from burning.

WARMING & COMFORTING

Vegetable satay noodles

GF DF V VG

Prep 30 minutes
Cook 15 minutes
Serves 4

| 400 g (14 oz) rice noodles |
| 1 tablespoon avocado oil |
| 1 onion, julienned |
| 2 garlic cloves, minced |
| 1 tablespoon grated fresh ginger |
| 2 carrots, julienned |
| 1 red capsicum (bell pepper), julienned |
| 200 g (7 oz) broccoli stems, julienned |
| 150 g (5½ oz) sugar-snap peas, julienned |
| 200 g (7 oz) firm tofu, julienned |
| sea salt |
| roasted peanuts, chopped, to serve |
| coriander (cilantro) leaves, to serve (optional) |
| lime wedges, to serve |

Satay sauce

| 60 g (2 oz/¼ cup) smooth peanut butter |
| 60 ml (2 fl oz/¼ cup) soy sauce |
| 1 tablespoon pure maple syrup |
| 1 tablespoon sriracha |
| 1 tablespoon lime juice |
| 125 ml (4 fl oz/½ cup) coconut milk |

There is something comforting about a bowl of creamy noodles, but this quick, warming version is also nutrient-packed, thanks to the addition of fresh vegetables and tofu.

Soak the rice noodles in a large amount of cold water. (This softens them up just enough for further cooking and prevents them breaking up when you stir-fry them.)

Prepare the satay sauce by whisking the peanut butter, soy sauce, maple syrup, sriracha, lime juice, coconut milk and 60 ml (2 fl oz/¼ cup) of water together in a small bowl until smooth. Set aside.

Heat the oil in a large saucepan over medium heat. Add the onion, garlic and ginger and sauté for 2–3 minutes, until softened and fragrant. Add the carrot, capsicum, broccoli, sugar-snap peas and tofu to the pan. Stir-fry the vegetables and tofu for about 5–6 minutes, until they are tender-crisp. Add the noodles to the pan, tossing to combine with the vegetables and tofu. Cook for another 2 minutes, ensuring the noodles are softened.

Pour the satay sauce over the vegetables and tofu, stirring to coat everything evenly. Let the mixture simmer for 2–3 minutes, until the sauce thickens slightly.

Taste and adjust the seasoning with salt, if necessary.

To serve, top with chopped peanuts and coriander leaves (if using) and add lime wedges on the side.

Hints For a different texture, swap the rice noodles for soba or udon noodles.

Add a teaspoon of tamarind paste for a tangier flavour in the sauce.

To enhance the tofu's texture, consider pressing it (see page 197) before julienning to remove excess moisture.

Add leftover cooked meat such as shredded chicken or brisket to this dish for a non-vegetarian option.

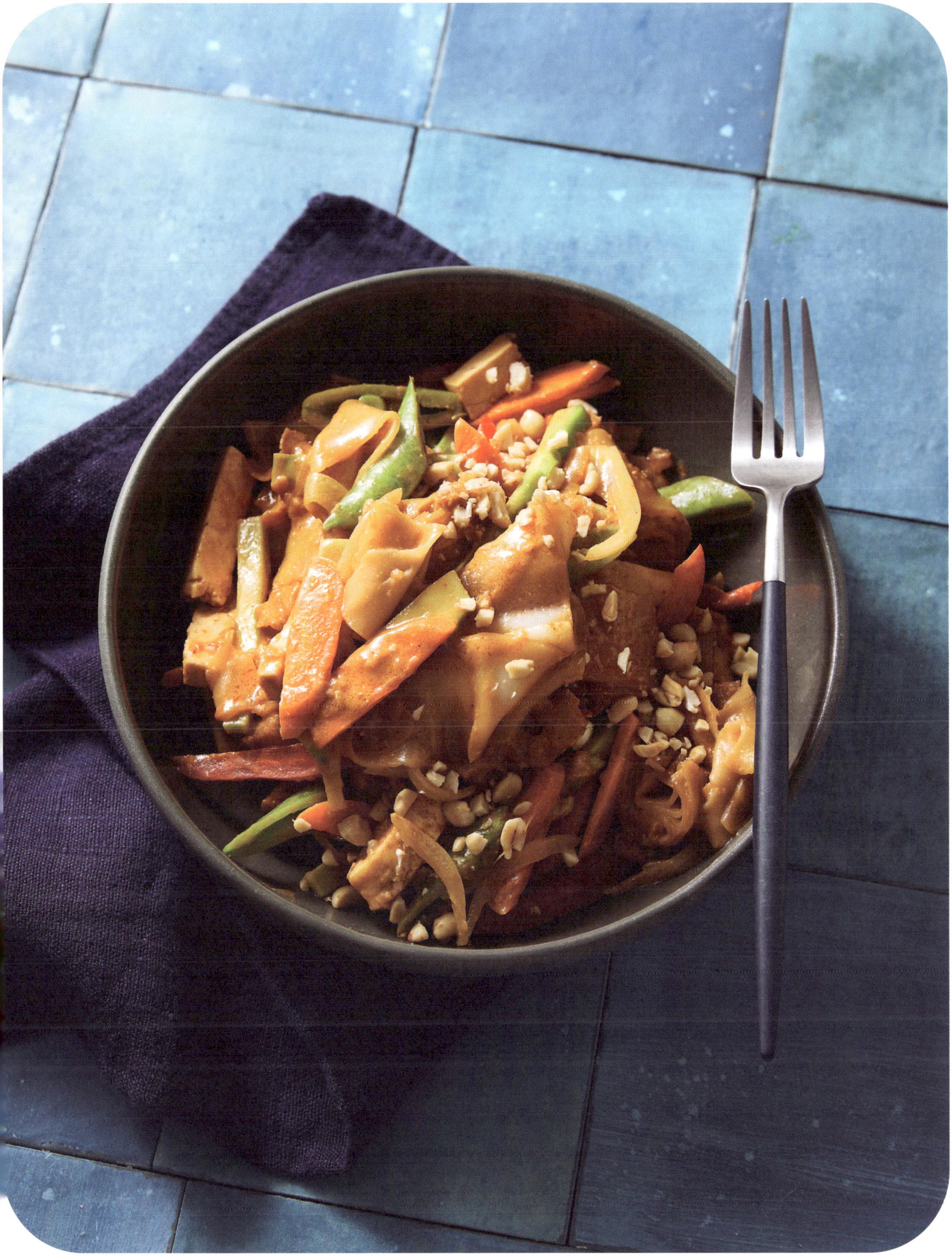

One-pan wonder

GF NF

Prep 30 minutes
Cook 20 minutes
Serves 4

2 tablespoons extra-virgin olive oil

4 pork sausages, casings removed and meat broken into pieces

1 large onion, sliced

3 garlic cloves, finely chopped

1 teaspoon oregano leaves, finely chopped, plus extra to serve

4 large field mushrooms, torn into pieces

200 g (7 oz) cherry tomatoes

4–6 large eggs

100 g (3½ oz) goat's cheese, crumbled (optional)

sea salt and freshly ground black pepper

crusty bread, buttered, to serve

I guarantee that you'll be returning to this simple, satisfying dish, which can be served for breakfast or brunch, for years to come. The field mushrooms supply a rich, earthy flavour and the minimal clean-up leaves you free to get on with your day.

Heat the olive oil in a large heavy-based frying pan over medium heat. Add the sausage pieces and cook, breaking them up further with a spatula, until browned, around 8–10 minutes. Add the onion and cook for 5 minutes, until softened. Stir in the garlic and oregano, cooking for an additional 1–2 minutes until fragrant.

Push the sausage mixture to the side of the pan to create space in the centre. Place the mushrooms and cherry tomatoes in the cleared area. Season with salt and pepper and cook for 5 minutes, until the mushrooms are golden and the tomatoes are just starting to blister.

Use the back of a spoon to make four to six small wells in the pan among the ingredients. Crack the eggs into the wells, ensuring they are evenly spaced. Sprinkle the crumbled goat's cheese around the pan (if using).

Reduce the heat to low and cover the pan. Cook for around 5 minutes, until the egg whites are set but the yolks remain runny. You may need to rotate the pan occasionally to ensure even cooking.

Remove the pan from the heat, top with the extra oregano and serve immediately with slices of buttered, crusty bread (or toast).

Hints Use a cast-iron pan for even heat distribution and to maintain the temperature.

If you prefer firmer egg yolks, cook the eggs for an additional 1–2 minutes, or until they reach your desired doneness.

For added flavour, sprinkle a pinch of smoked paprika or chilli flakes over the dish before serving.

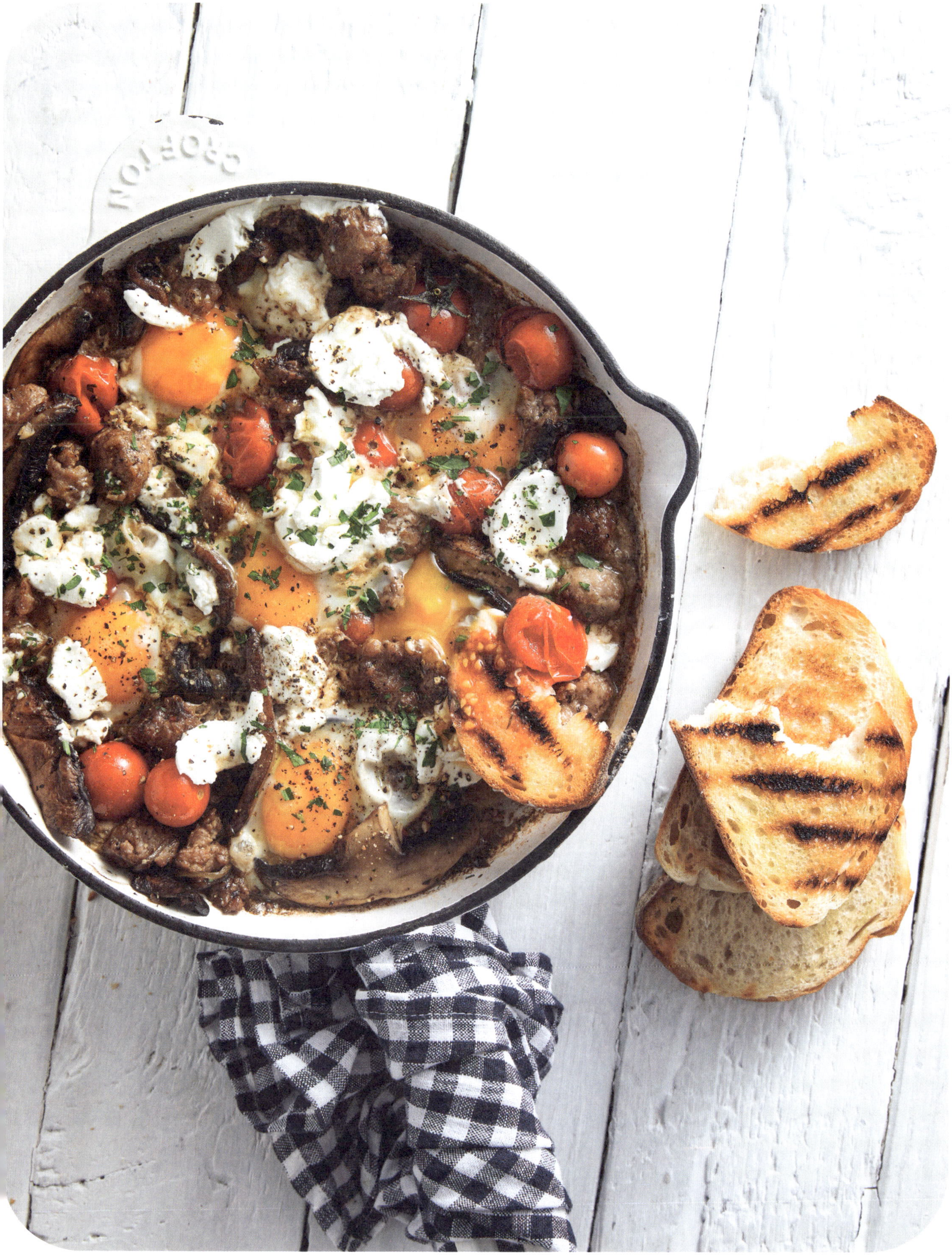
CROFTON

Choc, oat and raspberry muffins

NF V

Prep 15 minutes
Cook 20 minutes
Makes 12

½ avocado, mashed

120 ml (4 fl oz/½ cup) honey

60 g (2 oz/¼ cup) Greek-style yoghurt

60 ml (2 fl oz/¼ cup) coconut oil, melted

2 eggs

1 teaspoon vanilla extract

100 g (3½ oz/1 cup) rolled (porridge) oats

150 g (5½ oz/1 cup) wholemeal (whole-wheat) flour

1½ teaspoons baking powder

½ teaspoon bicarbonate of soda (baking soda)

¼ teaspoon ground cinnamon

¼ teaspoon salt

90 g (3 oz/½ cup) white chocolate chips

125 g (4½ oz/1 cup) fresh raspberries

Avocado is the hero in hiding here, creating a creamy richness that pairs perfectly with the sweetness of the raspberries and chocolate. Batch-prep and freeze these muffins, ready for when the snack cravings hit.

Preheat the oven to 180°C (360°F) and line a standard 12-hole muffin tin with paper liners.

Whisk the avocado, honey, yoghurt, melted coconut oil, eggs and vanilla extract together in a large bowl until smooth. Add the rolled oats, flour, baking powder, bicarbonate of soda, cinnamon and salt to the wet ingredients. Stir until just combined. Gently fold in the white chocolate chips and raspberries, being careful not to overmix.

Divide the batter evenly among the muffin holes, filling each about three-quarters full.

Bake for 18–20 minutes, or until a toothpick inserted into the centre comes out clean.

Allow the muffins to cool in the tin for 5 minutes before transferring them to a wire rack to cool completely.

Hints For a nutty twist, substitute 25 g (1 oz/¼ cup) of the rolled oats with ground almonds.

If using frozen raspberries, do not thaw them before adding to the batter to prevent bleeding.

These muffins freeze well, stored in an airtight container, for up to 3 months.

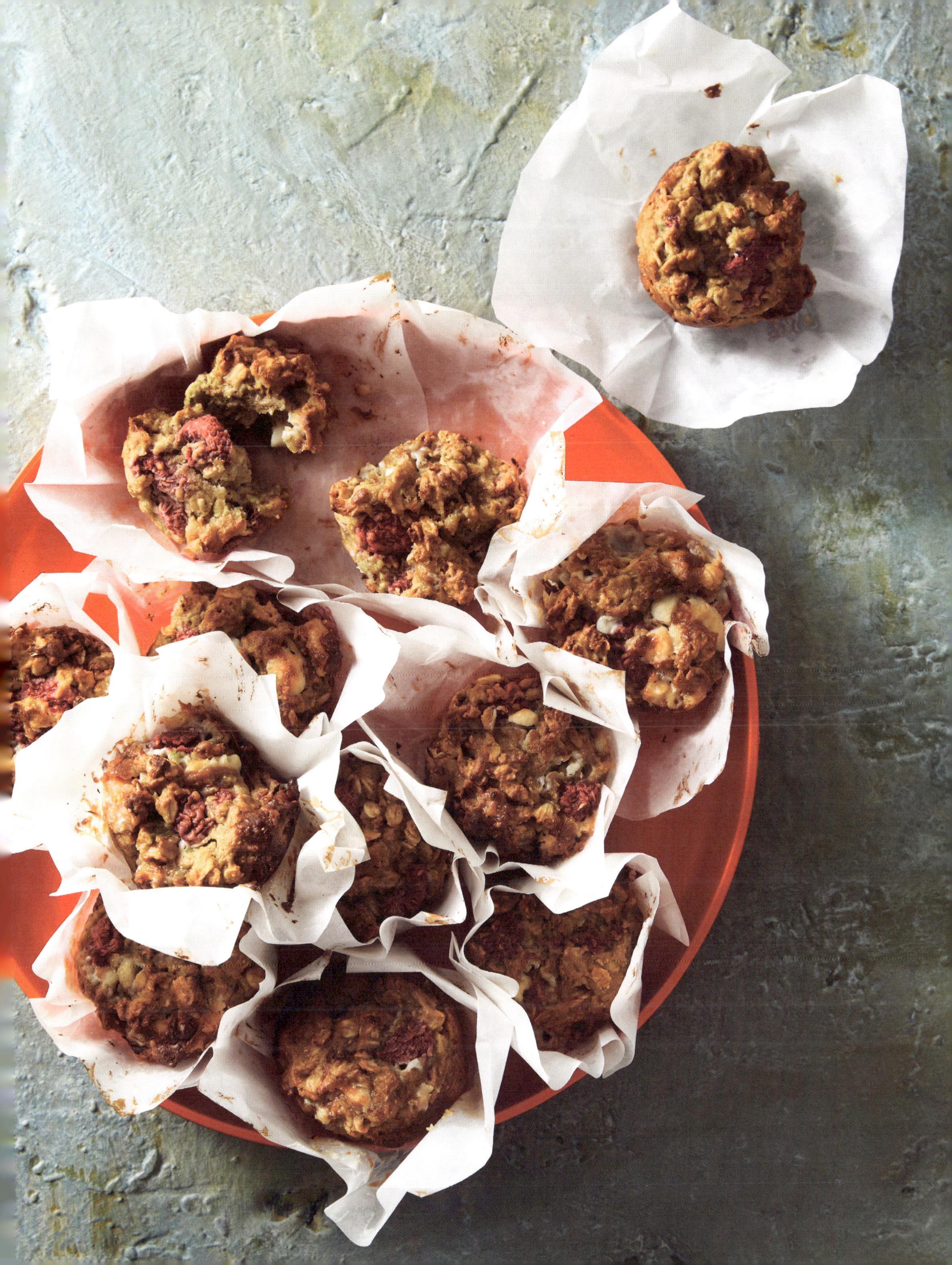

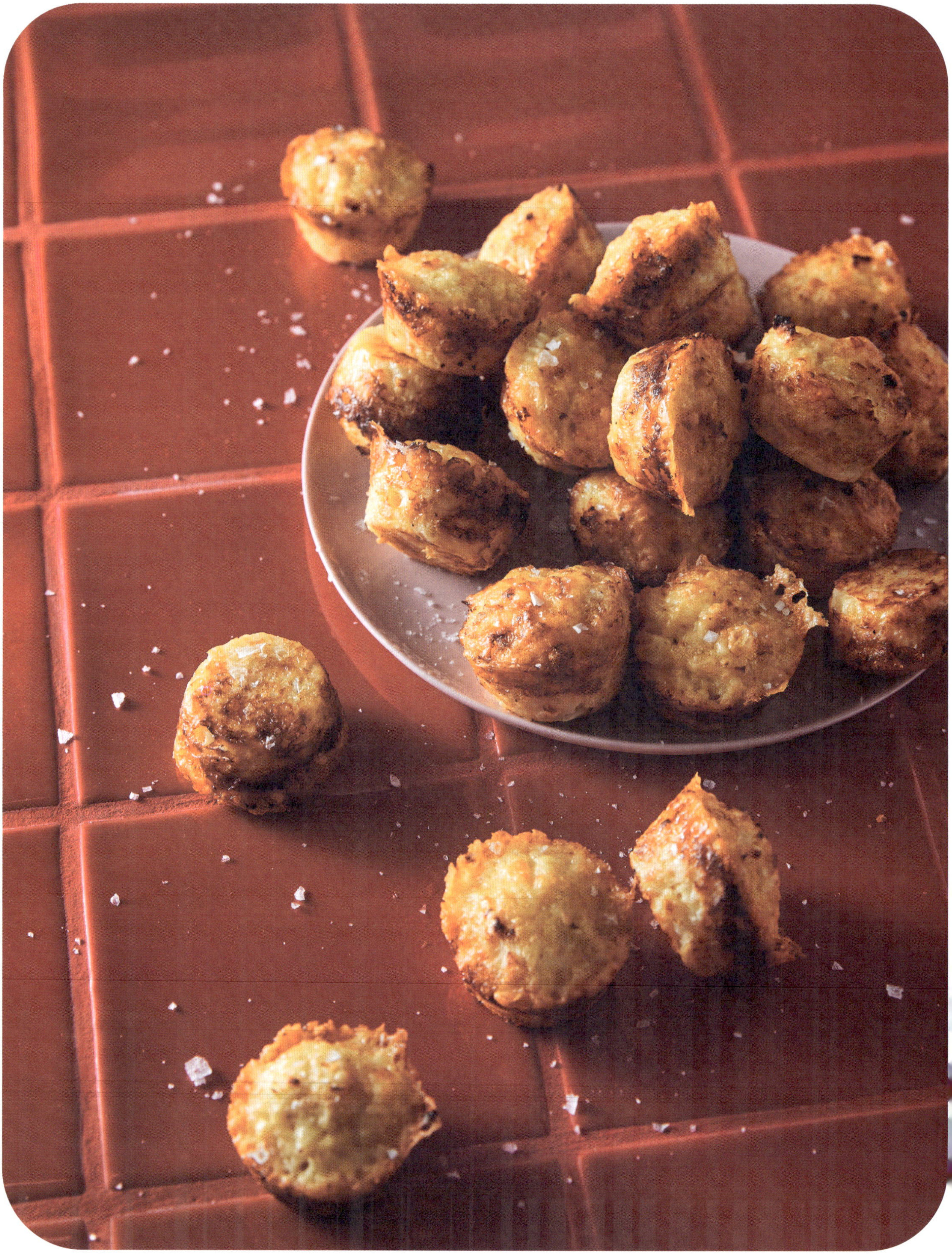

Cauliflower cheese bites

NF V

Prep 40 minutes
Cook 35 minutes
Makes 24

1 cauliflower, cut into florets

90 g (3 oz/¾ cup) cheddar, grated, plus 30 g (1 oz/¼ cup) more

15 g (½ oz/¼ cup) Japanese breadcrumbs

2 large eggs, beaten

25 g (1 oz/¼ cup) parmesan, grated

½ teaspoon garlic powder

sea salt and freshly ground black pepper

olive-oil spray

I make these when cauliflowers are cheap at the grocery store. But be warned – the blend of crispy cauliflower and cheesy goodness make them an addictive snack.

Preheat the oven to 200°C (390°F) and lightly spray a mini muffin tin with olive oil.

Steam the cauliflower florets until tender, about 8–10 minutes. Drain well and allow them to cool slightly. Alternatively, microwave them in a covered bowl for 5 minutes.

Mash the cauliflower in a large bowl (or use a food processor) until broken down but still slightly chunky, like rice. Add the 90 g (3 oz/¾ cup) of cheddar, the breadcrumbs, eggs, parmesan, garlic powder and some salt and pepper, and stir until well combined.

Divide the mixture between the muffin holes and top with a small sprinkle of the remaining cheddar.

Lightly spray the bites with olive-oil spray.

Bake for 20 minutes, or until golden and crispy.

Serve warm, as they are or with your favourite dipping sauce.

Hints For extra crispiness, turn the bites halfway through baking.

Add a pinch of chilli flakes to the mixture for a spicy kick.

These bites freeze well; store them in an airtight container for up to 3 months. Reheat in the oven to regain crispiness.

WARMING & COMFORTING

Tahini maple caramel and choc coconut banana splits

GF V

Prep 20 minutes
Cook 10 minutes
Serves 4

65 g (2¼ oz/¼ cup) tahini
160 ml (5½ fl oz) pure maple syrup
100 g (3½ oz) 70% dark chocolate, chopped
2 tablespoons coconut oil, melted
4 bananas, split in half lengthways
4 scoops of vanilla ice cream (or your favourite flavour)
70 g (2½ oz/½ cup) crushed peanuts

Rich, nutty tahini and sweet maple syrup combine to make a lip-smacking caramel sauce for these decadent banana splits. Make them to use up any uneaten bananas.

Whisk the tahini and maple syrup together in a small bowl until smooth and well combined. Set aside.

Melt the dark chocolate in a microwave-safe bowl in 20-second intervals, stirring between each, until fully melted and smooth. Whisk in the coconut oil until well combined.

Place pieces of split banana into each serving bowl. Add a scoop of ice cream, then drizzle the tahini maple caramel over the ice cream, followed by the dark chocolate. Sprinkle crushed peanuts on top.

Serve immediately before the chocolate shell hardens.

Hints Use room temperature tahini and maple syrup to ensure they mix together smoothly.

The dark chocolate magic shell will harden quickly once it touches the cold ice cream, so drizzle it right before serving.

For an extra touch, sprinkle some sea salt flakes over the banana splits to enhance the flavour of the toppings.

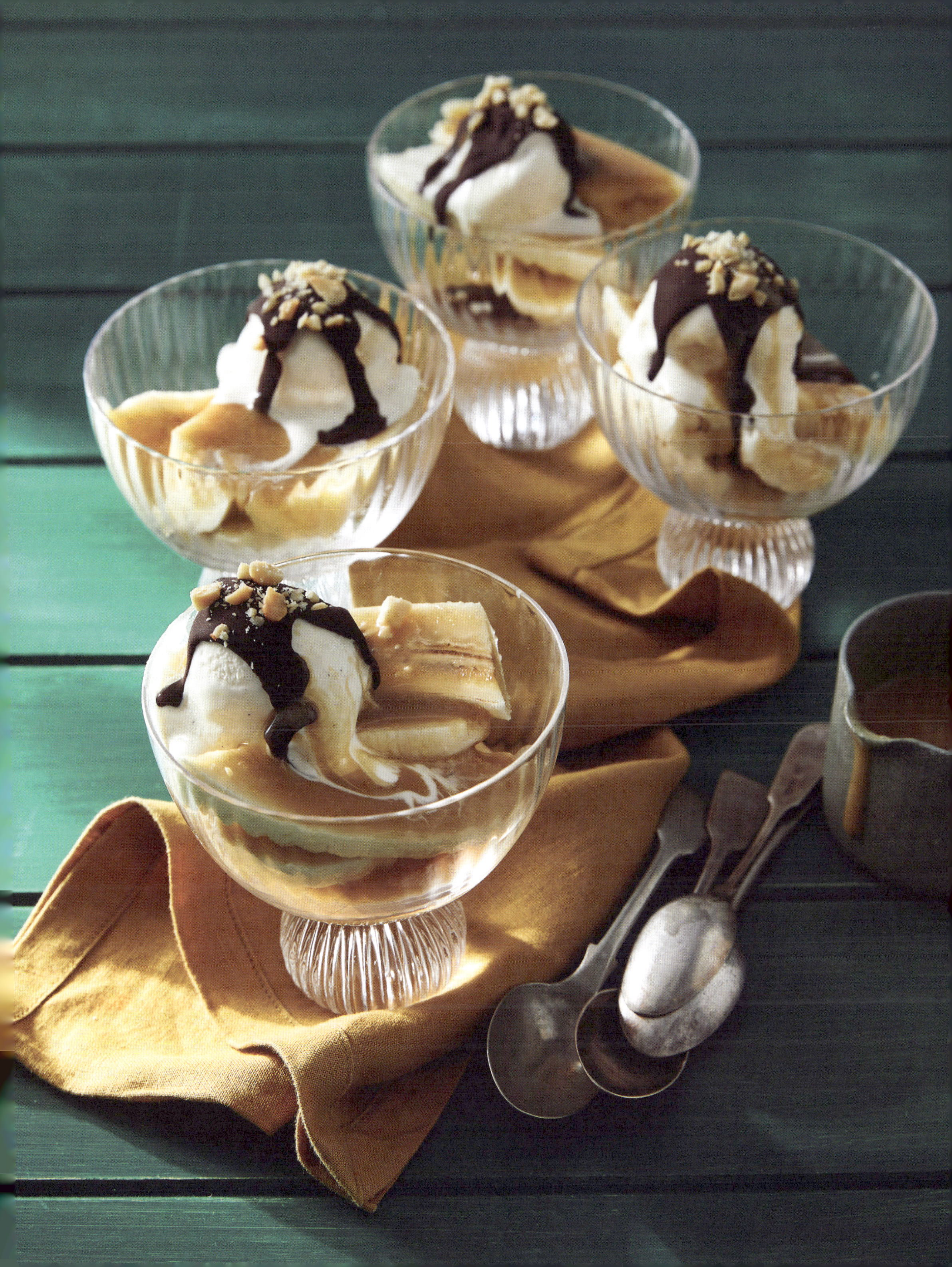

Week 2 menu

Power prep

Veggie-loaded bolognese sauce
Whole roast chicken
Home-made tomato passata
Chilli jam marinade

Dinners

No-fuss vegetable lasagne
Two-way bolognese:
Mexi-spice tray bake or Sweet potato shepherd's pies
Roast chicken with garlic, spinach and dill rice
Chicken pie with artichokes and olives
Marinated lamb with caponata
Chilli jam minced beef with rice and dressed vegetable pickles
Chicken rice mountains and Greek salad

Breakfasts

Toasted cheese soldiers with dippy eggs
Classic French toast with cinnamon and maple butter

Snack

Cheeseburger triangles

Sweet

Ricotta berry tart

Week 2 shopping list

Fruit & vegetables

- [ ] 90 g (3 oz) bean sprouts
- [ ] 4 carrots
- [ ] 1 large green capsicum (bell pepper)
- [ ] 1 large + 1 medium red capsicum (bell peppers)
- [ ] 2 celery stalks
- [ ] 1 bunch coriander (cilantro) (optional)
- [ ] 1 large + 1 medium Lebanese (short) cucumber
- [ ] 1 bunch dill
- [ ] 400 g (14 oz) baby spinach leaves
- [ ] 1 small + 1 medium eggplant (aubergine)
- [ ] 3 garlic bulbs
- [ ] 10 cm (4 in) piece of fresh ginger
- [ ] 2 large leeks
- [ ] 6 lemons
- [ ] 200 g (7 oz) mushrooms
- [ ] 2 large + 3 medium onions
- [ ] 1 red onion
- [ ] 1 tablespoon oregano leaves
- [ ] 1 bunch flat-leaf (Italian) parsley
- [ ] 400 g (14 oz) pumpkin (winter squash)
- [ ] 1 bunch rosemary
- [ ] 1 small bunch spring onions (scallions)
- [ ] 1 teaspoon tarragon leaves
- [ ] 2 large tomatoes
- [ ] 2 large + 3 medium zucchini (courgettes)

Pantry & baking

- [ ] 400 g (14 oz) tinned white beans
- [ ] 200 g (7 oz) tinned lentils
- [ ] 80 g (2¾ oz) pine nuts
- [ ] 400 g (14 oz) jasmine rice
- [ ] 400 g (14 oz) basmati rice
- [ ] 95 g (3¼ oz) soft brown sugar
- [ ] 1 teaspoon white (granulated) sugar
- [ ] 2 tablespoons taco seasoning
- [ ] 130 g (4½ oz) tomato paste (concentrated puree)
- [ ] 1.6 kg (3½ lb) tinned crushed tomatoes
- [ ] 8 large tortillas
- [ ] 125 ml (4 fl oz) red wine (optional)

Fridge

- [ ] 250 g (9 oz) cheddar
- [ ] 200 g (7 oz) crème fraîche
- [ ] 4 eggs
- [ ] 100 g (3½ oz) feta
- [ ] 6 fresh lasagne sheets
- [ ] 60 ml (2 fl oz) milk
- [ ] 150 g (5½ oz) mozzarella
- [ ] 170 g (6 oz) green olives
- [ ] 95 g (3¼ oz) kalamata olives
- [ ] 50 g (1¾ oz) parmesan
- [ ] 250 g (9 oz) ricotta

Meat & poultry

- [ ] 750 g (1 lb 11 oz) minced (ground) beef
- [ ] 2 × 1.4–1.6 kg (3 lb 1 oz–3½ lb) whole chickens
- [ ] 2 × large chicken breasts
- [ ] 4 lamb chump chops
- [ ] 250 g (9 oz) minced (ground) veal

Freezer

- [ ] 375 g (13 oz) filo pastry sheets
- [ ] 100 g (3½ oz) frozen spinach

Veggie-loaded bolognese sauce

Prep 15 minutes
Cook 1 hour
Makes 1.5–2 kg
(3 lb 5 oz–4 lb 6 oz)

2 tablespoons extra-virgin olive oil
1 onion, finely chopped
2 garlic cloves, crushed
250 g (9 oz) minced (ground) beef
250 g (9 oz) minced (ground) veal
2 carrots, finely diced
2 celery stalks, finely diced
1 zucchini (courgette), grated
1 red capsicum (bell pepper), finely diced
200 g (7 oz) mushrooms, finely chopped
2 tablespoons tomato paste (concentrated puree)
400 g (14 oz) tinned crushed tomatoes
125 ml (4 fl oz/½ cup) beef stock
125 ml (4 fl oz/½ cup) red wine (optional)
1 teaspoon dried oregano
1 teaspoon dried basil
1 bay leaf
60 ml (2 fl oz/¼ cup) milk
sea salt and freshly ground black pepper

(GF) (NF)

Batch-cooking a beautiful rich bolognese sauce will set you up for many stress-free dinners. This quantity is more than enough to make the Mexi-spice tray bake (page 114) and the Sweet potato shepherd's pies (page 117). But why not double it and freeze half for another week?

Heat the olive oil in a large saucepan over medium heat. Add the onion and garlic and sauté for 2–3 minutes, until softened. Add the minced beef and veal and cook, breaking it up with a spoon, for 7–10 minutes, or until browned.

Stir in the carrot, celery, zucchini, capsicum and mushrooms and cook for 5–7 minutes, until the vegetables begin to soften.

Add the tomato paste, cook for 1–2 minutes, then stir in the tinned tomatoes, beef stock, red wine (if using), oregano, basil and bay leaf. Season with salt and pepper.

Simmer the sauce on low heat for 45–60 minutes, stirring occasionally.

Remove the bay leaf, stir in the milk and cook for a further 10 minutes.

Allow the sauce to cool completely before storing in an airtight container in the fridge for up to 3 days or freeze for up to 3 months.

Hints For a vegetarian version, replace the minced beef and veal with a mixture of finely chopped porcini mushrooms (rehydrate the dried mushrooms before chopping) and tinned brown lentils (drained). Cook as per the method, omitting the beef stock and the milk. Instead, use vegetable stock, plus the liquid from rehydrating the porcini mushrooms, and finish with a splash of balsamic vinegar.

For extra richness, add a small piece of parmesan rind to the sauce during simmering (remove before serving).

This bolognese can be doubled and frozen for later use, making it a great meal-prep option.

THE WEEKLY GROCERY SHOP

Whole roast chicken

Prep 15 minutes
Cook 1 hour
Makes 2 meals for 4 people

2 × 1.4–1.6 kg (3 lb 1 oz–3½ lb) whole chickens

juice of 2 lemons

1 tablespoon extra-virgin olive oil, plus extra if needed

sea salt

Hint Leftover roast chicken can be shredded and used in a variety of dishes, such as salads, sandwiches or soups.

Roast chickens are so versatile! Use one for a classic roast (page 118) and save the other for pie (page 120). Don't forget to reserve and freeze the bones to make Chicken bone broth (page 139).

The night before roasting, place the chickens on a wire rack in the fridge, uncovered, to dry out the skin. This ensures extra-crispy skin during roasting.

The next day, preheat the oven to 180°C (360°F).

Remove the chickens from the fridge and let them come to room temperature. Drizzle the lemon juice over the chickens, rubbing it into the skin, then rub them generously with the olive oil and season well with salt. Place the squeezed lemon halves into the chicken cavities.

Place the chickens in a roasting tin and roast for 50–60 minutes, or until the chickens are fully cooked. (They should reach an internal temperature of 75°C /170°F in the thickest part of the thigh.)

Once roasted, remove the chickens from the oven and let them rest for 10 minutes. Use one chicken for Roast chicken with garlic, spinach and dill rice (page 118) and set aside the other for another meal, reserving the pan juices.

Store the roast chicken in an airtight container in the fridge for up to 4 days or freeze for up to 3 months.

(GF) (NF) (DF)

WARMING & COMFORTING

Home-made tomato passata

Prep 10 minutes
Cook 2 hours
Makes 700 ml (23½ fl oz/2¾ cups)

2 tablespoons extra-virgin olive oil
½ onion, finely chopped
1 carrot, grated
2–3 garlic cloves, chopped
800 g (1 lb 12 oz) tinned crushed tomatoes
1 bay leaf
1 teaspoon sea salt
white pepper

I believe that making your own passata – watching it simmer away in the knowledge that you are producing a classic staple that can be used across many meals – releases endorphins. Embrace your inner nonna and use it for No-fuss vegetable lasagne (page 112) and Marinated lamb with caponata (page 122).

Heat the olive oil in a saucepan over medium heat. Add the onion and carrot and cook until the onion is transparent, around 5 minutes. Add the garlic and cook until fragrant, around 1 minute more.

Add the tomatoes and 400 ml (13½ fl oz) of water. Stir to combine, then add the bay leaf and season with salt and white pepper.

Bring to a simmer, reduce the heat to low and cook for 1–2 hours, stirring occasionally.

Allow to cool completely before transferring to portioned airtight containers. Refrigerate for up to 1 week or freeze for up to 3 months.

(GF) (NF) (DF) (V) (VG)

Chilli jam marinade

Prep 5 minutes
Cook 7 minutes
Makes 750–875 ml
(25½–29½ fl oz/3–3½ cups)

250 g (9 oz/1 cup) sambal oelek
95 g (3¼ oz/½ cup) soft brown sugar
125 ml (4 fl oz/½ cup) rice vinegar
80 ml (2½ fl oz/⅓ cup) tamari or soy sauce
80 ml (2½ fl oz/⅓ cup) fish sauce
8 garlic cloves, minced
6 cm (2½ in) piece of fresh ginger, minced
80 ml (2½ fl oz/⅓ cup) coconut oil or extra-virgin olive oil
2 tablespoons avocado oil

Sweet and spicy, this marinade is as delicious dolloped on eggs or a burger as it is added to a stir-fry. (And it makes a great gift, too, dressed up in a fancy jar!) Use it to make Chilli jam minced beef with rice and dressed vegetable pickles (page 124), as well as Corn cobettes with cheese, chilli mayonnaise and lime (page 190).

Combine the ingredients in a large saucepan over medium heat. Simmer, stirring occasionally, for 5–7 minutes or until the sugar is dissolved and the mixture thickens slightly.

Allow to cool completely before transferring to portioned airtight containers. Refrigerate for up to 1 week or freeze for up to 3 months.

Hints When freezing, label portions with the date to keep track of freshness.

For a tasty salad dressing, mix 2 tablespoons of the chilli jam marinade with 80 ml (2½ fl oz/⅓ cup) of lime juice and 1 tablespoon of tamari until well combined.

(GF) (NF) (DF)

WARMING & COMFORTING

No-fuss vegetable lasagne

NF V

Prep 30 minutes
Cook 45 minutes
Serves 4

olive oil, for greasing
250 g (9 oz) ricotta
zest of 1 lemon
1 tablespoon chopped oregano leaves
50 g (1¾ oz/½ cup) parmesan, grated
2 garlic cloves, minced
500 ml (17 fl oz/2 cups) Home-made tomato passata (page 110) or store-bought passata (pureed tomatoes)
6 fresh lasagne sheets, cut into 5 cm (2 in) strips
400 g (14 oz) pumpkin (winter squash), thinly sliced
2 zucchini (courgettes), thinly sliced
1 small eggplant (aubergine), thinly sliced
100 g (3½ oz) frozen spinach, thawed and drained
150 g (5½ oz/1 cup) mozzarella, grated
sea salt

It's time to break the rules and go rogue. This fun take on a traditional lasagne is packed with vegetables and promotes freedom in the kitchen. Skip the layering and start scrunching!

Preheat the oven to 200°C (390°F). Grease a large casserole dish with olive oil.

Combine the ricotta, lemon zest, oregano, parmesan and garlic in a mixing bowl and season with salt. Set aside.

Pour half of the passata into the base of the prepared casserole dish, spreading it evenly.

Take the lasagne sheet strips and stand them upright in the tomato passata, scrunching them slightly to create ribbons. Alternate with the slices of pumpkin, zucchini and eggplant, also standing them upright between the lasagne sheets.

Nestle the spinach between the lasagne and vegetables, ensuring the dish is tightly packed.

Dollop the ricotta mixture in between the lasagne ribbons and vegetables, supporting the 'walls' and adding extra flavour.

Pour the remaining tomato passata over the top, making sure everything is evenly covered.

Top with the mozzarella, covering the surface evenly.

Bake for 45 minutes, or until the top is golden and bubbling.

Let the dish rest for a few minutes before serving.

Hints Use a mandoline to achieve uniformly sliced pumpkin, zucchini and eggplant pieces.

If making ahead, assemble the dish without baking, cover it with baking paper and store it in the fridge. Bake directly from the fridge, adding an extra 10 minutes to the cooking time.

Try adding a layer of sautéed mushrooms or sliced capsicum (bell pepper) for additional flavour and texture.

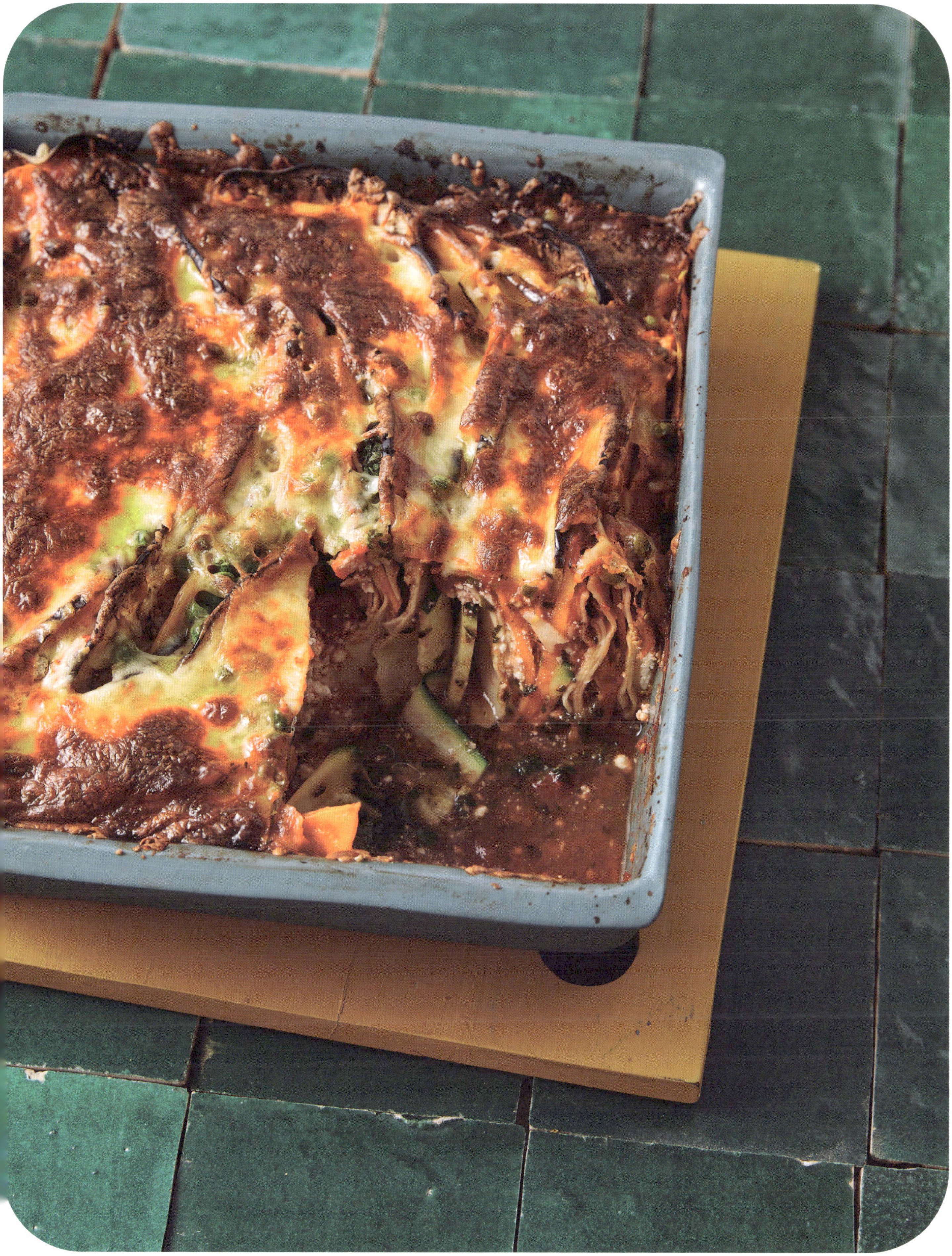

Two-way bolognese

On those days when kitchen motivation is low or time is short, a pre-prepared bolognese sauce will save you. These two fun takes on a bolognese-inspired dish (a tray bake and a pie) are so different that no one will guess they contain the same base ingredient.

Mexi-spice tray bake

(NF)

Prep 15 minutes
Cook 15 minutes
Serves 4

1 tablespoon taco seasoning

200 g (7 oz) tinned lentils, drained

500 g (1 lb 2 oz) Veggie-loaded bolognese sauce (page 108)

250 ml (8½ fl oz/1 cup) Home-made tomato passata (page 110) or store-bought passata (pureed tomatoes)

8 large store-bought or Home-made tortillas (page 199)

250 g (9 oz) cheddar, grated

coriander (cilantro) leaves, chopped, to serve (optional)

Preheat the oven to 200°C (390°F).

Mix the taco seasoning and lentils into the cooked bolognese sauce.

Spread half of the passata in the bottom of a casserole dish.

Fill the tortillas with the seasoned bolognese, roll them up and place them on top of the passata in the dish.

Top with the remaining passata and the grated cheese.

Bake for 30–40 minutes, until the cheese is melted and bubbling.

Top with the coriander (if using) to serve.

Hints Serve with sour cream and lime wedges on the side for an extra pop of flavour.

Add chopped jalapeños for a spicy kick.

For a healthier option, use wholemeal (whole-wheat) tortillas.

THE WEEKLY GROCERY SHOP

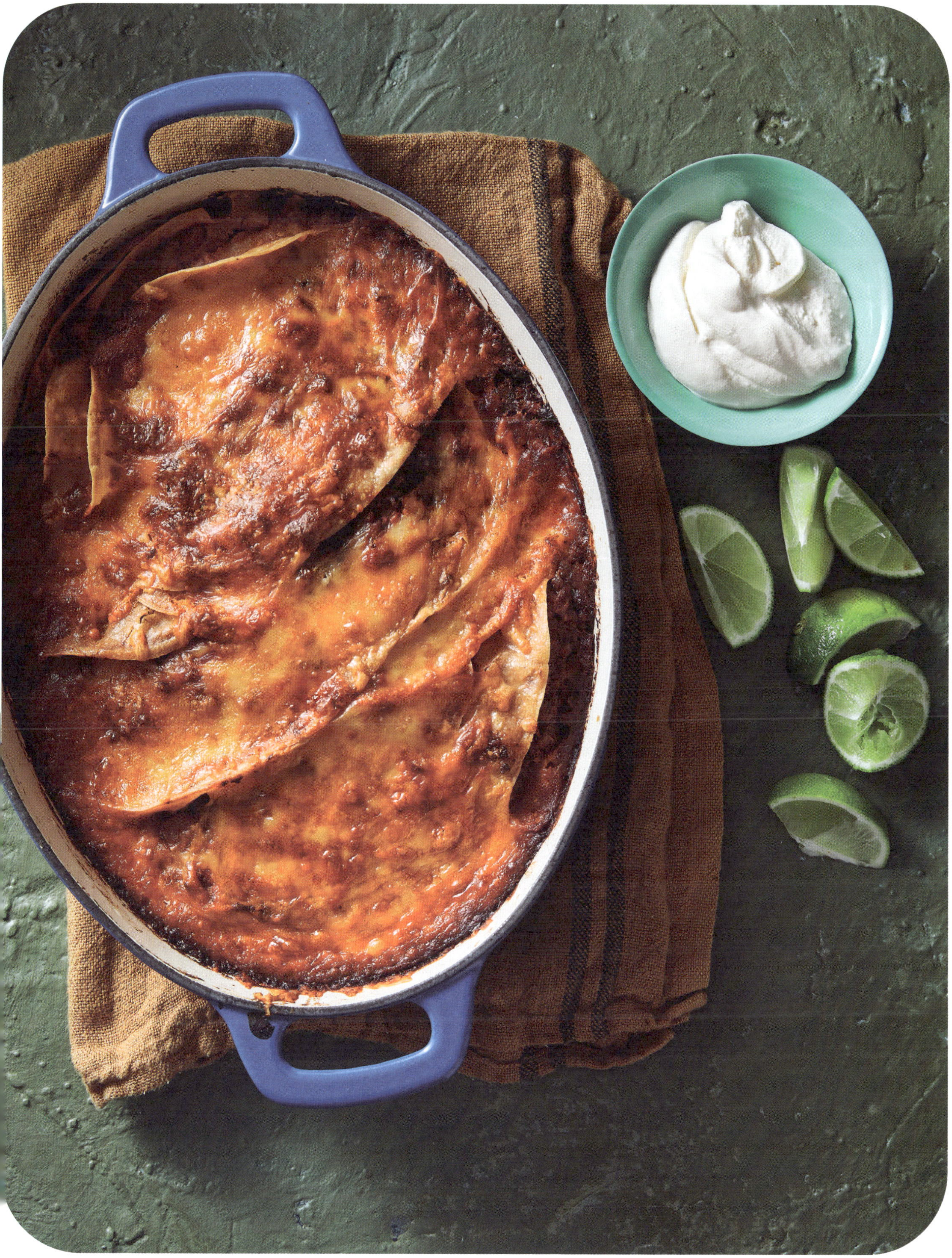

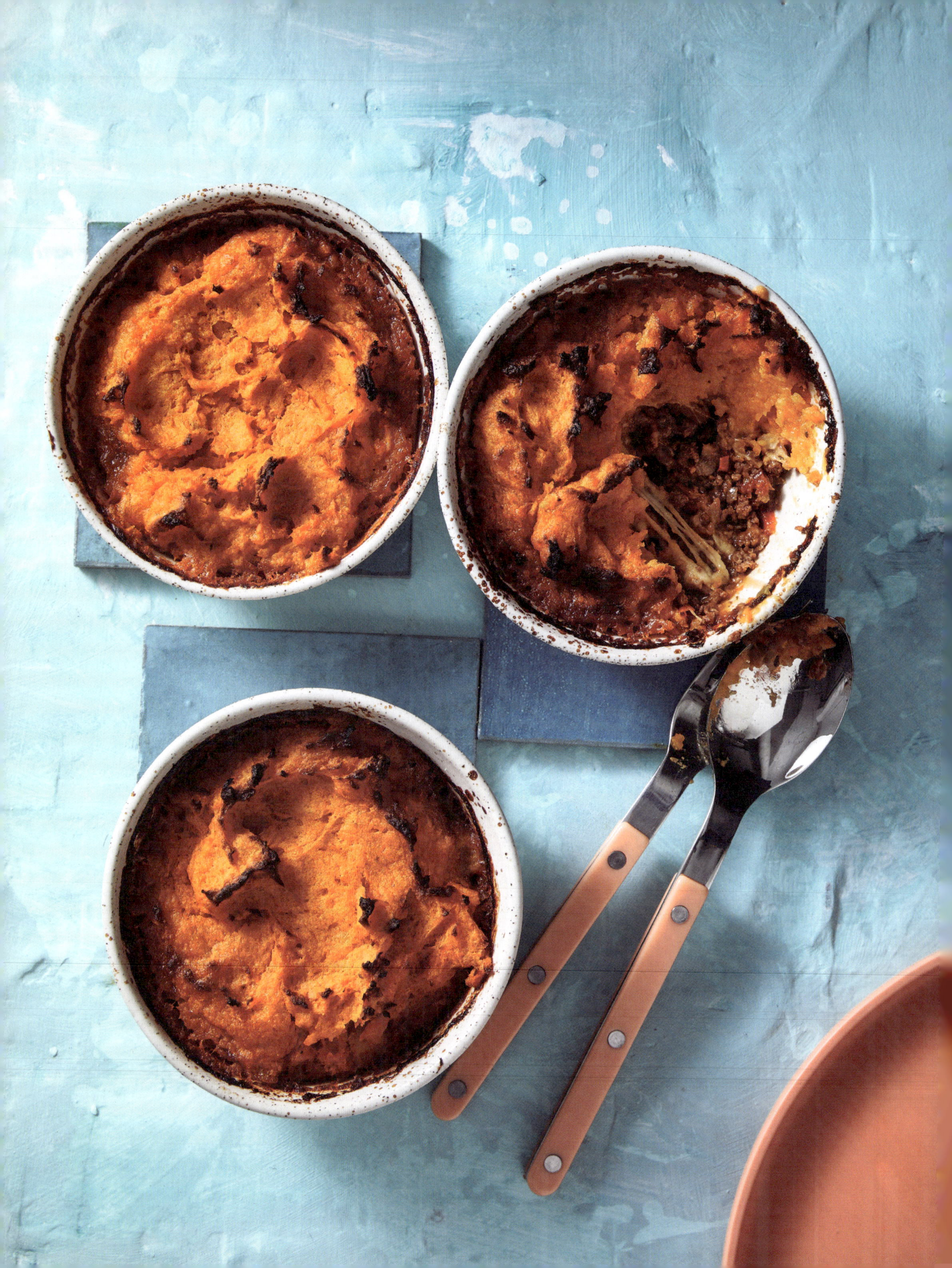

Sweet potato shepherd's pies

GF **NF**

Prep 40 minutes
Cook 1 hour
Serves 4

3 large potatoes, peeled and chopped

2 sweet potatoes, peeled and chopped

100 g (3½ oz) salted butter

500 g (1 lb 2 oz) Veggie-loaded bolognese sauce (page 108)

125 g (4½ oz) cheddar, grated

sea salt

Boil the potato and sweet potato in a large saucepan for 15–20 minutes, or until tender. Drain and very roughly mash the potato with the butter and season with salt.

Preheat the oven to 200°C (390°F).

Divide the bolognese sauce between four individual (250 ml/8½ fl oz/ 1 cup) ramekins, sprinkle with the grated cheese, then spoon the mashed potato on top. (This method will give you pies with a lovely melted cheese layer between the bolognese and the potato. But if you prefer your cheese crispy, spoon the mashed potato on top of the bolognese, then top with the grated cheese.)

Bake for 30 minutes, until the tops are golden, the potato is crispy and the filling is bubbling.

Note If you plan to cook this recipe instead of the Mexi-spice tray bake (page 114), you will need to add these ingredients to the weekly shopping list on page 107.

Hints Mix some smoked paprika or chopped chives into the mash.

Use a fork to rough up the mashed potato for a crispier top.

Instead of individual pies, make one large pie in a casserole dish (you may need to increase the baking time to 40 minutes to ensure the pie heats through).

WARMING & COMFORTING

Roast chicken with garlic, spinach and dill rice

GF NF DF

Prep 20 minutes
Cook 1 hour
Serves 4

2 tablespoons extra-virgin olive oil
2 large leeks, white and light green parts only, sliced
6 garlic cloves, minced
400 g (14 oz) tinned white beans, drained and rinsed
200 g (7 oz) baby spinach leaves, roughly chopped
400 g (14 oz/2 cups) basmati rice
1 litre (34 fl oz/4 cups) chicken stock or home-made Chicken bone broth (page 139)
1 bunch dill, chopped
zest of 1 lemon
1 × Whole roast chicken (page 109), hot, plus pan juices
sea salt and freshly ground black pepper

This is one of my favourite ways to enjoy a whole chicken: roasted with a simple yet sumptuous side.

Heat the olive oil in a large saucepan over medium heat. Add the leek and garlic and sauté for 5 minutes, until softened. Add the white beans and spinach leaves and cook for 2–3 minutes more, until the spinach is wilted. Stir in the rice, coating it well in the aromatics. Pour in the chicken stock, turn up the heat and bring it to a boil.

Reduce the heat to low, cover and simmer for 15–18 minutes, until the rice is cooked. Stir in the dill and lemon zest and season with salt and pepper, to taste.

Portion the warm roast chicken as you prefer, drizzle with the pan juices, and serve with the rice.

Hints If you would like extra juices for drizzling, extend the pan juices with a little chicken stock or stock (bouillon) powder mixed with hot water.

Use any leftover flavoured rice as a filling for stuffed capsicums (bell peppers) or a quick side dish.

Reserve and freeze the bones to make Chicken bone broth (page 139).

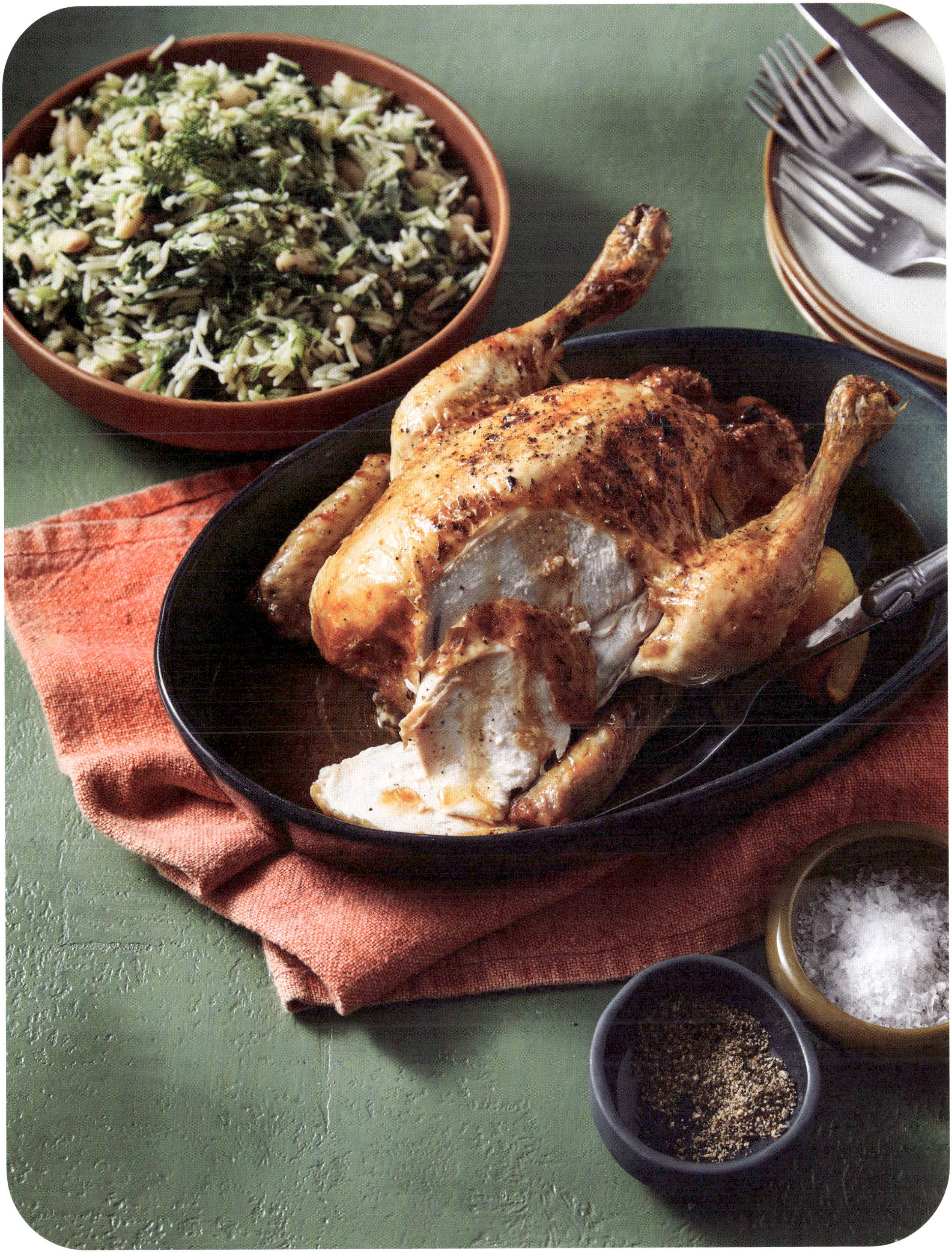

Chicken pie with artichokes and olives

NF

Prep 15 minutes
Cook 25 minutes
Serves 4

1 tablespoon extra-virgin olive oil, plus 3 teaspoons more

1 small onion, finely chopped

2 garlic cloves, minced

220 g (8 oz) artichoke hearts, quartered

60 g (2 oz) green olives, pitted and halved

1 × Whole roast chicken (page 109), shredded

200 g (7 oz) baby spinach leaves

1 tablespoon plain (all-purpose) flour

1 tablespoon Dijon mustard

200 g (7 oz) crème fraîche

1 teaspoon chopped tarragon leaves

125 ml (4 fl oz/½ cup) chicken stock or home-made Chicken bone broth (page 139)

8–10 sheets filo pastry, thawed

olive-oil spray

1 teaspoon sesame seeds

Use leftover roast chicken (page 109) to make this dish, which I like to serve with steamed greens or a simple side salad to complement the richness of the pie and sauce. When shredding the chicken, keep the bones and any skin or fatty offcuts to make Chicken bone broth (page 139).

Preheat the oven to 180°C (360°F). Lightly spray a casserole dish with olive-oil spray.

Heat 1 tablespoon of olive oil in a large frying pan over medium heat. Add the onion and garlic and sauté for 2–3 minutes, until softened. Stir in the artichoke hearts and olives, cooking for 3–4 minutes. Add the shredded chicken and spinach, stirring for 2–3 minutes, until the spinach wilts and the chicken is warmed through. Sprinkle the flour over the mixture and stir well, cooking for 1 minute. Add the Dijon mustard, crème fraîche, tarragon and chicken stock and stir until the mixture is smooth and well combined.

Strain the chicken mixture, then transfer it to the casserole dish.

Layer the filo pastry sheets on top of the chicken mixture, scrunching each sheet lightly as you go. Spray each sheet lightly with olive-oil spray and sprinkle with sesame seeds.

Bake for 20–25 minutes, or until the pastry is golden and crispy.

Serve the chicken pie hot with a green salad or steamed green beans on the side.

Hint Avoid overcooking the sauce after stirring in the flour or it may stick to the pan.

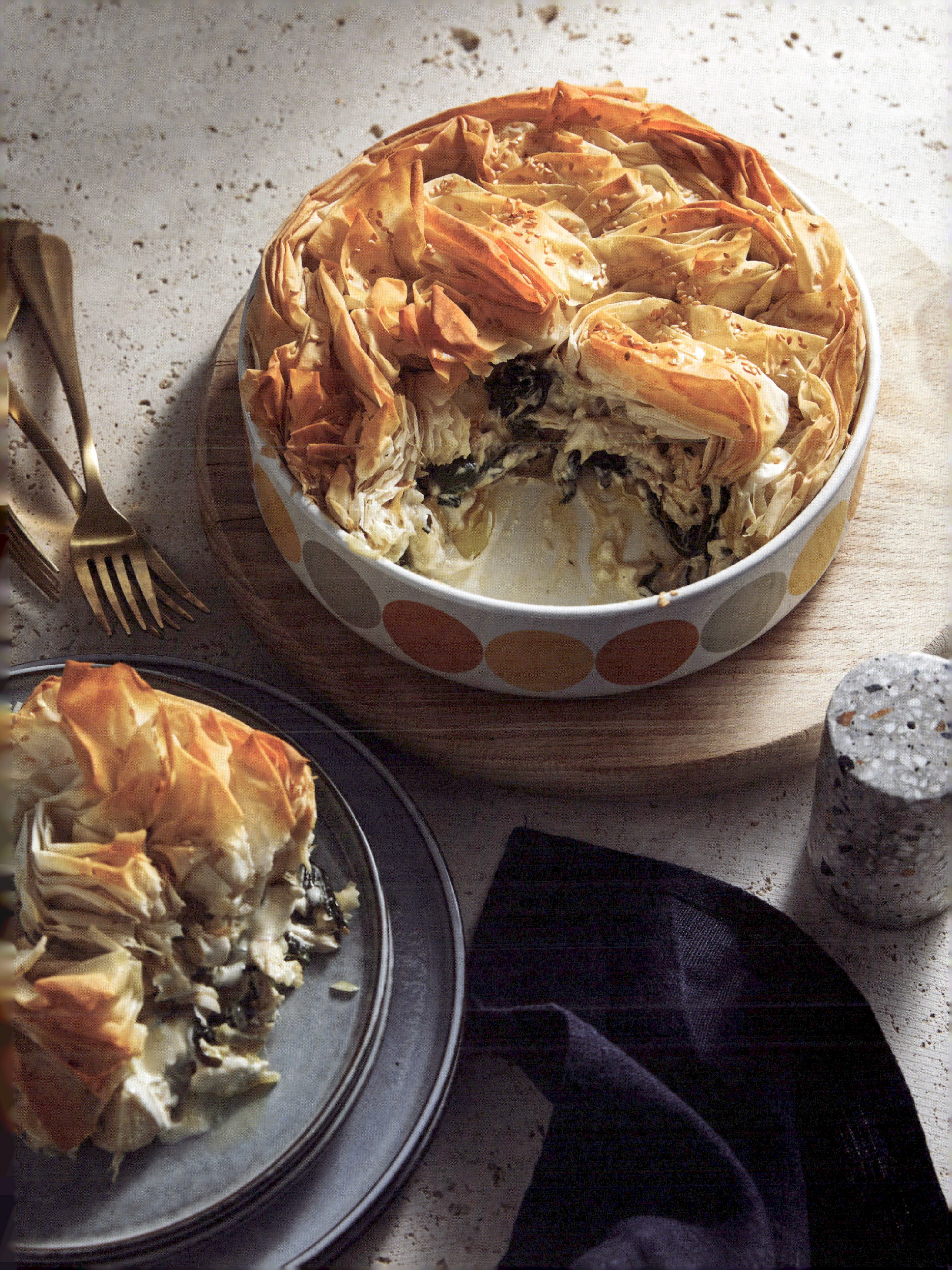

Marinated lamb with caponata

GF DF

Prep 20 minutes
Cook 40 minutes
Serves 4

4 lamb chump chops

2 tablespoons extra-virgin olive oil, plus 1 tablespoon more

1 large onion, diced

3 garlic cloves, minced

1 large red capsicum (bell pepper), diced

1 large green capsicum, diced

2 large zucchini (courgettes), diced

1 eggplant (aubergine), diced

2 tablespoons finely chopped rosemary leaves

3 tablespoons capers, rinsed and squeezed dry

110 g (4 oz) green olives, pitted and halved

1 × quantity Home-made tomato passata (page 110) or store-bought passata (pureed tomatoes)

sea salt and freshly ground black pepper

flat-leaf (Italian) parsley, finely chopped, to serve

pine nuts, toasted, to serve

lemon wedges, to serve (optional)

steamed rice, mashed potato or crusty bread, to serve

Marinade

2 tablespoons Dijon mustard

1 teaspoon freshly ground black pepper

2 garlic cloves, minced

juice of 1 lemon

Tender marinated lamb and succulent vegetables combine to produce an Italian-inspired dish that everyone will appreciate, especially on a wintry evening.

To make the marinade, mix the Dijon mustard, black pepper, garlic and lemon juice together in a small bowl. If not using straight away, cover and refrigerate.

When you're ready to cook, brush the marinade over the lamb chops. Heat 2 tablespoons of the olive oil in a large frying pan over medium–high heat. Add the lamb chops and brown them on both sides (about 3–4 minutes per side). Once browned, remove the chops from the pan and set aside.

In the same pan, using the remaining oil and juices from the lamb, start cooking the vegetables. Add the diced onion and cook for 2–3 minutes, until soft and translucent. Add the minced garlic and cook for another minute. Add the capsicum and zucchini and cook for 5 minutes, or until softened. Stir in the eggplant and continue cooking for 10 minutes more, or until the vegetables are tender. Season with salt and pepper and add the rosemary. Add the capers, olives, passata and 60 ml (2 fl oz/¼ cup) of water, stir well to combine and simmer for 30 minutes.

Return the browned lamb chops to the pan, along with any resting juices, nestling them into the caponata mixture. Cover the pan and simmer for an additional 10–15 minutes, until the lamb is tender and fully cooked.

Serve the lamb with the caponata sauce, parsley, pine nuts and lemon wedges (if using) alongside some steamed rice, mashed potato or crusty bread.

Hints Deglaze the pan with a splash of red wine after browning the lamb chops to lift any caramelised bits for extra depth in the caponata.

Letting the caponata simmer slowly with the lamb helps meld the flavours beautifully; don't rush this step.

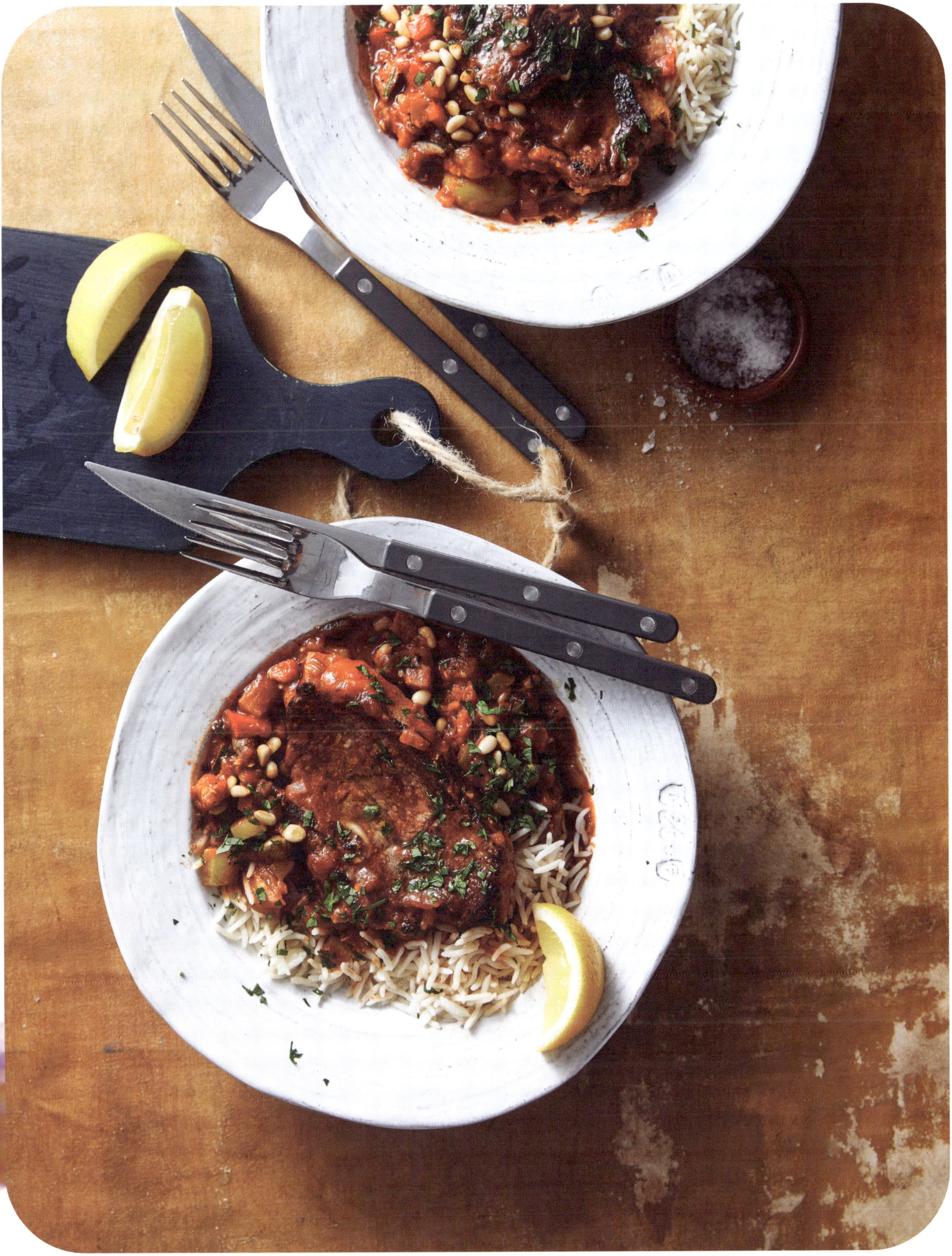

Chilli jam minced beef with rice and dressed vegetable pickles

GF NF DF

Prep 30 minutes
Cook 12 minutes
Serves 4

500 g (1 lb 2 oz) minced (ground) beef

125 ml (4 fl oz/½ cup) Chilli jam marinade (page 111)

1 tablespoon soy sauce

2 teaspoons fish sauce

1 tablespoon rice vinegar

2 teaspoons grated ginger

2 garlic cloves, crushed

2 tablespoons coconut oil

4 eggs

60 g (2 oz/¼ cup) spring onions (scallions), finely sliced

cooked jasmine rice, to serve

sesame seeds, to serve

Dressed vegetable pickles

1 large Lebanese (short) cucumber, julienned

1 carrot, julienned

90 g (3 oz) bean sprouts

1 tablespoon avocado oil

1 tablespoon soy sauce

1 tablespoon rice vinegar

1 tablespoon sesame seeds, toasted

1 tablespoon finely chopped spring onions (scallions)

2 teaspoons grated ginger

1 teaspoon white (granulated) sugar

Sweet and spicy beef with the freshness of quick-pickled vegetables is a match made (fast!) in heaven.

Combine the minced beef with chilli jam, soy sauce, fish sauce, rice vinegar, ginger and half the crushed garlic in a large bowl and mix well. Set aside.

Heat 1 tablespoon of the coconut oil in a large frying pan over medium heat and fry the eggs for 3–5 minutes, depending on how you like them done.

For the dressed vegetable pickles, toss the cucumber, carrot and bean sprouts with avocado oil, soy sauce, rice vinegar, sesame seeds, spring onion, ginger and sugar in a bowl, then set aside to allow the flavours to develop.

Heat the remaining coconut oil in a large frying pan over medium–high heat. Add the remaining garlic and the spring onion and sauté for 2 minutes, until fragrant. Add the marinated minced beef to the pan, breaking it up as it cooks. Stir-fry for 10 minutes over high heat, stirring frequently until the minced beef breaks down and is browned.

Serve the minced beef and dressed vegetable pickles on top of cooked rice and top with a fried egg and sesame seeds.

Hints For added spice, toss some thinly sliced fresh chilli into the minced beef while cooking.

Substitute rice with soba or udon noodles for a different texture.

Add some quick stir-fried veggies like bok choy (pak choy) or snow peas (mangetout) to the minced beef for extra nutrition.

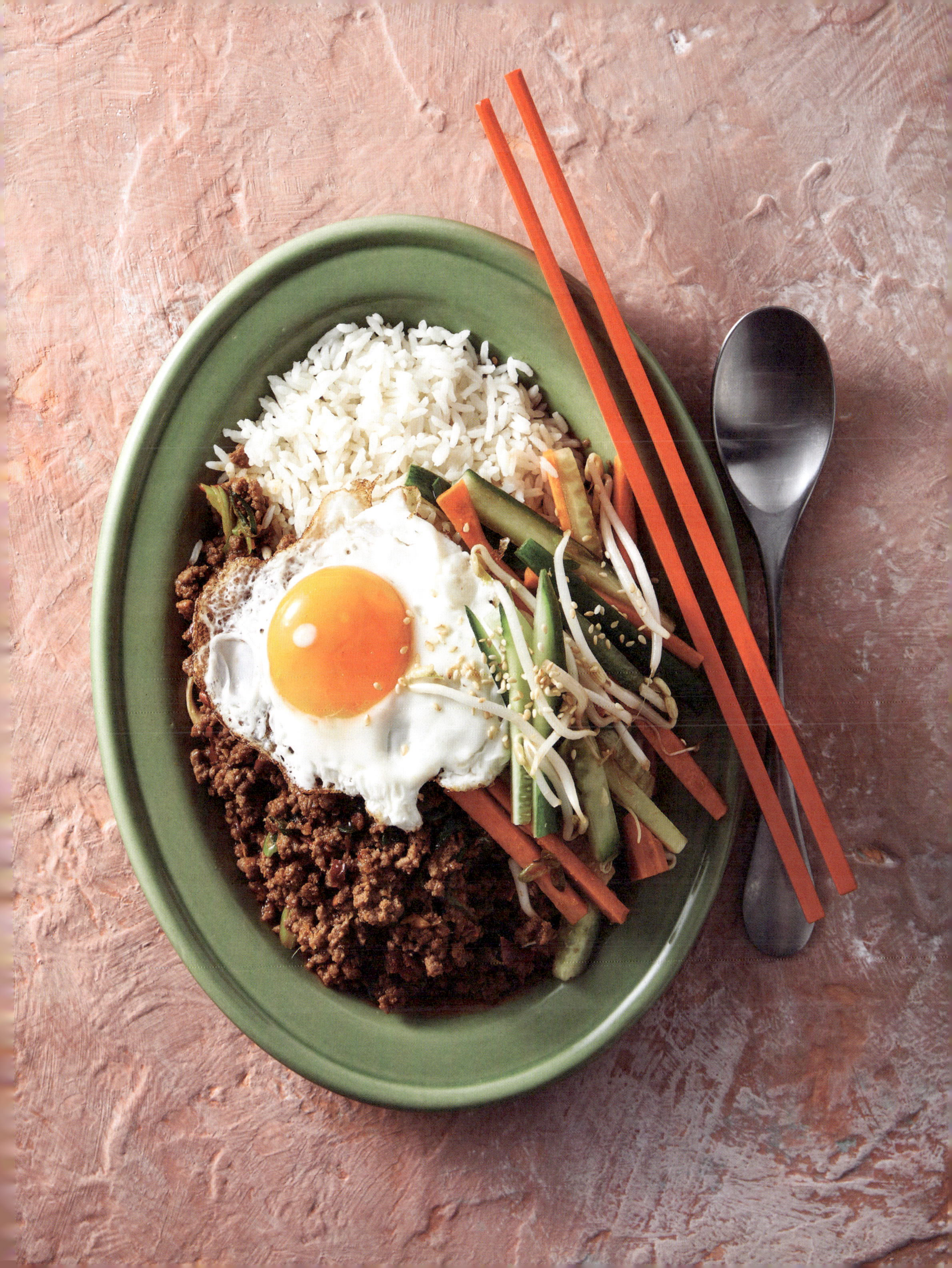

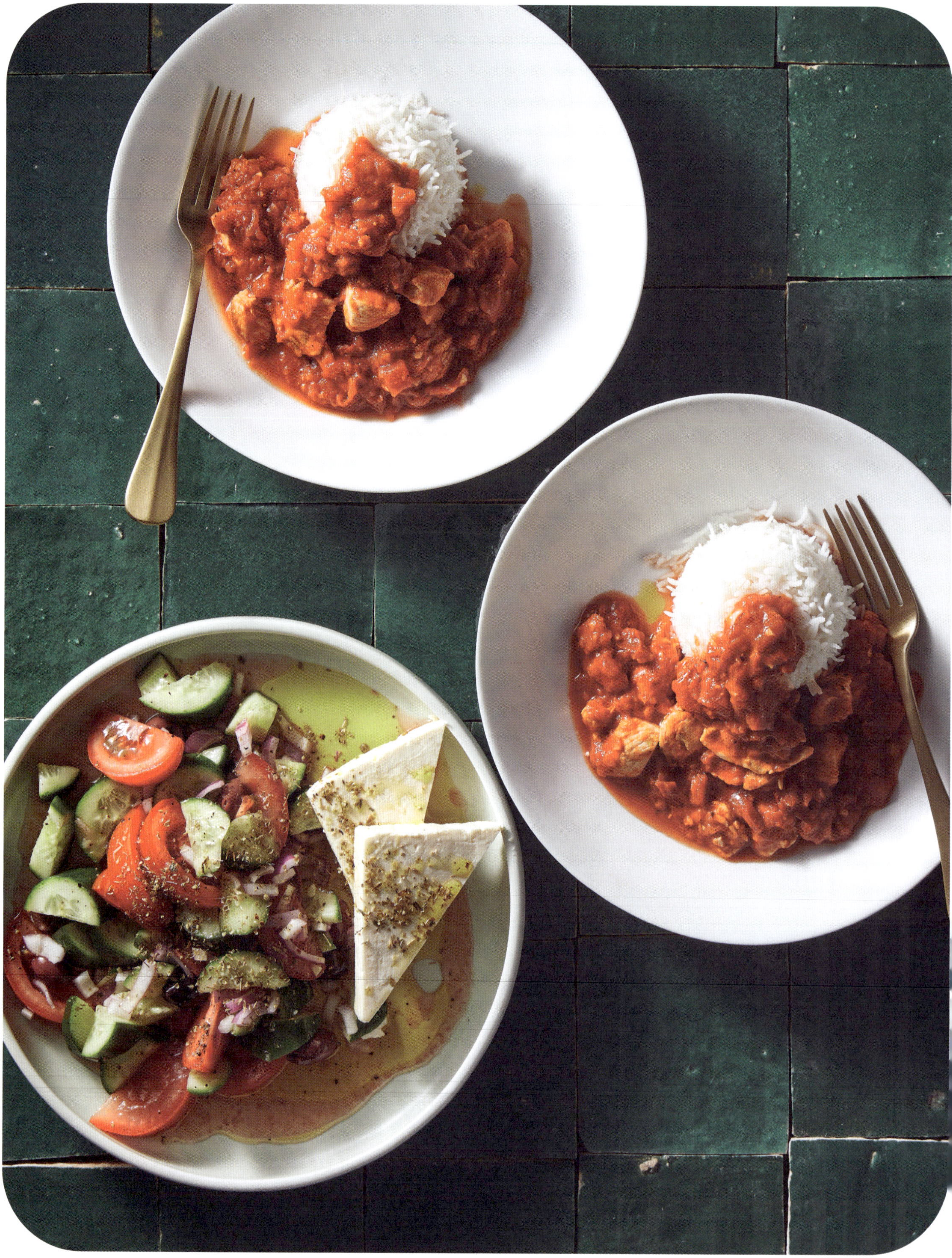

Chicken rice mountains and Greek salad

GF NF

Prep 30 minutes
Cook 3 hours 30 minutes
Serves 4

2 tablespoons extra-virgin olive oil
1 large onion, finely diced
3 garlic cloves, finely diced
2 × large chicken breasts, chopped into 3 cm (1¼ in) pieces
90 g (3 oz/⅓ cup) tomato paste (concentrated puree)
400 g (14 oz) tinned crushed tomatoes
sea salt and freshly ground black pepper
cooked jasmine rice, to serve

Greek salad

1 tablespoon white vinegar
3 tablespoons extra-virgin olive oil
1 teaspoon dried oregano
2 large tomatoes, chopped into wedges
1 Lebanese (short) cucumber, halved lengthways and sliced
1 red onion, diced
100 g (3½ oz) feta, cut into cubes or triangles
95 g (3¼ oz) kalamata olives

When I was growing up, my yiayia would make this dish weekly. The recipe is derived from her village in Greece. A simple yet warming meal, it's popular with children thanks to the rice mountains!

Heat the olive oil in a large saucepan over medium heat and add the onion and garlic. Sauté for 3–4 minutes, until translucent and fragrant. Add the chicken breast pieces and brown on all sides. Season with a generous amount of salt and pepper. Once the chicken is browned, add the tomato paste and tinned tomatoes. Stir to combine, then add 500 ml (17 fl oz/2 cups) of water. Stir again, reduce the heat to low and place the lid on the saucepan slightly ajar.

Cook the stew over low heat for at least 3 hours, stirring occasionally. If the liquid reduces too much, add an extra cup or two of water as needed. The stew is ready when the sauce is thick and creamy in consistency. Taste and adjust the seasoning if required.

To make the Greek salad, whisk the vinegar, olive oil and oregano in a small bowl until well combined. Place the chopped tomato, cucumber, red onion, feta and olives in a bowl. Pour the dressing over the salad and toss gently to combine.

To serve, pack the slightly cooled cooked rice into small cups, then invert each cup onto a plate to create a small mound of rice. Spoon the chicken stew over the rice and sprinkle with freshly ground black pepper. Serve with the Greek salad on the side.

Toasted cheese soldiers with dippy eggs

(NF) (V)

Prep 15 minutes
Cook 15 minutes
Serves 4

8 eggs
50 g (1¾ oz) salted butter, softened
8 slices of sourdough bread
1 garlic clove (optional)
200 g (7 oz) cheddar, grated
Tabasco sauce, to serve (optional)
chives, finely chopped, to serve (optional)

When you want breakfast for big kids and little kids alike, this two-in-one recipe fits the bill.

Preheat the oven grill (broiler) on high and line a baking tray with baking paper.

Bring a medium saucepan of water to a boil, then carefully lower the eggs into the boiling water and cook for 5–6 minutes for soft-boiled yolks. As soon as the eggs are ready, remove them from the pan and run them under cold water to stop the cooking process. Peel four of the eggs and place the remaining eggs in egg cups.

While the eggs are cooking, spread butter on one side of each slice of bread. Place the slices, buttered side up, on the baking tray and grill until golden, around 2–4 minutes. Remove the bread and rub the garlic clove over four of the slices (adults!). Flip all of the slices over and top with the grated cheese. Grill on the top shelf of your oven for 2 minutes, or until the cheese is melted and golden.

Cut the four non-garlicky grilled cheese slices into strips (soldiers) and serve alongside the eggs in egg cups for dipping.

Place the four peeled eggs onto the four remaining cheesy toasts. Cut the eggs open, drizzle with Tabasco sauce and top with chives, if using.

Hints Ensure the eggs are at room temperature before boiling to prevent cracking.

Use a sturdy bread that can hold up to the cheese and dipping without becoming soggy.

Experiment with different cheeses, like gruyere or parmesan, for varying flavours.

For extra umami, drizzle a little Worcestershire sauce over the cheese before grilling; for a tangy contrast, scatter some finely chopped sun-dried tomatoes under the cheese before grilling; or for a salty kick, place a thin slice of anchovy fillet under the cheese before grilling.

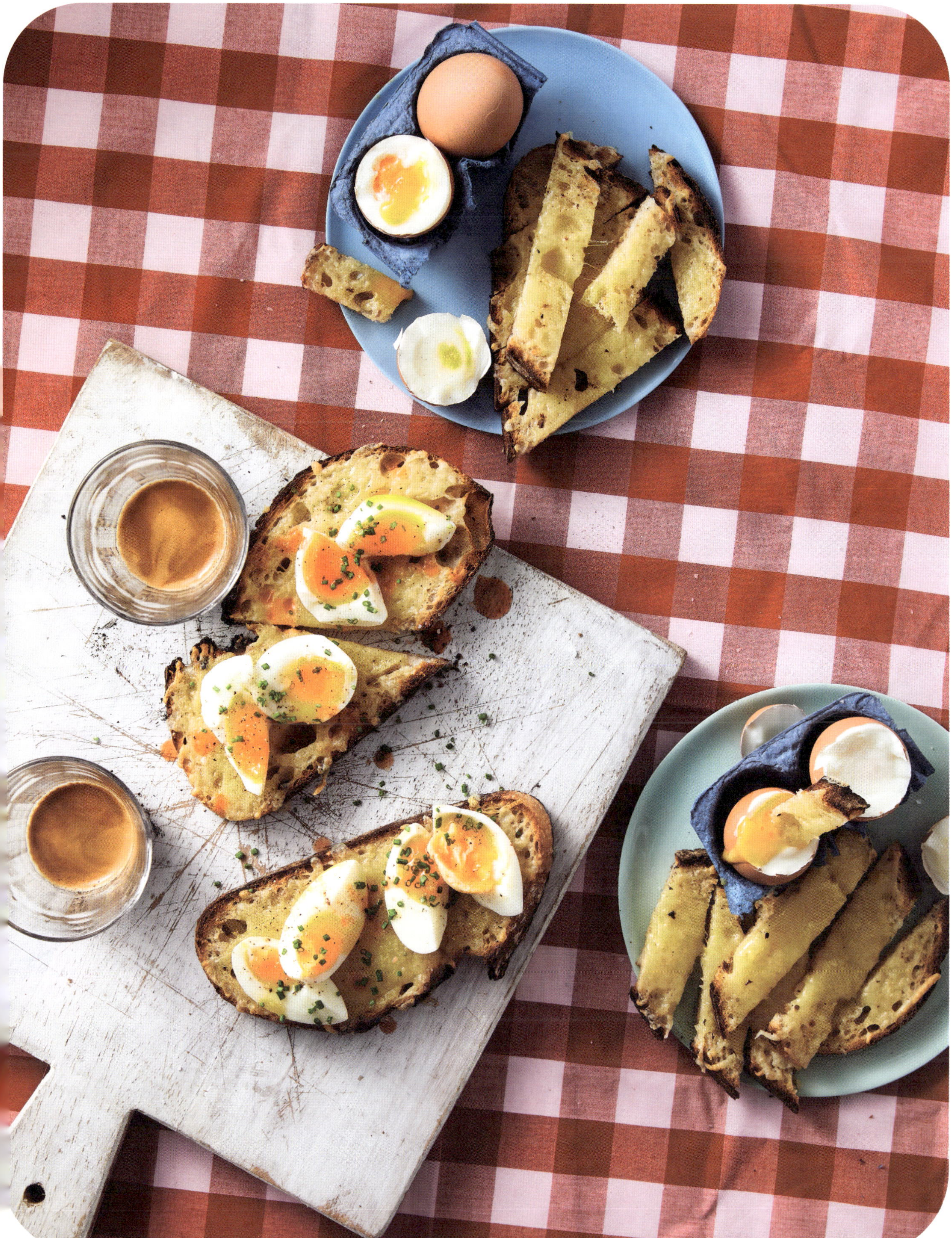

Classic French toast with cinnamon and maple butter

NF V

Prep 5 minutes
Cook 15 minutes
Serves 4

4 eggs
250 ml (8½ fl oz/1 cup) milk
1 teaspoon vanilla extract
1 tablespoon ground cinnamon
75 g (2¾ oz) unsalted butter, cut into thirds
4 slices thick-cut sourdough, crusts removed (optional)
sea salt
pure maple syrup, to serve

Maple butter

125 g (4½ oz) unsalted butter
60 ml (2 fl oz/¼ cup) pure maple syrup
sea salt

This easy Sunday-morning-worthy breakfast is a delicious way to use up day-old bread.

Whisk the eggs, milk, vanilla extract, cinnamon and a pinch of salt together in a shallow bowl.

Heat a large frying pan over medium heat and add a third of the butter. Allow it to melt and coat the pan.

Dip each slice of bread into the egg mixture, soaking both sides, then place the slices in the hot pan. Cook for 2–3 minutes on each side until golden brown and crisp, working in batches if necessary. Add more butter as needed between batches.

While the French toast is cooking, make the maple butter. Melt the butter in a small saucepan over low heat, then stir in the maple syrup and a pinch of salt. Allow it to gently warm through without boiling.

Serve the French toast warm, drizzled with maple syrup and a dollop of maple butter.

Hints Day-old bread will absorb the egg mixture better and result in the best texture.

If you prefer a sweeter French toast, add 1 tablespoon of caster (superfine) sugar to the egg mixture.

For an added twist, try adding a pinch of nutmeg or allspice to the egg mixture.

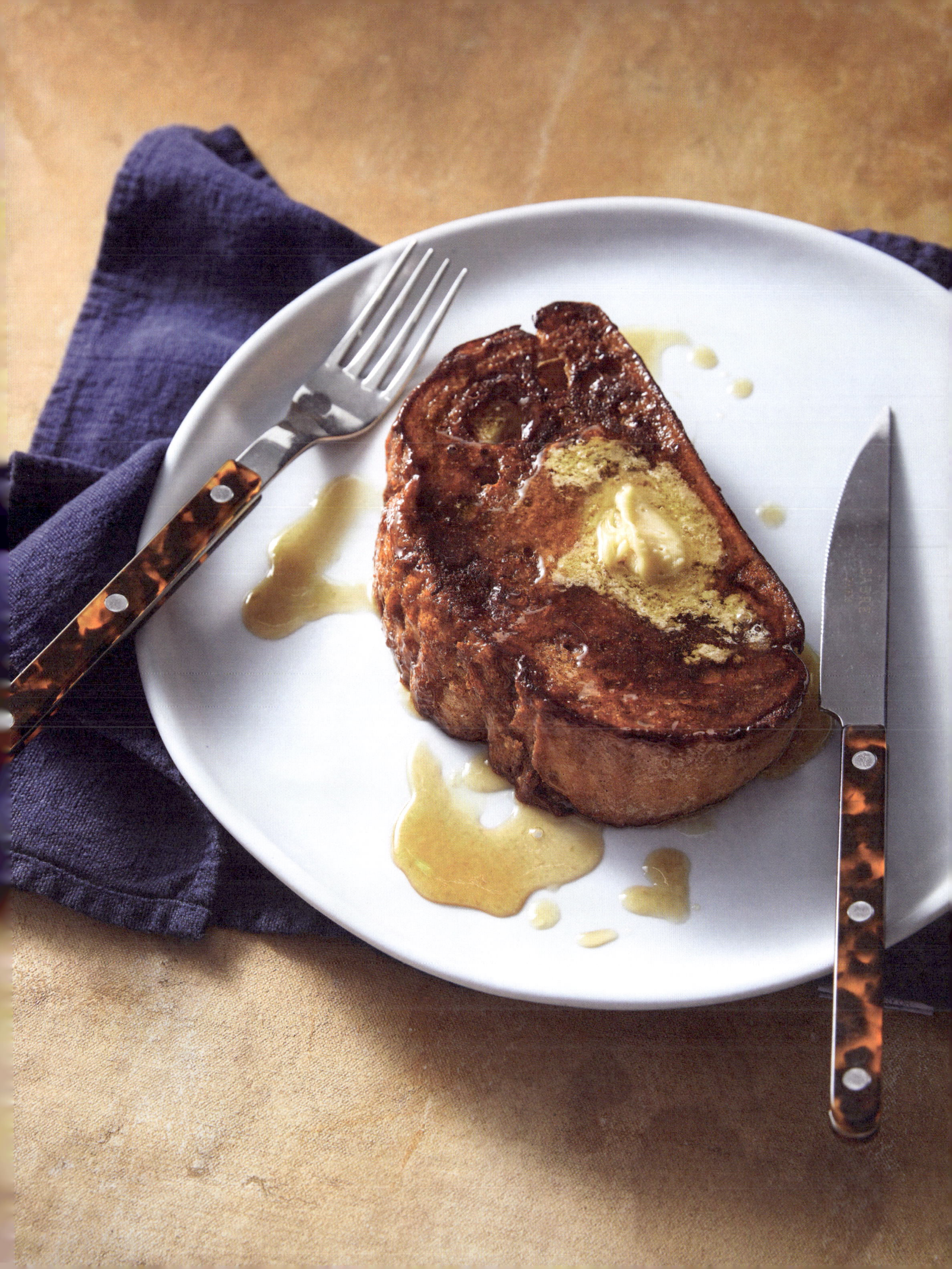

Cheeseburger triangles

NF

Prep 10 minutes
Cook 20 minutes
Serves 4

200 g (7 oz) ham, finely chopped
150 g (5½ oz) cheddar, grated
1 small onion, finely diced
1 tablespoon Dijon mustard
1 tablespoon tomato sauce (ketchup)
2 tablespoons finely chopped gherkins (pickles)
2 tablespoons mayonnaise
16 sheets filo pastry, thawed
2 tablespoons extra-virgin olive oil
1 egg, beaten (for egg wash)
sea salt

Burger sauce

125 g (4½ oz/½ cup) mayonnaise
2 tablespoons tomato paste (concentrated puree)
1 tablespoon Dijon mustard
1 tablespoon apple-cider vinegar
1 tablespoon finely chopped gherkins (pickles)
1 teaspoon garlic powder
½ teaspoon smoked paprika
¼ teaspoon freshly ground black pepper

You won't be able to eat just one – these cheeseburger triangles are so much better than a burger on the run.

Combine the burger sauce ingredients in a bowl and stir until well combined. Transfer to the fridge to allow the flavours to meld for at least 30 minutes.

Heat the oven to 200°C (390°F). Line a baking tray with baking paper.

Combine the ham, cheddar, onion, Dijon mustard, tomato sauce, gherkin and mayonnaise in a bowl and mix until well combined. Season with salt if needed.

Place two sheets of filo pastry on a clean surface. Lightly brush with olive oil, then fold it in half lengthways. Place two spoonfuls of the filling mixture near the bottom corner. Fold the pastry over to form a triangle, then continue folding to maintain the triangular shape. Repeat with the remaining filo sheets, olive oil and filling to make eight triangles.

Place the triangles on the baking tray. Brush the tops with beaten egg.

Bake for 15–20 minutes, or until the filo pastry is golden brown and crispy.

Let the triangles cool slightly before serving.

Hints Prepare the filling ahead of time and store it in the fridge for up to 4 days until ready to use.

When buying ham, look for a preservative-free option that doesn't contain added nitrates.

Substitute ham with sautéed mushrooms or roasted vegetables for a vegetarian option.

Serve with additional burger sauce or gherkins for extra flavour.

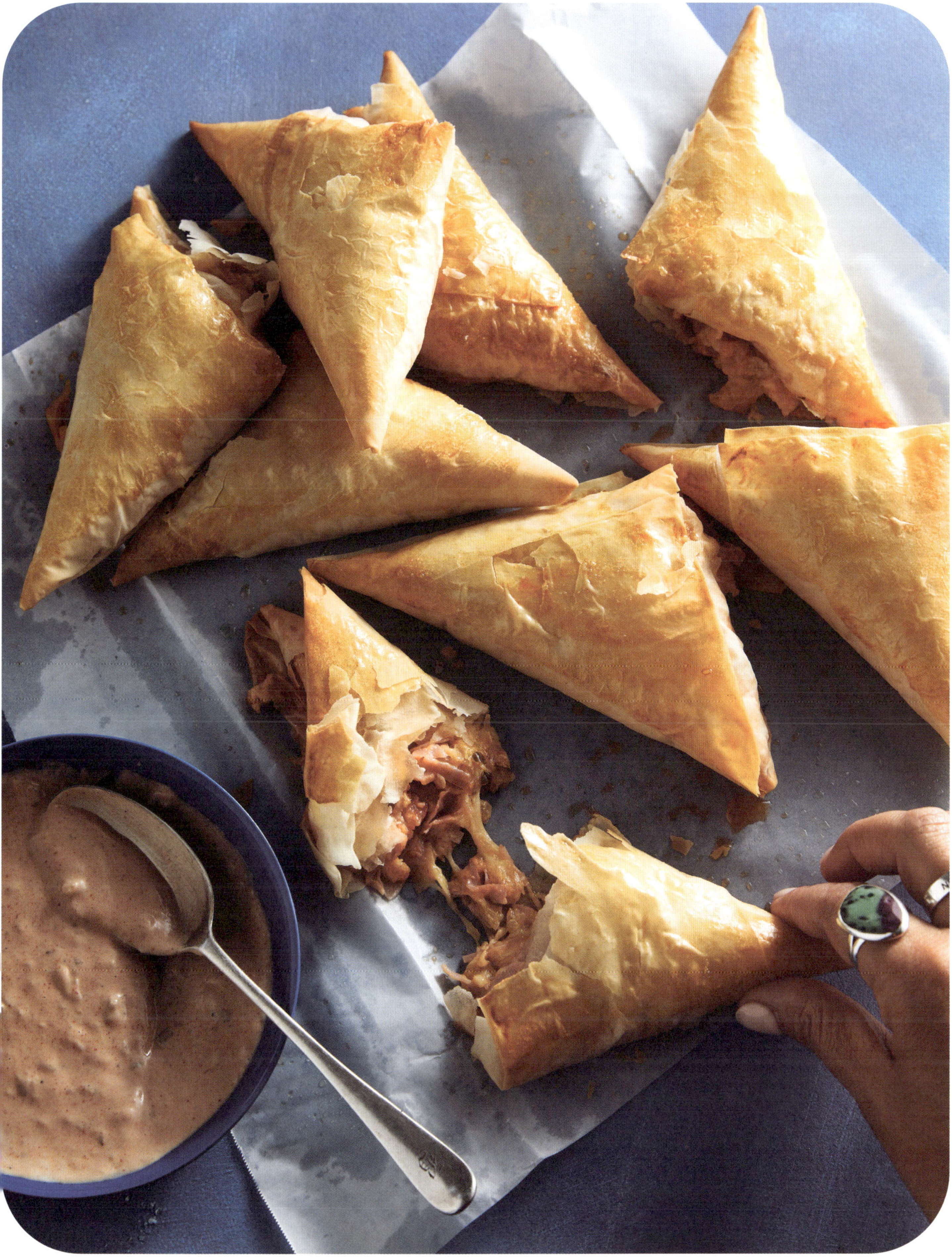

Ricotta berry tart

(NF) (V)

Prep 15 minutes
Cook 30 minutes
Serves 4

250 g (9 oz) ricotta
2 tablespoons honey
1 teaspoon ground cinnamon
½ teaspoon vanilla extract
200 g (7 oz) mixed berries (fresh or frozen)
1 tablespoon cornflour (cornstarch)
1 tablespoon soft brown sugar
27 × 36 cm (10¾ × 14¼ in) sheet butter puff pastry, thawed
1 egg, beaten (for egg wash)
sea salt
icing (confectioners') sugar, for dusting

This pretty sweet treat is so easy to whip up that the hardest part is waiting for the pastry to defrost!

Preheat the oven to 200°C (390°F) and line a baking tray with baking paper.

Mix the ricotta, honey, cinnamon, vanilla extract and a pinch of salt together in a bowl until smooth.

In a separate bowl, toss the berries with cornflour and brown sugar.

Lay the puff pastry on the baking tray. Spread the ricotta mixture evenly over the pastry, leaving a 2 cm (¾ in) border around the edges. Scatter the berry mixture on top of the ricotta mixture. Fold the edges of the pastry up, creating a rustic border. Brush the edges with beaten egg.

Bake for 25–30 minutes, or until the pastry is golden and crisp.

Allow the tart to cool slightly before dusting with icing sugar.

Hints Use mixed berries, like raspberries, blackberries and blueberries, for a variety of flavours and textures.

If using frozen berries, thaw them first and drain (and retain) the excess juice to avoid a soggy tart. Heat the juice in a small saucepan over medium heat for 10 minutes to reduce it, then serve it with the tart.

Serve warm with a dollop of whipped cream or vanilla ice cream for an extra indulgence.

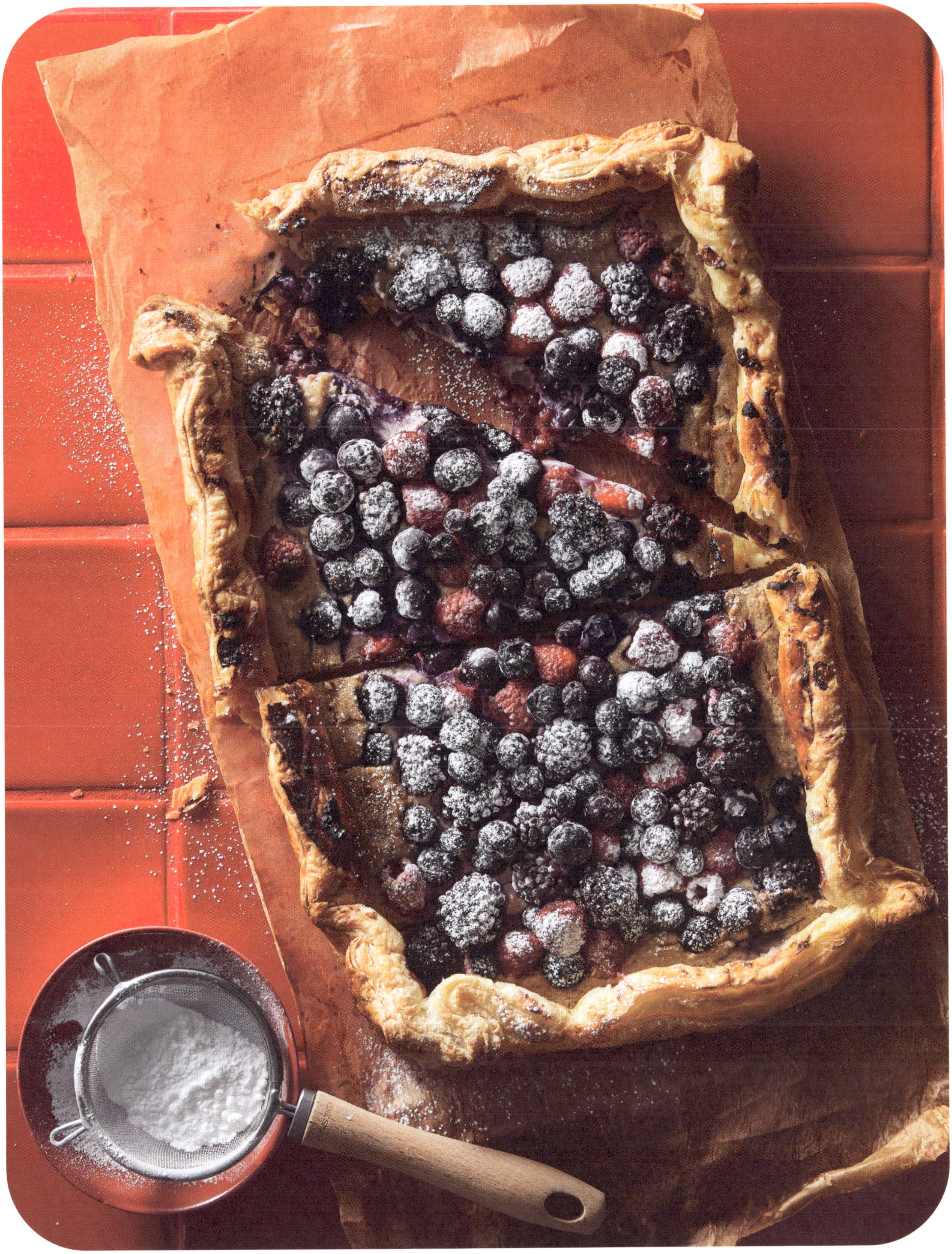

Week 3 menu

Power prep

Fish croquettes
Chicken bone broth
Slow-cooked lamb shoulder
Tomato coconut dal

Dinners

Pumpkin and sage mac 'n' cheese
Fish croquettes with yoghurt tartare sauce
Greek lamb with orzo
Lamb tagine with couscous
Grilled steak with stroganoff sauce
Tomato coconut dal with baked fish
Hoisin meatloaf with potato gratin

Breakfasts

Spiced egg and tomato flatbreads
Choc peanut porridge

Snack

As-you-like-it popcorn seasoning

Sweet

Sticky date mini cakes

Week 3 shopping list

Fruit & vegetables

- [ ] 400 g (14 oz) green beans
- [ ] 2 celery stalks
- [ ] 1 bunch coriander (cilantro) (optional)
- [ ] 1 bunch dill
- [ ] 4 garlic bulbs
- [ ] 5 cm (2 in) piece of fresh ginger
- [ ] 10 lemons
- [ ] 1 bunch mint
- [ ] 200 g (7 oz) mushrooms
- [ ] 4 onions
- [ ] 2 red onions
- [ ] 1 bunch oregano
- [ ] 1 bunch flat-leaf (Italian) parsley
- [ ] 150 g (5½ oz) baby peas
- [ ] 750 g (1 lb 11 oz) + 3 large potatoes
- [ ] 400 g (14 oz) pumpkin (winter squash)
- [ ] 1 bunch rosemary
- [ ] 1 bunch sage
- [ ] 1 bunch spring onions (scallions)
- [ ] 1 sweet potato

Meat & poultry

- [ ] 6 × bacon rashers (slices)
- [ ] 6 × 200 g (7 oz) firm white fish fillets, skinless and boneless
- [ ] 2 × 1.5 kg bone-in lamb shoulders
- [ ] 500 g (1 lb 2 oz) minced (ground) pork
- [ ] 1 × 600 g (1 lb 5 oz) skirt, flank or flat iron steak
- [ ] 200 g (7 oz) hot smoked trout (optional)
- [ ] 500 g (1 lb 2 oz) minced (ground) veal

Freezer

- [ ] 200 g (7 oz) frozen peas

Pantry & baking

- [ ] 70 g (2½ oz) toasted slivered almonds
- [ ] 100 g (3½ oz) dried apricots
- [ ] 120 g (4½ oz) Japanese breadcrumbs
- [ ] 400 ml (13½ fl oz) tinned coconut milk
- [ ] 185 g (6½ oz) pearl couscous
- [ ] 4 flatbreads (if not using home-made)
- [ ] 250 g (9 oz) red lentils
- [ ] 300 g (10½ oz) macaroni
- [ ] 60 g (2 oz) mayonnaise
- [ ] 400 g (14 oz) orzo
- [ ] 50 g (1¾ oz) tomato paste (concentrated puree)
- [ ] 800 g (1 lb 12 oz) tinned crushed tomatoes
- [ ] 300 g (10½ oz) tinned tuna, trout or salmon
- [ ] 250 ml (8½ fl oz) white wine

Fridge

- [ ] 90 g (3 oz) salted butter
- [ ] 125 g (4½ oz) cheddar
- [ ] 170 g (6 oz) gruyere, comté or smoked cheddar
- [ ] 250 ml (8½ fl oz) thick (double/heavy) cream
- [ ] 4 eggs
- [ ] 700 ml (23½ fl oz) milk
- [ ] 100 g (3½ oz) parmesan
- [ ] 200 g (7 oz) sour cream
- [ ] 400 g (14 oz) Greek-style yoghurt

Home freezer

- [ ] frozen leftover roast chicken bones (from 1–2 chickens) and any skin or fatty offcuts (see page 139)

Fish croquettes

Prep 30 minutes
Cook 15 minutes
Makes 24

600 g (1 lb 5 oz) peeled potatoes, diced
300 g (10½ oz) firm white fish fillets, skinless and boneless
300 g (10½ oz) tinned tuna, trout or salmon, drained and flaked
200 g (7 oz) hot smoked trout, flaked (optional)
200 g (7 oz) frozen peas, thawed
4 spring onions (scallions), finely sliced
20 g (¾ oz/⅓ cup) flat-leaf (Italian) parsley, chopped
zest of 2 lemons
2 eggs, beaten
45 g (1½ oz/¾ cup) Japanese breadcrumbs
2 tablespoons plain (all-purpose) flour
60–125 ml (2–4 fl oz/¼–½ cup) extra-virgin olive oil, for frying
sea salt

(NF) (DF)

Use some of these nutritious croquettes for the Fish croquettes with yoghurt tartare sauce (page 144) and freeze the leftovers for another night – they're just as good served simply with a side of green beans, sweet potato fries or green salad.

Cook the potato in a large saucepan of salted boiling water until tender, about 10 minutes. Drain and mash until smooth. Set aside to cool slightly.

Poach the fish fillets in a frying pan in 60–80 ml (2–2½ fl oz/¼–⅓ cup) of simmering water for 3–4 minutes, until just cooked through. Drain and flake the fish, then set aside.

Combine the mashed potato, flaked fish, tinned fish, smoked trout (if using), peas, spring onion, parsley and lemon zest in a large mixing bowl and season with salt. Stir in the eggs, half of the breadcrumbs and the flour until the mixture holds together.

Shape the mixture into small croquettes, about the size of a golf ball, then flatten slightly.

Coat each croquette in the remaining breadcrumbs.

If using another day, freeze the croquettes at this stage. Thaw them in the fridge before cooking.

When ready to cook, heat the olive oil in a frying pan over medium heat. Fry the croquettes in batches until golden brown and crispy on both sides (about 3–4 minutes per side). Drain on paper towel.

Hints If the mixture is too wet to shape, add more breadcrumbs 1 tablespoon at a time until it firms up.

Leftover fish croquettes can be frozen for up to 3 months.

Chicken bone broth

Prep 15 minutes
Cook 2 hours 30 minutes
Makes 1.5–2 litres
(51–68 fl oz/6–8 cups)

frozen leftover roast chicken bones (from 1–2 chickens) and any skin or fatty offcuts (see page 109)

1–2 tablespoons extra-virgin olive oil

sea salt and freshly ground black pepper

1 onion, cut in half

1 garlic bulb, cut in half horizontally

2 celery stalks, cut into 2 cm (¾ in) chunks

small handful each of rosemary, flat-leaf (Italian) parsley and oregano leaves

zest of 1 lemon

125 ml (4 fl oz/½ cup) apple cider vinegar

Don't let your leftover chicken bones go to waste when you can make the ultimate comfort food: home-made chicken bone broth. Use it to make Greek lamb with orzo (page 146), or to flavour risottos, soups and stews. And when your immune system needs a boost, enjoy it as it is, from a mug.

Preheat the oven to 220°C (430°F). Line a baking tray with baking paper.

Take the chicken bones out of the freezer, toss them in the olive oil and season extremely well with salt and pepper.

Place the seasoned bones on the baking tray and roast for 20–30 minutes, until golden.

Once roasted, transfer the bones to a large stockpot, cracking the larger bones (legs, wings) to release more flavour and nutrients into the broth. Add the onion, garlic, celery, herbs, lemon zest, 1 teaspoon of black pepper, 1 teaspoon of sea salt and apple cider vinegar to the pot.

Cover the bones and vegetables with the apple cider vinegar and enough cold water to ensure everything is submerged.

Bring to a simmer over medium heat, then reduce the heat to low and continue to cook, with the lid slightly ajar, for about 2 hours, or until the bones turn pink.

Strain the golden chicken broth into a large bowl, discarding the solids, and season well.

Allow the broth to cool slightly before decanting into sterilised jars or airtight containers. Store in the fridge for up to 1 week or freeze for up to 3 months.

Hints For a deeper flavour, roast the garlic and onion in the oven along with the bones.

If you have other aromatics on hand, such as bay leaves or thyme, you can add them for extra flavour.

If you'd like a richer broth, after straining the broth into a bowl, return it to the stockpot and continue to cook it over a low heat, uncovered, for another 45 minutes, stirring occasionally.

(GF) (NF) (DF)

WARMING & COMFORTING

Slow-cooked lamb shoulder

Prep 15 minutes
Cook 4 hours
Makes 2 meals for 4 people

2 × 1.5 kg bone-in lamb shoulders
10 garlic cloves, sliced
4 sprigs rosemary
80 ml (2½ fl oz/⅓ cup) extra-virgin olive oil
1 tablespoon dried oregano
zest and juice of 4 lemons
250 ml (8½ fl oz/1 cup) white wine
500 ml (17 fl oz/2 cups) beef stock
sea salt and freshly ground black pepper

Set and forget this slow-cooked lamb shoulder and a few hours later, you'll have the basis for Greek lamb with orzo (page 146) and Lamb tagine with couscous (page 149).

Preheat the oven to 160°C (320°F).

Make small incisions all over the lamb shoulders and insert the garlic slices and rosemary sprigs into the cuts.

Rub the lamb with olive oil, oregano, lemon zest, salt and pepper.

Place both lamb shoulders in a large roasting tin. Squeeze the lemon juice over the lamb, then pour in the white wine and chicken stock. Cover the roasting tin tightly with baking paper and place in the oven.

Slow roast for 4 hours, basting occasionally with the pan juices. Remove the baking paper for the last 30 minutes to allow the lamb to brown.

Once the lamb is tender and falling off the bone, remove both shoulders from the oven and shred the meat using two forks.

Use the meat from one shoulder for Greek lamb with orzo (page 146) or Lamb tagine with couscous (page 149).

Store the shredded meat from the second shoulder in an airtight container in the fridge for up to 4 days or freeze for up to 3 months.

Hints If you prefer a richer flavour, use lamb stock instead of chicken bone broth.

You can add a pinch of ground cinnamon to the lamb before roasting for a subtle Greek twist.

(GF) (NF) (DF)

Tomato coconut dal

Prep 45 minutes
Cook 40 minutes
Serves 4

1 tablespoon extra-virgin olive oil

1 onion, finely chopped

3 garlic cloves, minced

1 tablespoon Curry paste (page 73)

250 g (9 oz/1 cup) red lentils, rinsed

1 sweet potato, peeled and diced

400 g (14 oz) tinned crushed tomatoes

400 ml (13½ fl oz) tinned coconut milk

500 ml (17 fl oz/2 cups) vegetable stock (or Chicken bone broth, page 139, if you don't need to keep this vegetarian/vegan)

Use this fragrant dal for a quick weeknight dinner with baked fish (page 152) or serve it on rice with a green leafy salad. This recipe makes enough to put a little aside for a satisfying breakfast of Spiced egg and tomato flatbreads (page 157).

Heat the olive oil in a large saucepan over medium heat. Add the onion and garlic and cook for 3–4 minutes, until softened. Stir in the curry paste and cook for a further minute until fragrant. Add the lentils, sweet potato, tomatoes, coconut milk and stock. Stir to combine and bring to a boil.

Reduce the heat to low and simmer, stirring occasionally, until the lentils and sweet potato are tender and the dal has thickened, about 25 minutes.

Put 125 ml (4 fl oz/½ cup) of the dal aside to make Spiced egg and tomato flatbreads (page 157) for brekkie later in the week.

If not using the dal straight away, allow it to cool, then store it in an airtight container in the fridge for up to 4 days or freeze for up to 3 months.

Hints Roast the sweet potato cubes beforehand for a slightly caramelised flavour.

Swap out the sweet potato for pumpkin (winter squash) if preferred.

(GF) (NF) (DF) (V) (VG)

WARMING & COMFORTING

Pumpkin and sage mac 'n' cheese

NF V

Prep 45 minutes
Cook 50 minutes
Serves 4

300 g (10½ oz) macaroni

2 tablespoons extra-virgin olive oil

1 red onion, finely diced

2 garlic cloves, minced

10 sage leaves, plus extra to serve

Roast pumpkin cubes

400 g (14 oz) peeled pumpkin (winter squash), cut into 3 cm (1¼ in) cubes

2 tablespoons extra-virgin olive oil

1 teaspoon ground cumin

½ teaspoon ground coriander

½ teaspoon smoked paprika

½ teaspoon ground cinnamon

sea salt

Mustard cheese sauce

50 g (1¾ oz) salted butter

3 tablespoons plain (all-purpose) flour

500 ml (17 fl oz/2 cups) milk

2 teaspoons Dijon mustard

125 g (4½ oz/1 cup) grated cheddar

50 g (1¾ oz/½ cup) grated parmesan

¼ teaspoon ground nutmeg

sea salt

In a twist on the classic, roast pumpkin elevates this dish into a warm, sweet and cheesy hug.

Preheat the oven to 200°C (390°F). Line a large baking tray with baking paper.

To make the roast pumpkin cubes, toss the pumpkin with the olive oil, cumin, coriander, smoked paprika, cinnamon and a generous pinch of salt in a large bowl until it is evenly coated. Spread the pumpkin in a single layer on the baking tray. Roast, turning halfway through, for 30–35 minutes, or until the pumpkin is tender and slightly caramelised.

While the pumpkin is roasting, cook the macaroni according to the package instructions. Drain and set aside.

To make the mustard cheese sauce, melt the butter in a medium saucepan over medium heat. Add the plain flour and whisk continuously for 2 minutes to form a roux. Gradually whisk in the milk, ensuring a smooth consistency. Continue to cook, stirring constantly, for about 5 minutes, or until the sauce thickens. Remove the pan from the heat and stir in the Dijon mustard, cheddar, parmesan and nutmeg. Season to taste with salt.

When the pumpkin is ready, heat the olive oil in a large frying pan over medium heat. Add the red onion and cook for 5 minutes, or until softened. Add the garlic and sage leaves, frying until the sage is crisp and the garlic is fragrant, about 2 minutes. Add the roast pumpkin cubes and gently toss with the onion, garlic and sage. Set aside.

To make the crumb topping, combine the breadcrumbs, parmesan and melted butter in a small bowl. Sprinkle this crumb mixture evenly on top of the macaroni.

Preheat the oven grill (broiler) to high.

Combine the cooked macaroni with the pumpkin mixture in a large mixing bowl. Pour the mustard cheese sauce over the top and mix everything together until well combined. Transfer the mixture to a large casserole dish.

Place the dish on the top shelf of the oven to grill for 5–7 minutes, or until the top is golden brown and crispy.

Serve with a few extra sage leaves and grated parmesan if desired.

Crumb topping

30 g (1 oz/½ cup) Japanese breadcrumbs

2 tablespoons grated parmesan, plus extra to serve

20 g (¾ oz) salted butter, melted

Hints Cook more pumpkin than you need and use the surplus later in the week in salads or grain bowls. Store leftover pumpkin cubes in an airtight container in the fridge for up to 1 week or freeze in portions for up to 3 months.

For extra crunch, add some toasted pine nuts or walnuts to the crumb topping mixture.

The dish can be made ahead: assemble the macaroni and cheese, then cover and refrigerate. When ready to serve, add the crumb topping and grill.

WARMING & COMFORTING

Fish croquettes with yoghurt tartare sauce

(NF)

Prep 20 minutes
Cook 10 minutes
Serves 4

80–125 ml (2½–4 fl oz/⅓–½ cup) extra-virgin olive oil, for frying

8 × Fish croquettes (page 138), thawed if frozen

lemon wedges, to serve

Yoghurt tartare sauce

185 g (6½ oz/¾ cup) Greek-style yoghurt

60 g (2 oz/¼ cup) mayonnaise

2 tablespoons capers, rinsed, squeezed dry and finely chopped

2 tablespoons finely chopped gherkins (pickles)

1 tablespoon lemon juice

1 teaspoon Dijon mustard

1 tablespoon finely chopped dill

sea salt

Perfect for a weeknight meal or the next time you're entertaining, these make-ahead croquettes are as a versatile as they are delicious.

For the yoghurt tartare sauce, combine the yoghurt, mayonnaise, capers, gherkins, lemon juice, Dijon mustard and dill in a small bowl. Season with salt to taste, then set aside.

Heat the olive oil in a frying pan over medium heat. Fry the thawed croquettes until golden brown and heated through, about 3–4 minutes on each side. Drain on paper towel.

Serve the croquettes with the yoghurt tartare sauce, lemon wedges and a side of steamed green beans or a Greek salad (see page 127).

Hint If you're short on time, you can fry the croquettes straight from frozen; just increase the cooking time by a few minutes per side.

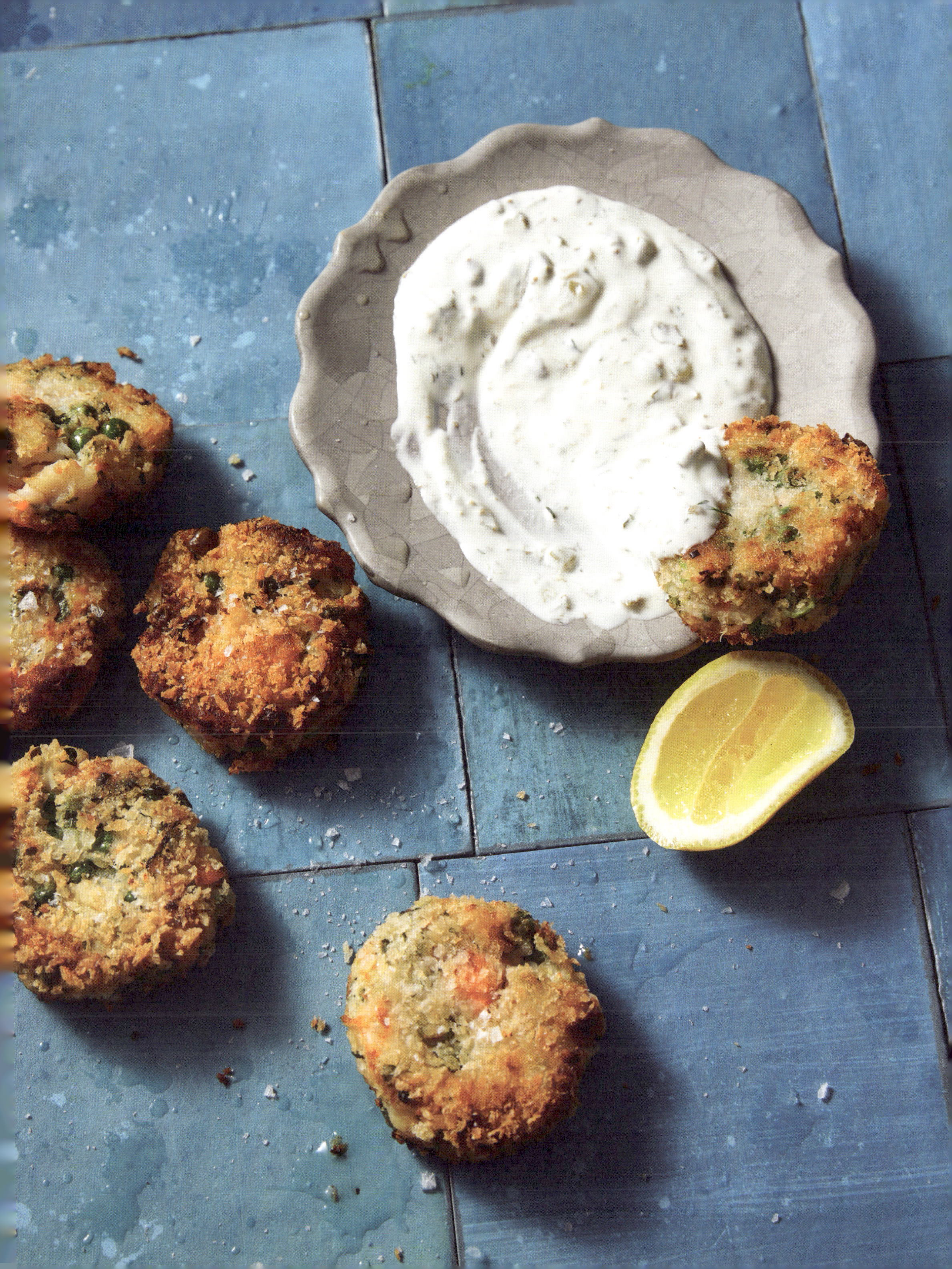

Greek lamb with orzo

NF DF

Prep 20 minutes
Cook 10 minutes
Serves 4

400 g (14 oz) orzo

1 × Slow-cooked lamb shoulder (page 140), meat shredded and warmed

baby peas, to serve

lemon zest, to serve

flat-leaf (Italian) parsley, chopped, to serve

sea salt and freshly ground black pepper

The orzo beautifully absorbs the flavour-soaked juicy lamb in this dish, which the little ones will love as much as the bigger ones.

Preheat the oven to 160°C (320°F).

Cook the orzo in a large saucepan of salted boiling water according to package instructions. Drain and set aside.

Spoon some of the lamb pan juices into the pasta and stir to combine.

Serve the warm shredded lamb over the orzo with some baby peas. Top with lemon zest, plenty of parsley and salt and pepper.

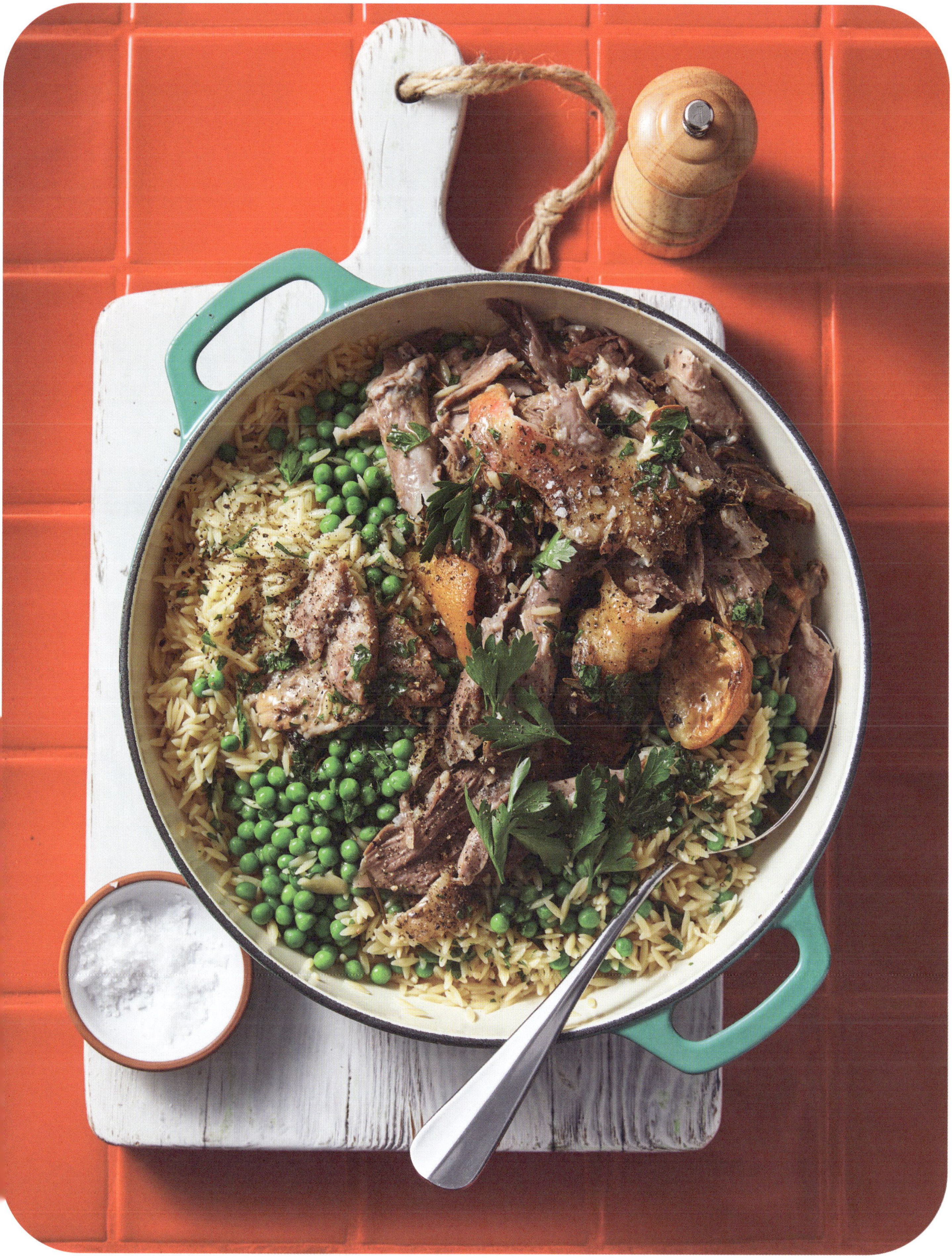

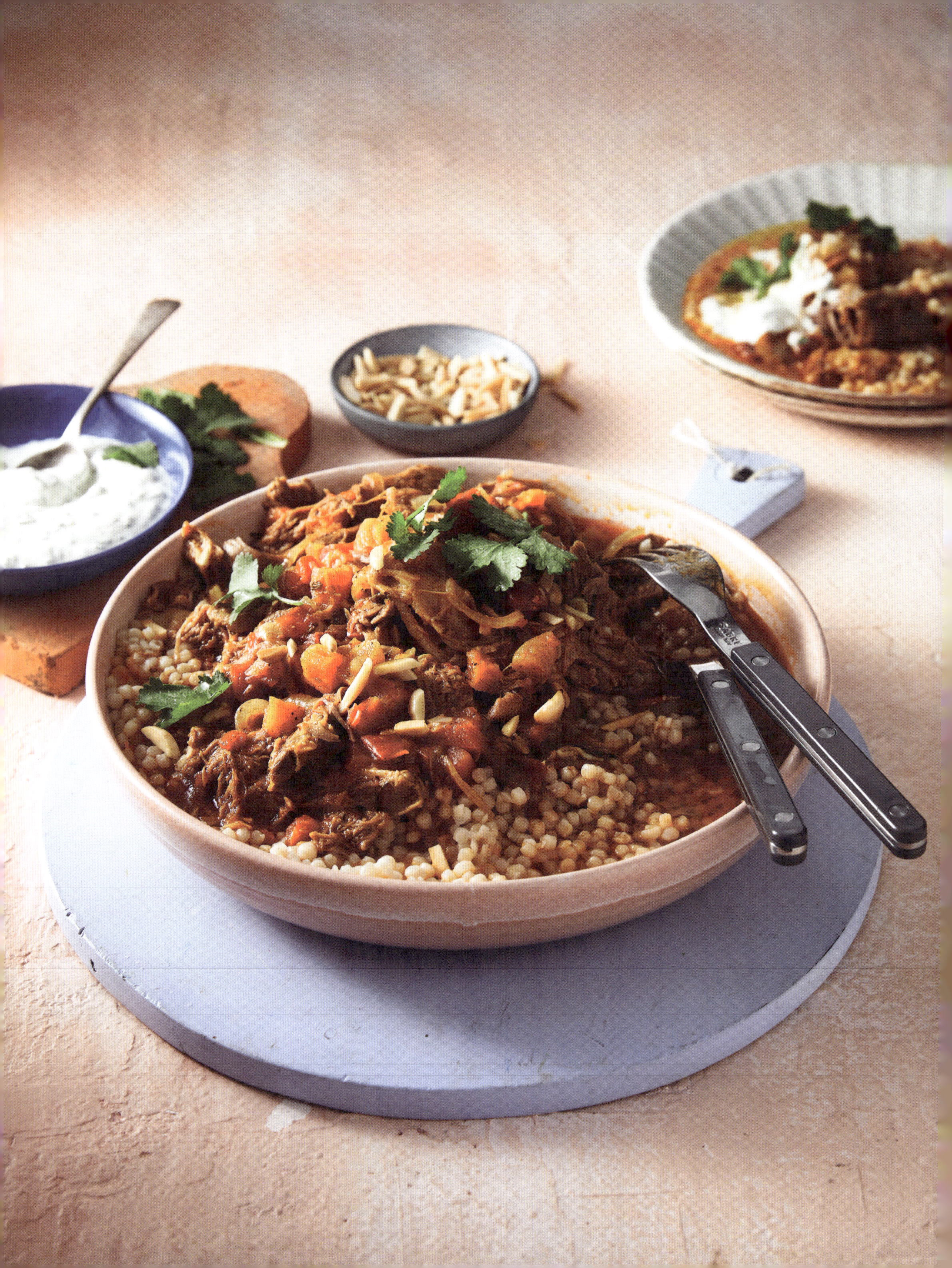

Lamb tagine with couscous

(DF)

Prep 45 minutes
Cook 30 minutes
Serves 4

| 1 tablespoon extra-virgin olive oil |
| 1 onion, finely sliced |
| 2 garlic cloves, crushed |
| 1 teaspoon each ground cumin, coriander, cinnamon |
| ½ teaspoon ground ginger |
| ¼ teaspoon each ground turmeric, paprika |
| 500 g (1 lb 2 oz) leftover shredded Slow-cooked lamb shoulder (page 140) |
| 400 g (14 oz) tinned diced tomatoes |
| 1 tablespoon tomato paste (concentrated puree) |
| 200 ml (7 fl oz) Chicken bone broth (page 139) or chicken stock |
| 100 g (3½ oz) dried apricots, chopped |
| 185 g (6½ oz/1 cup) pearl couscous |
| 2 tablespoons chopped mint leaves |
| 2 tablespoons chopped coriander (cilantro) leaves, plus extra to serve (optional) |
| 50 g (1¾ oz) toasted slivered almonds, plus extra to serve |

Citrus yoghurt dressing

| 125 g (4½ oz/½ cup) Greek-style yoghurt |
| juice of ½ lemon |
| 2 tablespoons chopped mint leaves |
| 2 tablespoons chopped coriander (cilantro) leaves (optional) |
| sea salt |

The array of spices in this dish turns your leftover Slow-cooked lamb shoulder (page 140) into a sumptuous meal that, alongside pearl couscous and a citrus yoghurt dressing, transports your dinner table to Morocco.

Heat the olive oil in a large saucepan over medium heat. Add the onion and garlic and sauté for 2–3 minutes, until softened. Add the ground cumin, coriander, cinnamon, ginger, turmeric and paprika and stir for 30–60 seconds, until fragrant. Stir in the shredded lamb, coating it with the spices. Pour in the tomatoes, tomato paste and stock and stir to combine.

Bring to a simmer, then add the apricots. Cover and cook for 20 minutes, stirring occasionally.

While the lamb is simmering, prepare the couscous according to the package instructions. Fluff with a fork and stir in the chopped mint and coriander leaves (if using).

For the dressing, mix the yoghurt, lemon juice, mint and coriander leaves in a small bowl and season with salt.

Stir the almonds into the lamb tagine just before serving.

Serve the lamb on top of the couscous and top with the dressing, extra almonds and coriander leaves.

Hints If you prefer a richer flavour, use lamb stock instead of chicken bone broth.

For extra sweetness, add a handful of sultanas (golden raisins) to the couscous.

For a bit of heat, include a pinch of chilli flakes.

WARMING & COMFORTING

Grilled steak with stroganoff sauce

GF NF

Prep 45 minutes
Cook 45 minutes
Serves 4

1 × 600 g (1 lb 5 oz) skirt, flank or flat iron steak
2 tablespoons extra-virgin olive oil
1 onion, finely sliced
2 garlic cloves, minced
200 g (7 oz) mushrooms, sliced
1 tablespoon Dijon mustard
1 tablespoon Worcestershire sauce
1 tablespoon tomato paste (concentrated puree)
1 teaspoon paprika
250 ml (8½ fl oz/1 cup) beef stock
200 g (7 oz) sour cream
20 g (¾ oz) salted butter
2 tablespoons chopped flat-leaf (Italian) parsley
sea salt and freshly ground black pepper
pasta or mashed potato, to serve
seasonal green vegetables, to serve

When you have a hungry family who can't wait for dinner, this classic stroganoff will save the day.

Preheat the barbecue or a chargrill pan to high heat.

Season the steak with salt and pepper and rub with 1 tablespoon of the olive oil. Grill or fry the steak for 4–5 minutes on each side for medium-rare, or adjust to your preferred doneness. Remove from the heat, cover with baking paper and allow it to rest.

In a large saucepan, heat the remaining olive oil over medium heat. Add the onion and cook for 5 minutes, until softened. Add the garlic and mushrooms and cook for 15 minutes, until the mushrooms are golden and tender. Stir in the Dijon mustard, Worcestershire sauce, tomato paste and paprika. Pour in the beef stock and bring to a simmer. Allow the sauce to simmer for 5 minutes to reduce slightly, then stir in the sour cream until well combined. Taste and adjust the seasoning with salt and pepper if needed.

Slice the rested steak into thin strips and nestle them into the pan with the stroganoff sauce. Add the butter and allow it to melt into the sauce, then sprinkle in the parsley.

Serve the stroganoff steak with pasta or mashed potato alongside your choice of seasonal green vegetables.

Hints For a richer sauce, you can add a splash of brandy or cognac before adding the stock.

If you prefer a thicker sauce, mix a little flour with the beef stock before adding it to the pan.

This dish can be prepared ahead by making the sauce up to 3 days in advance and reheating it before serving with freshly grilled steak.

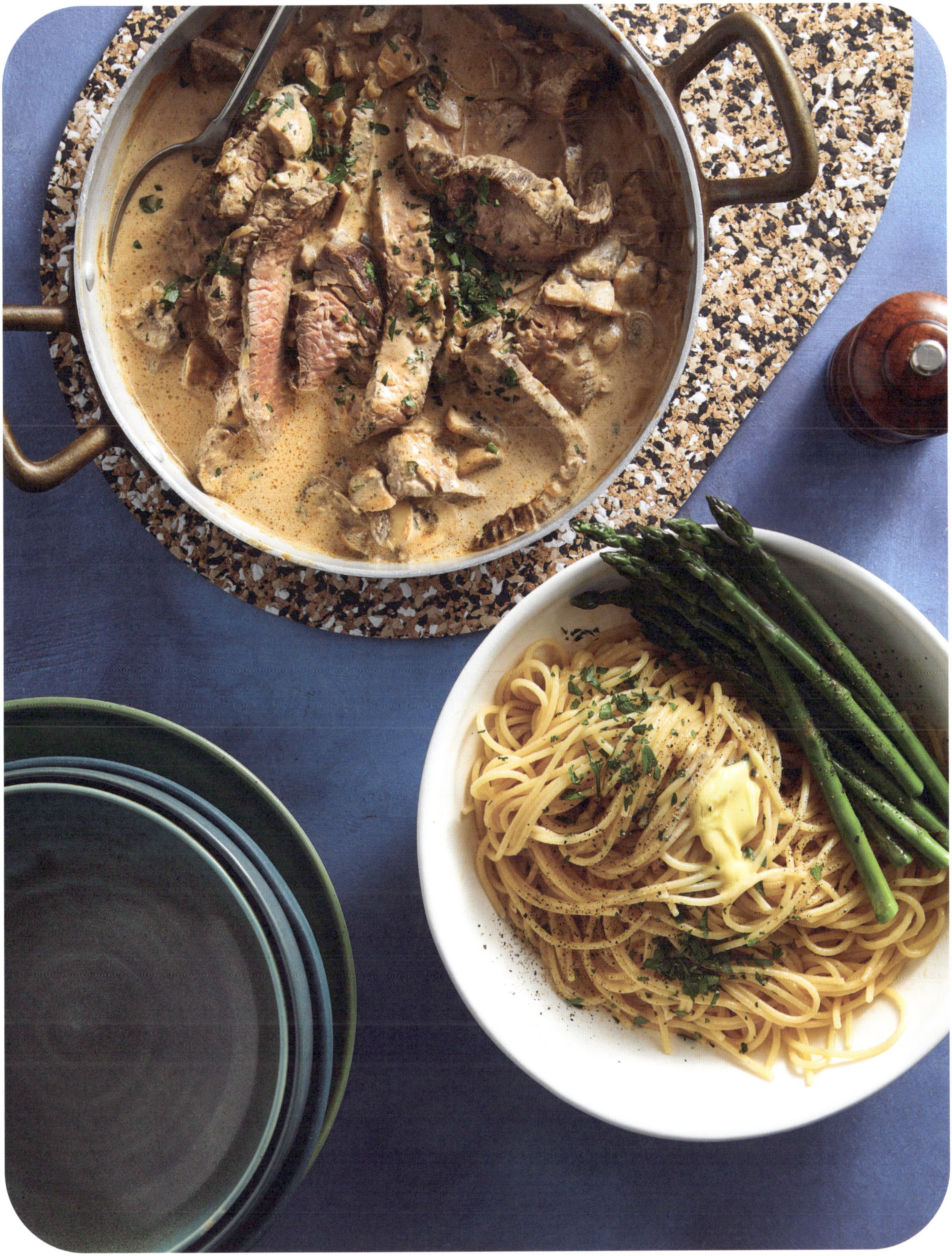

Tomato coconut dal with baked fish

GF NF V

Prep 40 minutes
Cook 15 minutes
Serves 4

4 × 200 g (7 oz) firm white fish fillets, skinless and boneless

½ teaspoon paprika

sea salt and freshly ground black pepper

extra-virgin olive oil, to drizzle and serve

1 × quantity Tomato coconut dal (page 141)

basmati rice, to serve

greek-style yoghurt, to serve

coriander (cilantro) sprigs, to serve (optional)

lemon wedges, to serve

Subtly spiced, this nutrient-packed one-dish dinner makes an easy yet elegant evening meal. Any type of firm white fish will work; use what is available.

Preheat the oven to 180°C (360°F).

Season the fish fillets with paprika, salt and a little olive oil.

Place the dal in a shallow ovenproof dish and nestle the fillets into the dal.

Bake for 12–15 minutes, or until the fish is just cooked through and softly poached.

Serve with basmati rice and a dollop of yoghurt topped with some black pepper and a drizzle of olive oil. Add coriander (if using) and lemon wedges on the side.

Hint Add a splash of lime juice to the yoghurt for a tangy twist.

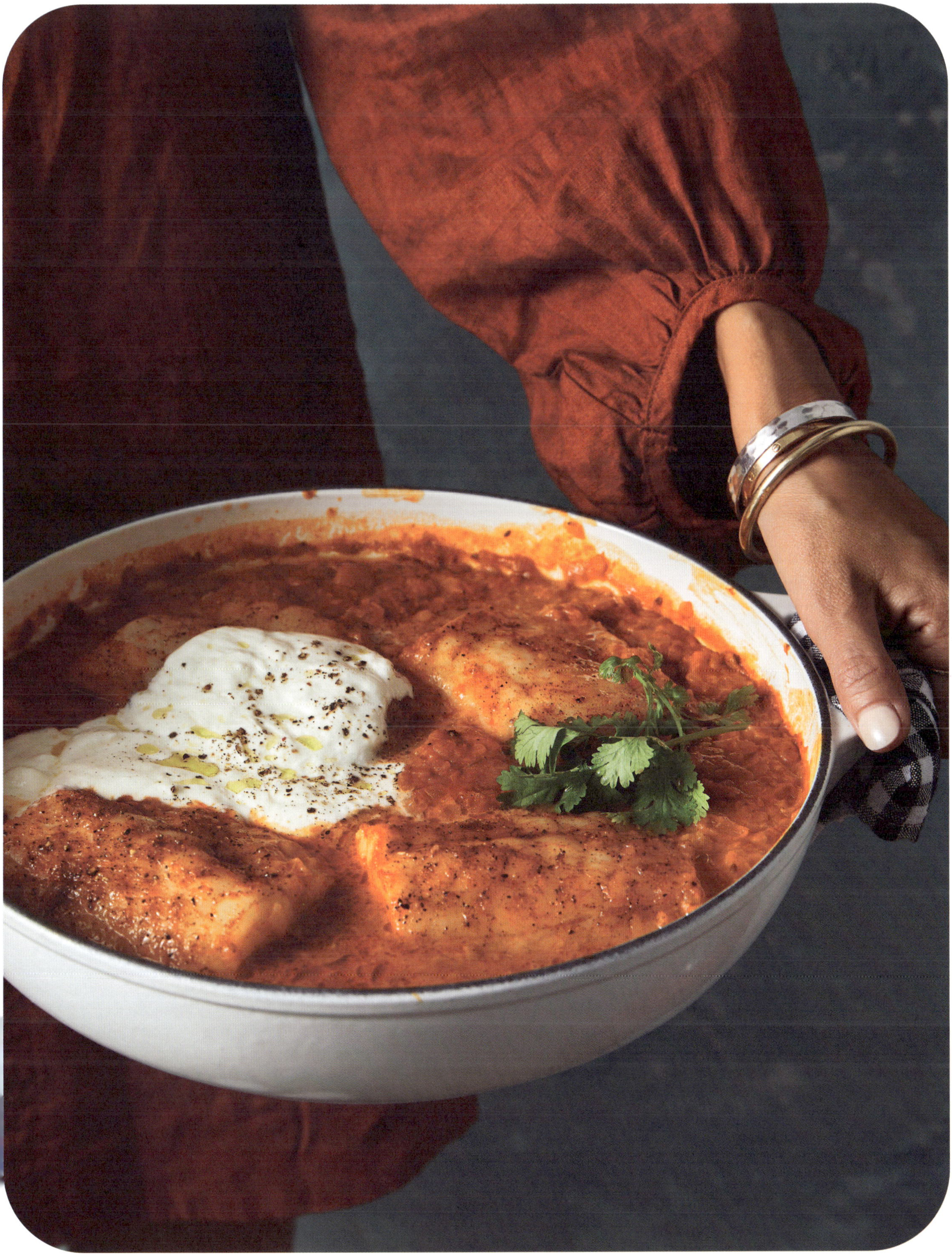

Hoisin meatloaf with potato gratin

NF

Prep 1 hour 40 minutes
Cook 1 hour 30 minutes
Serves 4–6

green beans, blanched, to serve

chilli sauce, to serve (optional)

Potato gratin

3 large potatoes, peeled and thinly sliced

2 tablespoons extra-virgin olive oil, plus extra for greasing

2 garlic cloves, crushed

3 spring onions (scallions), finely chopped

170 g (6 oz/1⅓ cups) gruyere, comté or smoked cheddar, grated

250 ml (8½ fl oz/1 cup) thick (double/heavy) cream

Meatloaf

1 × quantity Hoisin sauce (page 73) or store-bought

2 tablespoons soy sauce

2 teaspoons sichuan peppercorns, crushed (optional)

2 teaspoons freshly grated ginger

1½ teaspoons avocado oil

2 teaspoons rice vinegar

¾ teaspoon honey

45 g (1½ oz/¾ cup) Japanese breadcrumbs, soaked in 185 ml (6 fl oz/¾ cup) milk

2 eggs

4 garlic cloves, minced

500 g (1 lb 2 oz) minced (ground) veal

500 g (1 lb 2 oz) minced (ground) pork

6 × bacon rashers (slices)

If you have never tried meatloaf, now is the time. This version brings the classic dish into the modern world.

Preheat the oven to 200°C (390°F). Line a baking tray with baking paper and grease a casserole dish with the extra olive oil.

For the potato gratin, combine the potato in a large bowl with the olive oil, garlic, spring onion and 110 g (4 oz/1 cup) of the cheese. Toss well, then layer the potato evenly in the casserole dish.

Pour the cream over the potato, cover with baking paper and bake for 45 minutes, or until the potato is tender.

While the gratin is baking, prepare the meatloaf. Combine the hoisin sauce, soy sauce, peppercorns (if using), ginger, avocado oil, rice vinegar and honey in a food processor and blend until a fine paste forms. Transfer the paste to a large bowl and mix it with the breadcrumbs soaked in milk, eggs, garlic, minced veal and pork until well combined.

Use your hands to form the mixture into a log shape and place it on the baking tray.

Remove the potato gratin from the oven (leaving the baking paper in place) and reduce the oven temperature to 200°C (390°F). Place the meatloaf in the oven and bake for 30 minutes.

Remove the meatloaf from the oven and top it with the slices of bacon. Take the baking paper off the gratin, sprinkle the remaining cheese on top, then return it to the oven at the same time as the meatloaf and cook for a further 10 minutes. When ready, the bacon on the meatloaf should be crisp on the edges and the cheese on the gratin should be melted and golden.

Serve the bacon-topped meatloaf with the potato gratin, green beans and chilli sauce (if using) on the side.

Hints When buying bacon, look for a preservative-free option that doesn't contain added nitrates.

Leftover meatloaf makes a delicious sandwich filling.

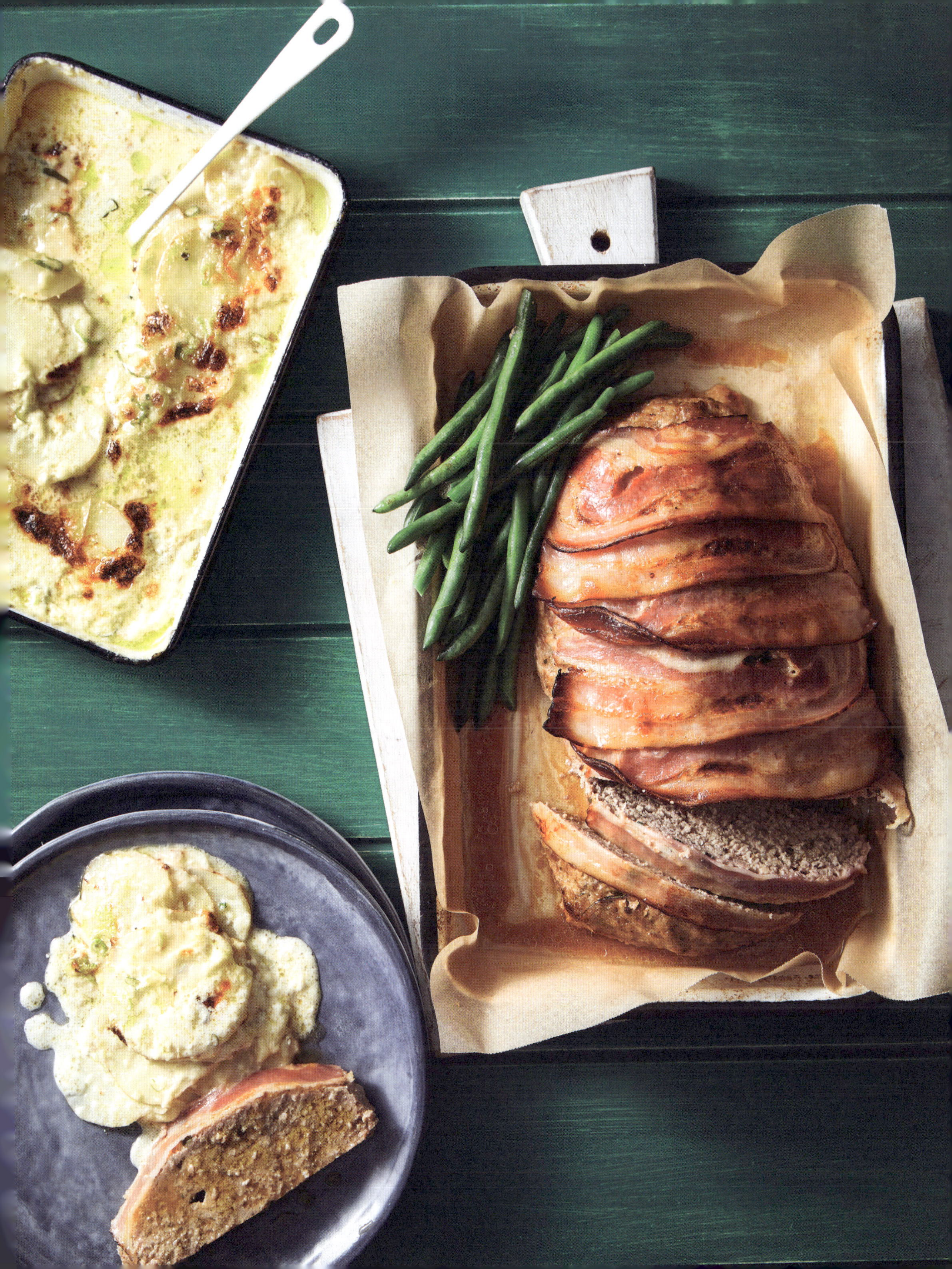

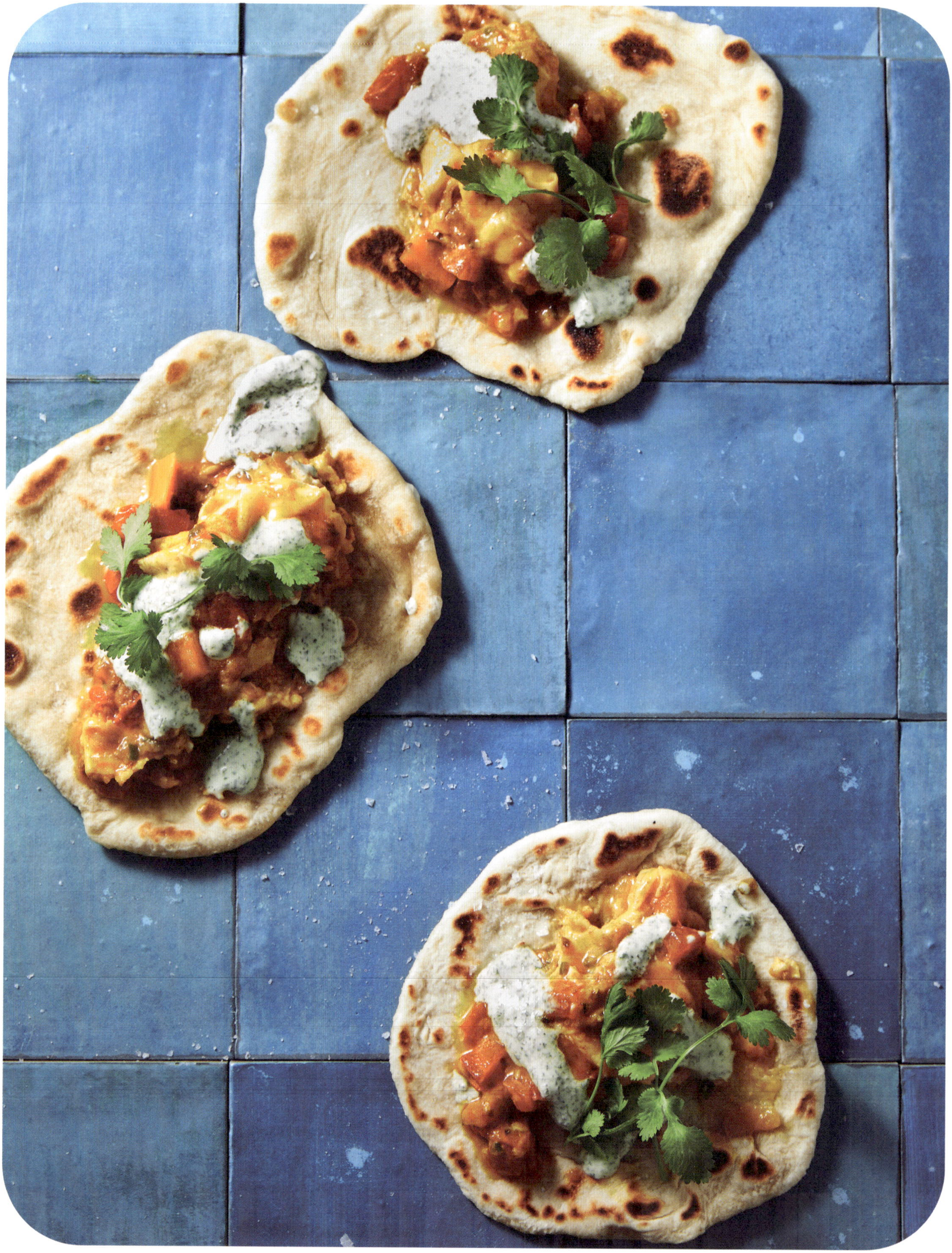

Spiced egg and tomato flatbreads

NF V

Prep 15 minutes
Cook 15 minutes
Serves 4

2 tablespoons extra-virgin olive oil

1 teaspoon ground cumin

½ teaspoon ground turmeric

½ teaspoon chilli flakes (optional)

1 green chilli, finely chopped (optional)

2 tomatoes, diced

125 ml (4 fl oz/½ cup) Tomato coconut dal (page 141)

8 eggs, beaten and seasoned with salt

7 g (¼ oz/¼ cup) coriander (cilantro) leaves, chopped, plus extra to serve (optional)

½ quantity Home-made flatbreads (page 226) or 4 store-bought

Yoghurt sauce

15 g (½ oz/¼ cup) mint leaves

15 g (½ oz/¼ cup) coriander leaves (optional)

120 g (4½ oz/½ cup) Greek-style yoghurt

This is a flavour combination you won't know you needed until you've tried it!

Heat the olive oil in a non-stick pan over medium heat. Add the cumin, turmeric, and chilli flakes and green chilli (if using) and stir until fragrant, about 30 seconds. Add the tomato and cook until softened, about 2 minutes. Add half of the dal and stir until warmed through. Pour the eggs into the pan, stirring gently with a spatula to create soft curds. Continue to stir until the eggs are softly scrambled but not dry. Remove from the heat and stir in the coriander (if using).

To make the yoghurt sauce, place the mint, coriander (if using) and yoghurt in a food processor and blend until smooth.

Warm the flatbreads in a dry pan or microwave.

Spread the remaining dal on the flatbreads, then spoon the tomato scrambled egg on top, garnish with extra coriander (if using) and serve immediately. Alternatively, roll the filled flatbreads up and wrap them in baking paper for an on-the-go breakfast.

Hints For extra flavour, sprinkle some crumbled feta over the scrambled egg before wrapping.

Add a handful of spinach to the scrambled egg for some extra greens.

You can use any leftover dal or curry you have on hand for this recipe.

WARMING & COMFORTING

Choc peanut porridge

GF DF V

Prep 15 minutes
Cook 10 minutes
Serves 4

200 g (7 oz/2 cups) rolled (porridge) oats
1 litre (34 fl oz/4 cups) almond milk
2 tablespoons Dutch (unsweetened) cocoa powder
½ teaspoon vanilla extract
2 tablespoons honey
60 g (2 oz/¼ cup) smooth peanut butter
¼ teaspoon sea salt
banana, sliced, to serve
dark chocolate chips, to serve (optional)
roasted peanuts, chopped, to serve (optional)

This could just as easily be dessert as breakfast. The best part is, it's as nutritious as it is delicious.

Combine the oats and 300 ml (10 fl oz) of water in a bowl and soak for 20 minutes (or overnight).

Place the soaked oats in a medium saucepan over medium heat with 750 ml (25½ fl oz/3 cups) of the almond milk, cocoa powder, vanilla and 1 tablespoon of the honey. Cook for 10 minutes, stirring occasionally, until the oats are creamy and tender. Stir in the peanut butter and sea salt until well combined. Gradually add the remaining almond milk, adjusting to your desired consistency.

Divide the porridge into bowls and top with the sliced banana. Drizzle with the remaining honey and top with dark chocolate chips and roasted peanuts, if using.

Hints For a richer flavour, substitute almond milk with coconut milk.

If you prefer a sweeter porridge, add an extra tablespoon of honey.

For a vegan version, substitute honey with pure maple syrup and make sure the chocolate is at least 70% cocoa.

To make the porridge extra creamy, stir in a splash of thick (double/heavy) cream just before serving.

THE WEEKLY GROCERY SHOP

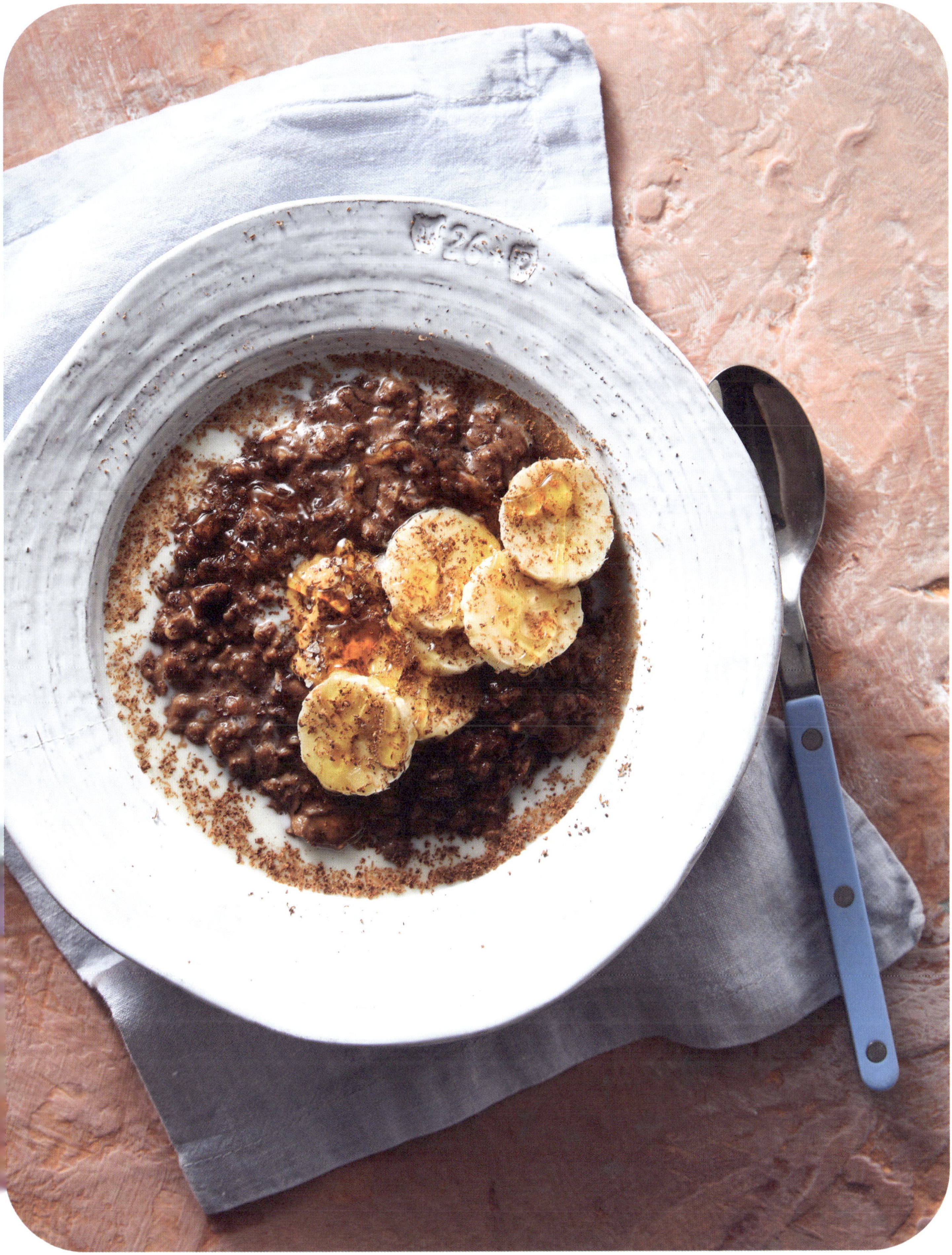

As-you-like-it popcorn seasoning

GF | NF | DF | V | VG

Once you've made your own popcorn seasoning, you'll never buy it again. Try out these easy recipes, then choose your own adventure. The options are endless!

Prep 15 minutes
Serves Enough seasoning for 4–6 servings

Sour cream and chives seasoning

15 g (½ oz/¼ cup) nutritional yeast
2 tablespoons dried chives
½ teaspoon onion powder
½ teaspoon garlic powder
½ teaspoon dried dill
sea salt

Combine all the ingredients in a blender or spice grinder. Blend until it forms a fine powder. Adjust salt to taste. Store in an airtight container and use as required.

Sweet and tangy seasoning

4 tablespoons caster sugar
2 teaspoons sea salt

Mix the ingredients thoroughly in a small bowl. Adjust salt to taste. Store in an airtight container and use as required.

Barbecue chicken seasoning

2 tablespoons smoked paprika
1 tablespoon onion powder
1 tablespoon garlic powder
1 tablespoon nutritional yeast
1 teaspoon dried oregano
1 teaspoon dried thyme
½ teaspoon cayenne pepper (adjust for heat preference)
1 teaspoon soft brown sugar
½ teaspoon mustard powder
sea salt

Combine all the ingredients in a blender or spice grinder. Blend until smooth and well combined. Adjust salt to taste. Store in an airtight container and use as required.

Hints If you prefer a finer powder, blend for longer or use a fine mesh sieve to remove any larger pieces.

Feel free to tweak the seasonings to match your preferred flavour intensity.

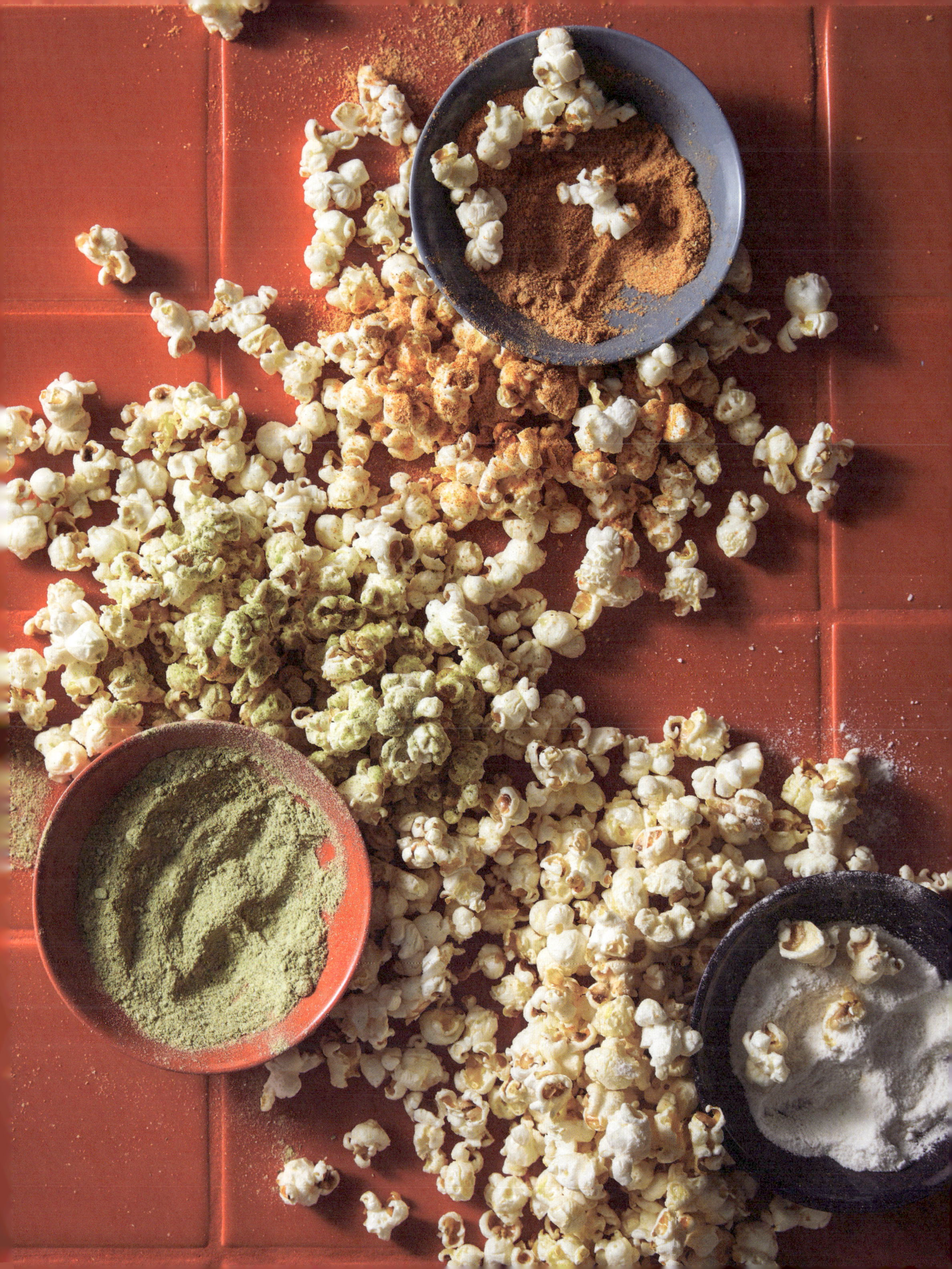

Sticky date mini cakes

NF V

Prep 45 minutes
Cook 25 minutes
Makes 12

200 g (7 oz) pitted dates, roughly chopped

1 teaspoon bicarbonate of soda (baking soda)

250 ml (8½ fl oz/1 cup) boiling water

100 g (3½ oz) unsalted butter, softened, plus extra for greasing

150 g (5½ oz) coconut sugar or soft brown sugar

2 eggs, lightly beaten

1 teaspoon vanilla extract

200 g (7 oz) wholemeal (whole-wheat) flour

1½ teaspoons baking powder

sea salt

Easy caramel sauce

100 g (3½ oz) coconut sugar or soft brown sugar

50 g (1¾ oz) unsalted butter

100 ml (3½ fl oz) thick (double/heavy) cream

1 teaspoon vanilla extract

sea salt

Brown sugar whipped cream

300 ml (10 fl oz) thick (double/heavy) cream

2 tablespoons soft brown sugar

½ teaspoon vanilla extract

Choosing a favourite recipe is like choosing a favourite child – don't do it. (But I'll give you a hint – this one.) These mini cakes are decadent, yet so easy to make.

Place the chopped dates in a bowl with the bicarbonate of soda. Pour the boiling water over the dates and set aside to soften for 10 minutes.

Preheat the oven to 180°C (360°F). Grease a standard 12-hole muffin tin with the extra butter.

Cream the butter and sugar together in a bowl using an electric mixer until light and fluffy. Add the eggs and vanilla extract to the butter mixture, beating well. Gently fold in the softened date mixture, flour, baking powder and a pinch of salt until just combined.

Divide the batter evenly between the muffin holes. Bake for 20–25 minutes, or until a skewer inserted into a muffin centre comes out clean. Allow the muffins to cool slightly in the tin before transferring them to a wire rack.

For the easy caramel sauce, combine the sugar, butter, cream and vanilla extract in a small saucepan over medium heat. Cook, stirring constantly, for 5–7 minutes, until the sugar dissolves and the sauce thickens slightly. Stir in a pinch of salt, to taste, then set aside to cool.

For the brown sugar whipped cream, whisk the cream, brown sugar and vanilla extract in a large bowl using an electric mixer until soft peaks form. Keep chilled until ready to serve.

Serve the sticky date mini cakes with a drizzle of caramel sauce and a dollop of brown sugar whipped cream.

Hints Substitute a portion of the flour with almond meal for a nuttier flavour.

Store the mini cakes in an airtight container in the fridge for up to 1 week or freeze for up to 3 months. Store the caramel sauce in the fridge for up to 1 week; warm before serving. Reheat frozen mini cakes for 10–15 minutes at 160°C (320°F).

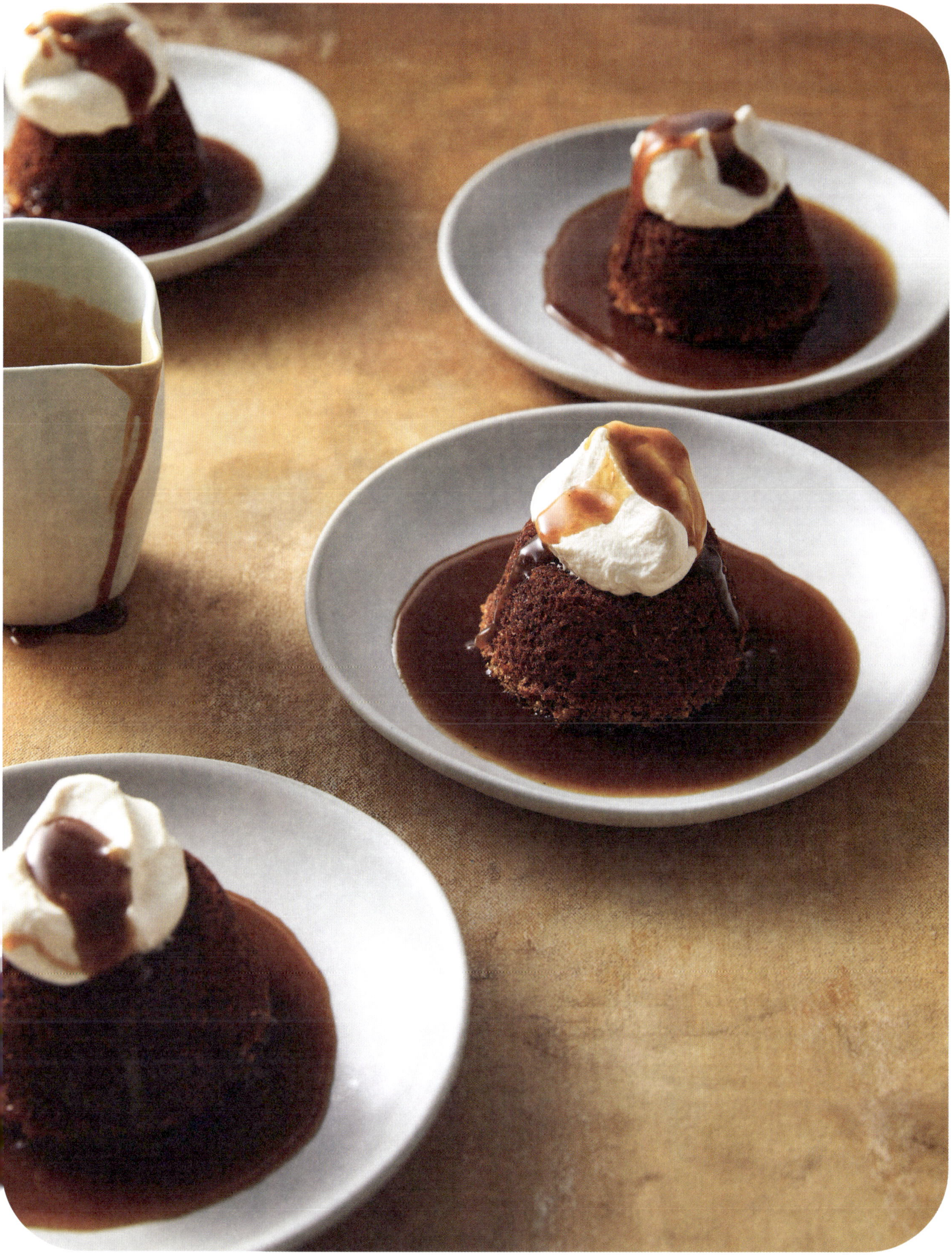

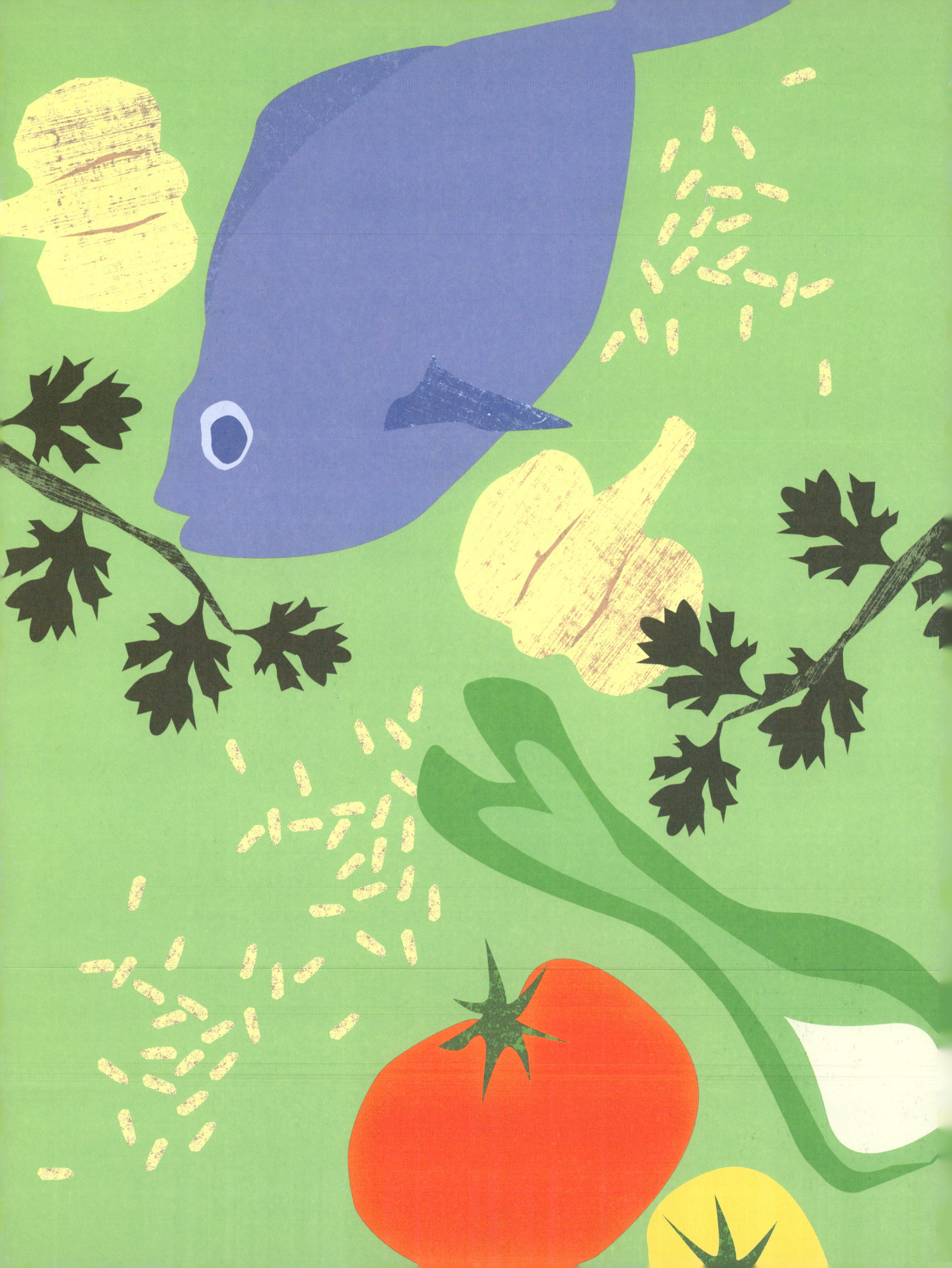

Light & fresh

During the warm months, I prefer to prepare lighter, quicker meals that require less time in the kitchen. I enjoy making the most of seasonal produce in fresh, vibrant salads and using the barbecue or grill to cook veggies and easy proteins. Whenever we can, we love to dine outdoors.

See page 74 for a key to the dietary symbols used on the recipes.

Week 1 menu

Power prep

Lemon mayonnaise
Seasoned beef mince
Herb dressing
Butterflied roast chicken

Dinners

Butterflied roast chicken with lemon potatoes
Chicken, noodle and cabbage salad
Caprese smash burgers
Crusted pork fillet with juicy roast tomatoes
Spinach spiral pie with lemon mayonnaise
Summer tuna pasta salad
Beef koftas with grilled haloumi, zucchini and broccoli salad

Breakfasts

BLT omelette tray
Home-made granola

Snack

Corn cobettes with cheese, chilli mayonnaise and lime

Sweet

Carrot cake energy bites

Week 1 shopping list

Fruit & vegetables

- [ ] 2 bunches basil
- [ ] 1 bunch Thai basil
- [ ] 125 g (4½ oz) bean sprouts
- [ ] 200 g (7 oz) young green beans
- [ ] 1 large head of broccoli
- [ ] 1 green or red cabbage
- [ ] 2 large carrots
- [ ] 1 bunch coriander (cilantro) (optional)
- [ ] 1 bunch dill
- [ ] 1 garlic bulb
- [ ] 2.5 cm (1 in) piece of fresh ginger
- [ ] 8 lemons
- [ ] 1 iceberg lettuce
- [ ] 1 lime
- [ ] 1 bunch mint
- [ ] 1 small onion
- [ ] 2 small red onions
- [ ] 2 bunches flat-leaf (Italian) parsley
- [ ] 1 kg (2 lb 3 oz) baby (chat) potatoes
- [ ] 80 g (2¾ oz) mixed salad leaves
- [ ] 6 spring onions (scallions)
- [ ] 9 large tomatoes
- [ ] 300 g (10½ oz) cherry tomatoes on the vine
- [ ] 500 g (1 lb 2 oz) heirloom or mixed tomatoes
- [ ] 2 zucchini (courgettes)

Meat & poultry

- [ ] 1 kg (2 lb 3 oz) minced (ground) beef
- [ ] 2 × whole butterflied chickens
- [ ] 2 × 350 g (12½ oz) pork fillets

Pantry & baking

- [ ] 60 g (2 oz) toasted slivered almonds
- [ ] 2 baguettes
- [ ] 120 g (4½ oz/1½ cups) coarse, fresh sourdough breadcrumbs (about 3 slices of sourdough bread)
- [ ] 25 g (1 oz) fresh breadcrumbs
- [ ] 190 g (6½ oz) couscous
- [ ] 500 g (1 lb 2 oz) rigatoni
- [ ] 400 g (14 oz) soba or udon noodles
- [ ] 1 teaspoon white (granulated) sugar
- [ ] 425 g (15 oz) tinned tuna in olive oil
- [ ] 8 wooden skewers

Fridge

- [ ] 4 eggs
- [ ] 400 g (14 oz) haloumi
- [ ] 60 ml (2 fl oz) milk
- [ ] 350 g (12½ oz) mozzarella
- [ ] 75 g (2¾ oz) parmesan
- [ ] 500 g (1 lb 2 oz) ricotta
- [ ] 125 g (4½ oz) Greek-style yoghurt

Freezer

- [ ] 750 g (1 lb 11 oz) filo pastry sheets
- [ ] 1 kg (2 lb 3 oz) frozen spinach

Lemon mayonnaise

Prep 3 minutes
Makes 340 ml (11½ fl oz/1⅓ cups)

1 large egg, at room temperature
1 tablespoon Dijon mustard
1 tablespoon lemon juice
1 teaspoon finely grated lemon zest
1 small garlic clove, minced (optional)
250 ml (8½ fl oz/1 cup) avocado oil
sea salt and freshly ground black pepper

Upgrade the Spinach spiral pie (page 180) with this tangy mayonnaise, use it to dress the chopped salad for Caprese smash burgers (page 176), or simply drizzle it over freshly steamed green beans.

In a tall, narrow container that fits the head of your hand-held blender, add the egg, Dijon mustard, lemon juice and zest, garlic (if using) and oil. Place the blender at the bottom of the container, ensuring it covers the egg yolk, and turn the blender on at its highest setting. Keep the blender stationary for about 10–15 seconds, until you see the mayonnaise start to emulsify at the bottom. Slowly lift the blender upwards through the mixture, allowing the oil to be incorporated gradually until you have a thick, creamy mayonnaise.

Season with salt and pepper, to taste.

Serve immediately or store in an airtight container in the fridge for up to 1 week.

Hints For best results, ensure all your ingredients, especially the egg, are at room temperature.

If you don't have a hand-held blender, you can make the mayonnaise using a whisk by adding the first five ingredients to a large mixing bowl and whisking until completely combined. Then begin to add the oil, ½ teaspoon at a time, whisking well to emulsify, until you have added about 60 ml (2 fl oz/¼ cup) of the oil. Then add the remaining oil in a steady stream while continuing to whisk.

You can adjust the thickness by adding a small amount of water or more lemon juice if needed.

For an extra twist, add a pinch of smoked paprika or some herbs.

(GF) (NF) (DF) (V)

Seasoned beef mince

Prep 15 minutes
Makes 2 meals for 4 people

25 g (1 oz/¼ cup) fresh breadcrumbs

60 ml (2 fl oz/¼ cup) milk

1 kg (2 lb 3 oz) minced (ground) beef

1 small onion, finely grated

3 garlic cloves, minced

15 g (½ oz/¼ cup) flat-leaf (Italian) parsley, finely chopped

15 g (½ oz/¼ cup) basil leaves, finely chopped

1 teaspoon dried oregano

1 teaspoon ground cumin

1 teaspoon ground coriander

½ teaspoon smoked paprika

½ teaspoon chilli flakes (optional)

25 g (1 oz/¼ cup) parmesan, grated

1 large egg, lightly beaten

2 tablespoons extra-virgin olive oil

sea salt and freshly ground black pepper

Prepping your beef ahead of time not only enhances the flavour of the meat, it makes Caprese smash burgers (page 176) and Beef koftas (page 184) into ultra-quick, tasty meals.

Soak the breadcrumbs in the milk until soft, about 15 minutes. (Or, to prepare ahead, you can soak the breadcrumbs overnight in the fridge.)

Combine the minced beef, onion, garlic, fresh herbs, oregano, cumin, coriander, smoked paprika, chilli flakes (if using) and parmesan in a large mixing bowl. Add the milky breadcrumbs and the egg to the mixture and season generously with salt and pepper.

Pour the olive oil in and use your hands to mix everything together until well combined – but do not overwork the beef.

Divide the seasoned beef into two portions. Place in airtight containers and refrigerate for up to 2 days or freeze for up to 3 months.

Hints Use Japanese breadcrumbs for a lighter texture in the beef mince mixture.

For a stronger flavour, let the seasoned beef mince sit in the fridge for at least 1 hour before using.

(NF)

LIGHT & FRESH

Herb dressing

Prep 15 minutes
Makes 750 ml (25½ fl oz/3 cups)

120 g (4½ oz/2 cups) of your favourite herbs, finely chopped

2 garlic cloves, minced

2 tablespoons capers, rinsed, squeezed dry and finely chopped

2 tablespoons Dijon mustard

zest and juice of 1 lemon

60 ml (2 fl oz/¼ cup) red-wine vinegar

125 ml (4 fl oz/½ cup) extra-virgin olive oil

½ teaspoon chilli flakes (optional)

1 teaspoon honey

sea salt and freshly ground black pepper

The fresh herbs in this dressing make it ideal for dressing up grilled meats or vegetables, and the capers work magic in a potato salad. Or mix it with mayonnaise for a more-ish dipping sauce.

Combine the fresh herbs, garlic and capers in a large mixing bowl. Add the Dijon mustard, lemon zest and juice, red-wine vinegar and olive oil and whisk until well combined.

Stir in the chilli flakes (if using) and honey, then season generously with salt and pepper. Taste the sauce and adjust the seasoning as needed.

If a thinner consistency is desired, add more olive oil or lemon juice.

Use immediately or store in an airtight container or jar in the fridge for up to 1 week. (You'll need to shake it up before serving.)

(GF) (NF) (DF) (V) (VG)

Hints For a milder flavour, reduce the amount of garlic or capers.

Herbs like flat-leaf (Italian) parsley, mint, basil and dill work well in this dressing.

This sauce can be made a day in advance and stored in the fridge to allow the flavours to meld.

To make a creamy dressing, blend the sauce with a small amount of Greek-style yoghurt or sour cream.

Butterflied roast chicken

Prep 5 minutes
Cook 40 minutes
Makes 2 meals for 4 people

2 × whole butterflied chickens, at room temperature

juice of 1 lemon

sea salt

This easy, cook-once-use-twice recipe results in two delicious chicken dinners: a roast with lemon potatoes (page 172) and a noodle salad (page 175).

Preheat the oven to 220°C (430°F).

Place the butterflied chickens on a large baking tray. Pat them dry with paper towel, then drizzle them with lemon juice and season with salt.

Roast the chickens for 1 hour, or until the skin is golden brown and the juices run clear when pierced at the thickest part.

When the chicken is done, remove it from the oven and let it rest for 10 minutes before using.

Allow the second chicken to cool before storing it in an airtight container in the fridge for up to 3 days or freezing for up to 3 months.

(GF) (NF) (DF)

LIGHT & FRESH

Butterflied roast chicken with lemon potatoes

GF NF

Prep 15 minutes
Cook 45 minutes
Serves 4

1 kg (2 lb 3 oz) baby (chat) potatoes, cut into three rounds
2 tablespoons extra-virgin olive oil
juice of ½ lemon
500 g (1 lb 2 oz) heirloom or mixed tomatoes, sliced
1 small red onion, thinly sliced
200 g (7 oz) mozzarella, torn into pieces
1 bunch basil, leaves torn
250 ml (8½ fl oz/1 cup) Herb dressing (page 170)
1 × Butterflied roast chicken (page 171), hot
sea salt

Zesty potatoes combined with a punchy, fresh salad set the tone for a well-balanced midweek meal. Serve with your pre-prepared roast chicken and dinner couldn't be easier (or more popular).

Preheat the oven to 220°C (430°F).

Place the baby potatoes in a roasting tin, then drizzle them with olive oil and lemon juice. Season with salt and roast for 45 minutes, turning occasionally, until golden and crispy.

Meanwhile, combine the tomato, red onion, mozzarella and basil leaves in a large bowl. Drizzle half of the herb dressing over the salad and toss gently to coat.

Portion the hot roast chicken as you prefer. Drizzle as much as you like of the remaining herb dressing over the chicken and potatoes.

Serve immediately with any leftover dressing on the side.

Hints Ensure the potatoes are well coated in the lemon to achieve a crispy finish.

Use a variety of tomatoes for the salad to add colour and depth of flavour.

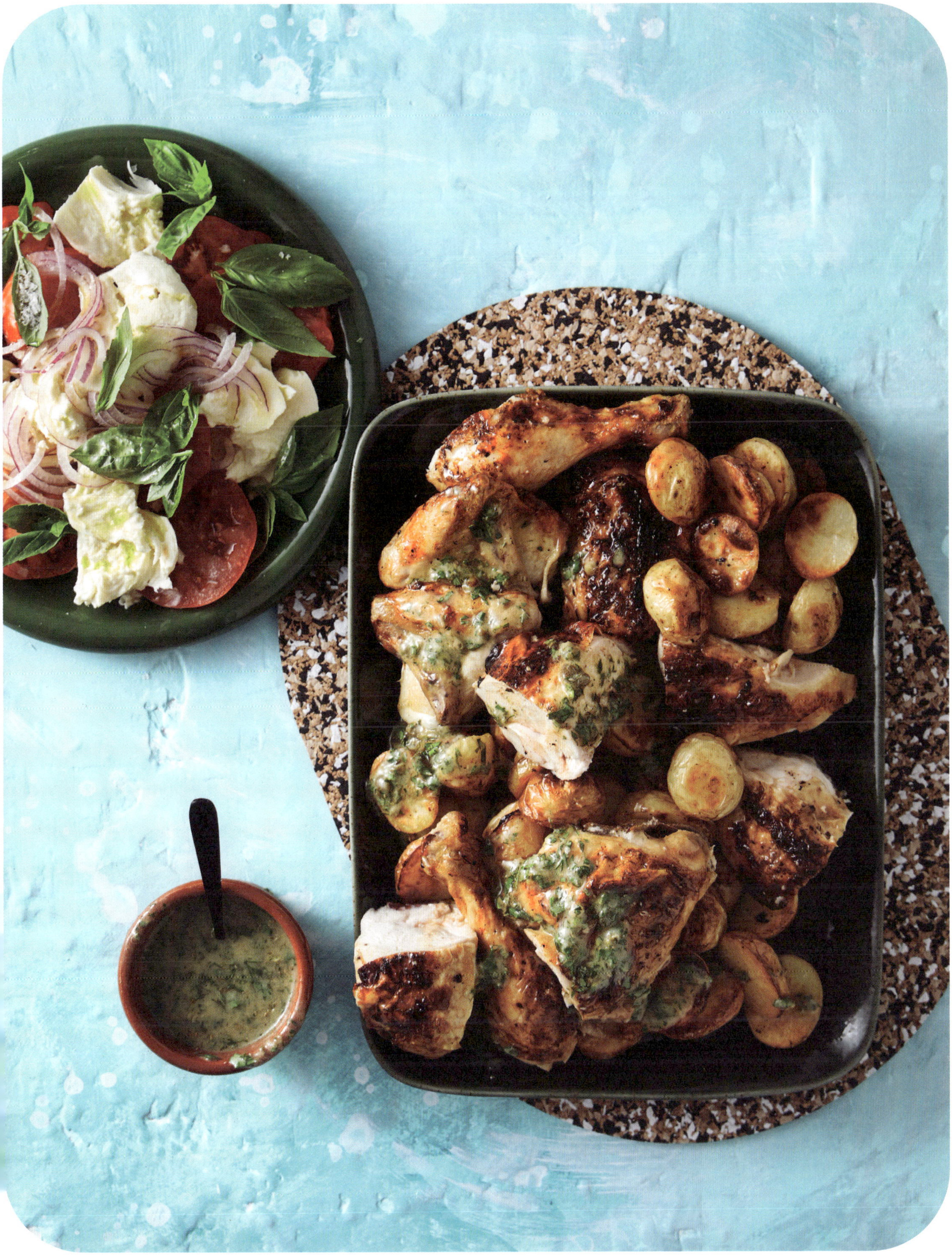

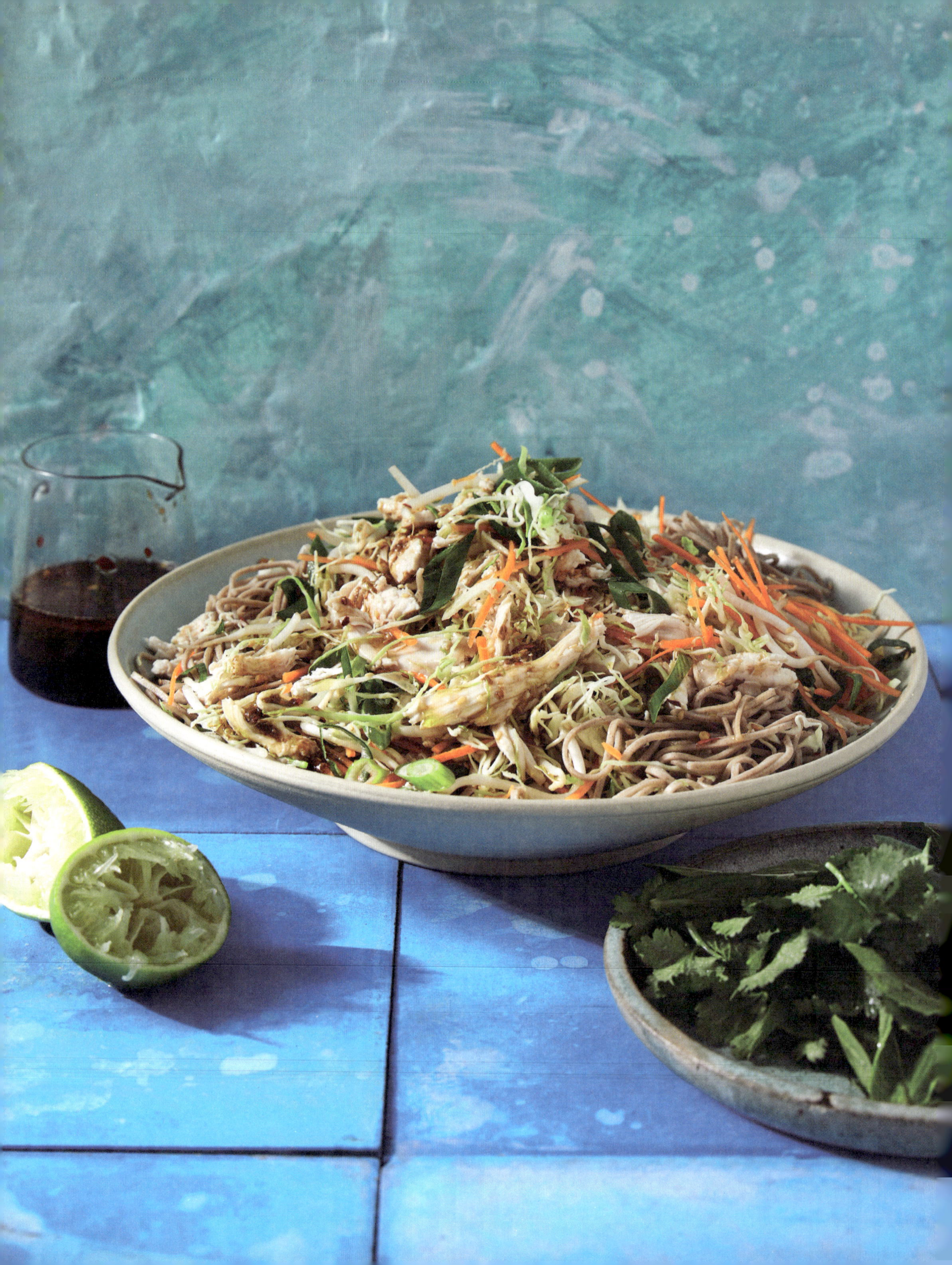

Chicken, noodle and cabbage salad

GF NF DF

Prep 25 minutes
Cook 10 minutes
Serves 4

400 g (14 oz) soba or udon noodles

350 g (12½ oz/2 cups) Butterflied roast chicken (page 170), shredded

½ green or red cabbage, shredded

2 large carrots, julienned

125 g (4½ oz/1¼ cups) bean sprouts

40 g (1½ oz/¼ cup) sesame seeds, toasted

15 g (½ oz/¼ cup) coriander (cilantro) leaves, chopped (optional)

15 g (½ oz/¼ cup) mint leaves, chopped

15 g (½ oz/¼ cup) Thai basil leaves, chopped

2 spring onions (scallions), chopped

Honey soy dressing

60 ml (2 fl oz/¼ cup) soy sauce

2 tablespoons rice vinegar

1 tablespoon honey

1 tablespoon grated fresh ginger

1 garlic clove, finely minced

1 teaspoon chilli flakes (optional)

juice of 1 lime

sea salt

Turn your leftover chicken into a vibrant summer salad – the combination of fresh vegetables, herbs and honey soy dressing creates a flavour explosion.

Cook the noodles according to the packet instructions, then drain and rinse under cold water. Set aside.

Combine the shredded chicken, cabbage, carrot, bean sprouts, sesame seeds, coriander (if using), mint, Thai basil and spring onion in a large mixing bowl.

In a separate small bowl, whisk the honey soy dressing ingredients together until well combined.

Add the noodles to the large mixing bowl with the chicken and vegetables. Pour the dressing over the salad and toss everything together until evenly coated.

Adjust the seasoning with more soy sauce or lime juice if needed.

Serve immediately or chill in the fridge for 15–20 minutes before serving as a cold salad.

Hints Add some chopped peanuts or cashews for an extra crunch.

This salad can be made ahead and stored in the fridge for up to 2 days; just add the herbs and dressing before serving to keep it fresh.

LIGHT & FRESH

Caprese smash burgers

(NF)

Prep 25 minutes
Cook 15 minutes
Serves 4

2 baguettes, cut in half lengthways and widthways

1 tablespoon Dijon mustard

150 g (5½ oz/1 cup) mozzarella, grated

500 g (1 lb 2 oz) Seasoned beef mince (page 169)

4 large tomatoes, thickly sliced

Chopped salad

½ iceberg lettuce, finely chopped

15 g (½ oz/¼ cup) dill, chopped

15 g (½ oz/¼ cup) basil leaves, chopped

170 ml (5½ fl oz/¾ cup) Lemon mayonnaise (page 168)

These burgers – beef patties smashed into cheese and bread then grilled – are the juiciest ever. Say goodbye to takeaway.

Preheat the oven grill (broiler) or a barbecue to medium–high heat. If using an oven grill (broiler), line a baking tray with baking paper.

Place the four bottom halves of the baguettes on the tray cut side up, then spread them with mustard. Sprinkle with the mozzarella. Place a quarter of the beef mince on top of each cheesy baguette and press firmly so that the mince spreads out to cover the cheese, sealing it in.

Grill the baguettes for 6–8 minutes, or until the beef mince is fully cooked and the cheese has melted, forming a crispy, golden crust on the bread. Alternatively, if barbecuing, place the baguettes meat-side down onto the barbecue.

While the meat is cooking, prepare the chopped salad by combining the lettuce, dill, basil and lemon mayonnaise in a bowl and mix well.

To assemble the burgers, top the meat with the tomato and a generous spoonful of the chopped salad. Place the plain baguette halves on top, pressing gently to keep everything together.

Hints Swap the mozzarella with a mix of provolone and parmesan for a different cheese profile.

If barbecuing the beef, add a handful of wood chips to the barbecue for a smokier flavour.

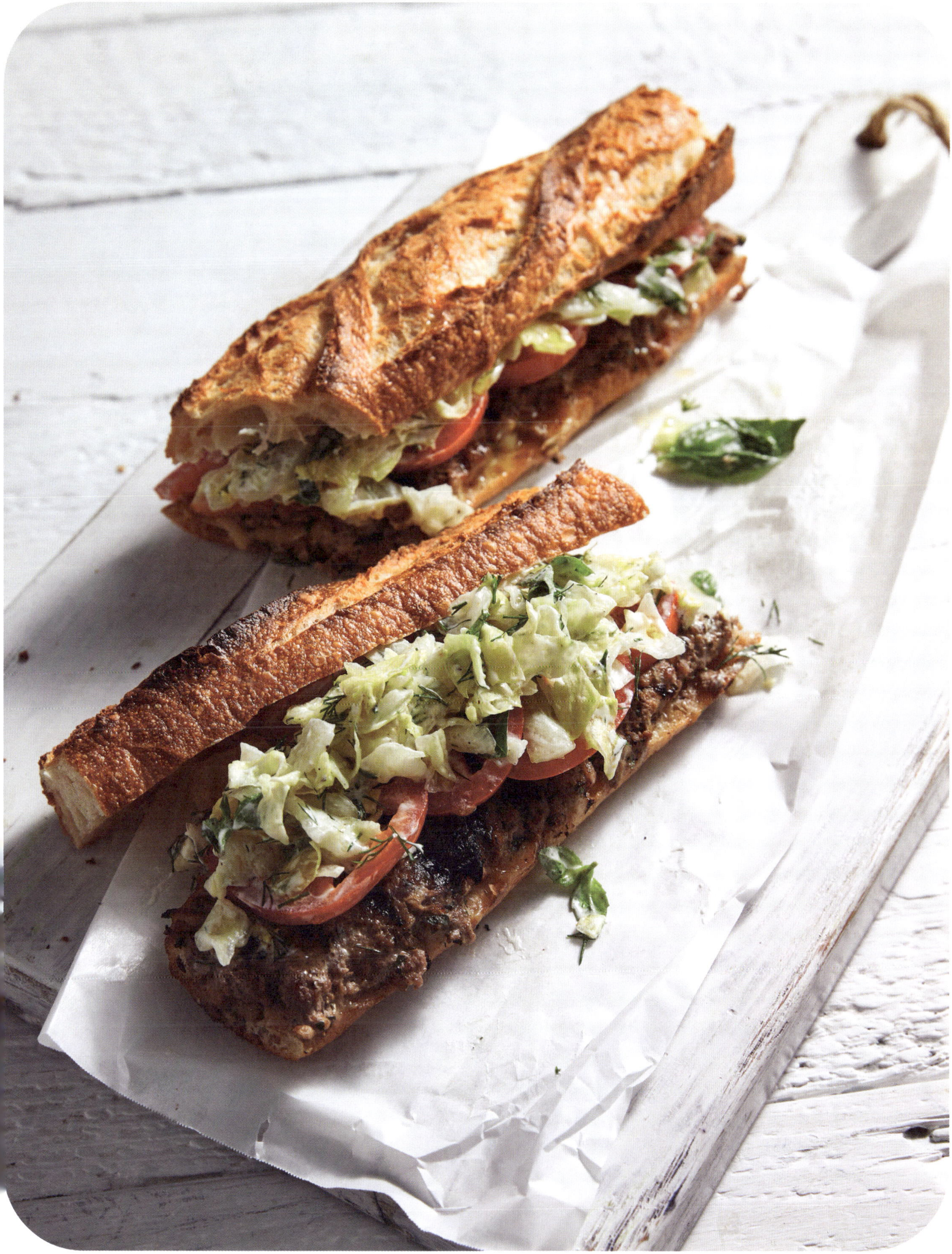

Crusted pork fillet with juicy roast tomatoes

NF

Prep 20 minutes
Cook 30 minutes
Serves 4

120 g (4½ oz/1½ cups) coarse, fresh sourdough breadcrumbs

15 g (½ oz/¼ cup) flat-leaf (Italian) parsley, finely chopped

50 g (1¾ oz/½ cup) parmesan, grated

1½ teaspoons finely grated lemon zest

2 garlic cloves, minced

1 tablespoon extra-virgin olive oil

2 × 350 g (12½ oz) pork fillets, trimmed

30 ml (1 fl oz) Dijon mustard

olive-oil spray

300 g (10½ oz) cherry tomatoes on the vine

sea salt and freshly ground black pepper

80 g (2¾ oz/2 cups) mixed salad leaves

125 ml (4 fl oz/½ cup) Herb dressing (page 170)

lemon wedges, to serve

Simple yet elegant, this dish is just as good for entertaining as it is for a weeknight dinner.

Preheat the oven to 200°C (390°F). Line a baking tray with baking paper.

Mix breadcrumbs, parsley, parmesan, lemon zest and garlic in a bowl. Drizzle in the olive oil and season with salt and pepper. Mix thoroughly until combined.

Place the pork fillets on the baking tray. Spread a thin layer of Dijon mustard on top of the pork, then firmly press the breadcrumb mixture onto the mustard-coated pork, ensuring an even layer. Lightly spray with olive-oil spray.

Roast the pork for 15 minutes.

Add the cherry tomatoes on the vine to the tray, lightly spraying them with olive-oil spray.

Continue roasting for an additional 10–12 minutes, or until the breadcrumb topping is golden and the pork is just cooked through.

Remove the pork from the oven, loosely cover it with baking paper, and allow it to rest for 5 minutes before slicing.

Place the salad leaves in a bowl, drizzle the herb dressing on top and toss to combine.

Serve the sliced pork with the roasted cherry tomatoes, lemon wedges and salad on the side.

Hints For a crunchier texture, use Japanese breadcrumbs instead of fresh breadcrumbs.

Substitute the parsley with basil or oregano for a different herb flavour.

If you prefer your pork more well-done, increase the cooking time by 2–3 minutes.

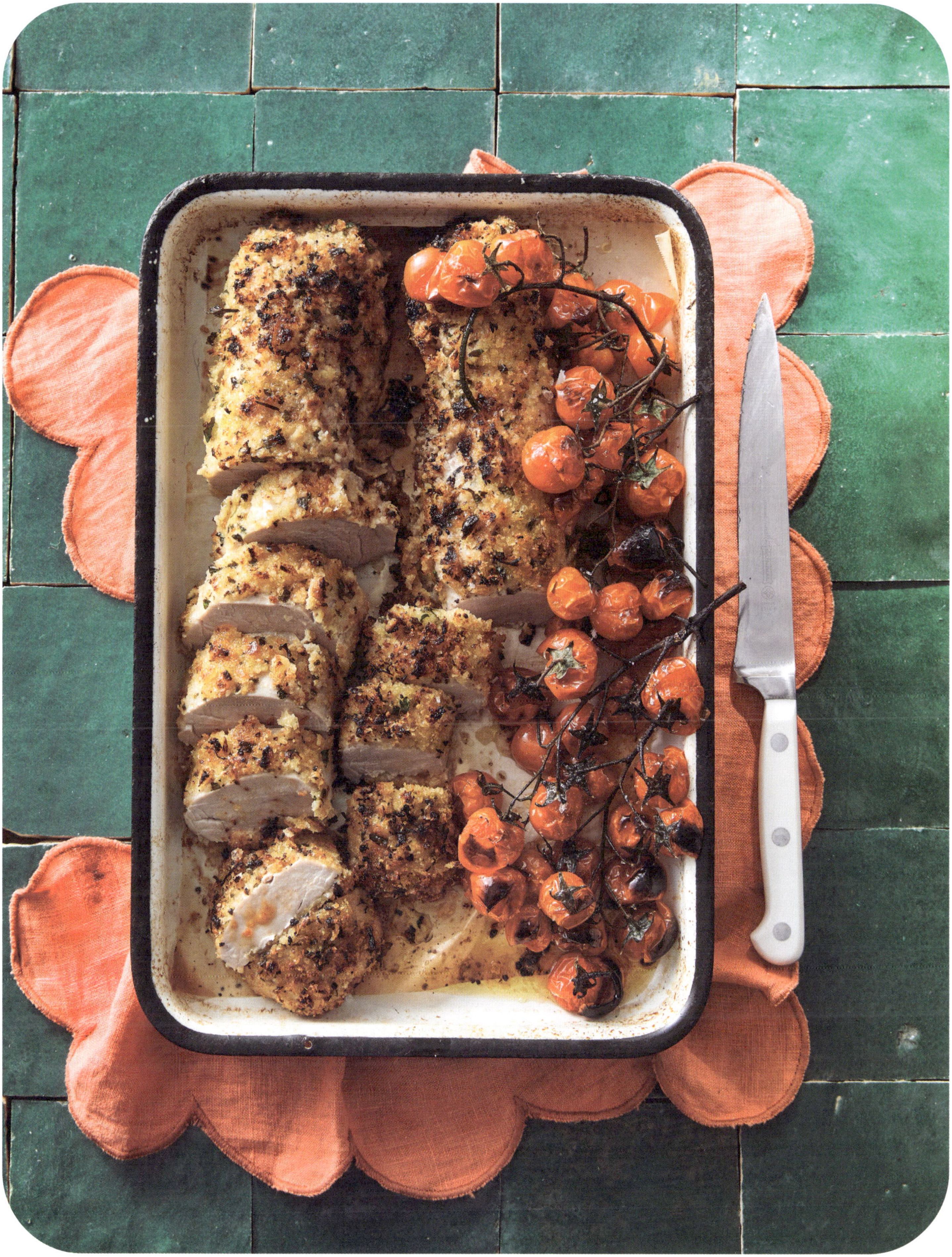

Spinach spiral pie with lemon mayonnaise

NF V

Prep 1 hour
Cook 45 minutes
Makes 2 pies
(2 meals for 4 people)

750 g (1 lb 11 oz) filo pastry sheets, thawed

125 ml (4 fl oz/½ cup) extra-virgin olive oil

1 × quantity Lemon mayonnaise, to serve (page 168)

Spinach ricotta filling

1 kg (2 lb 3 oz) frozen spinach, thawed and drained

500 g (1 lb 2 oz) ricotta

200 g (7 oz) haloumi, grated

25 g (1 oz/½ cup) dill, chopped

25 g (1 oz/½ cup) flat-leaf (Italian) parsley, chopped

15 g (½ oz/¼ cup) mint leaves, chopped

4 spring onions (scallions), finely chopped

zest of 1 lemon

¼ teaspoon ground nutmeg

2 eggs, lightly beaten

sea salt and freshly ground black pepper

sesame seeds, for sprinkling

With its flaky golden pastry and wholesome filling, this Mediterranean-inspired pie looks impressive but is simple to make and ideal for dinner during the warmer months.

Preheat the oven to 180°C (360°F). Line two large baking trays with baking paper.

Combine the spinach ricotta filling ingredients in a large bowl and season generously with salt and pepper. Mix until well combined.

To make the first pie, work with half the filo pastry sheets and half the filling. Place a sheet of filo pastry on a clean surface and brush lightly with olive oil. Layer another sheet on top and brush again with olive oil. Repeat until you have four sheets stacked.

Spoon a thin line of the spinach and ricotta mixture along one long edge of the filo stack. Carefully roll the stacked filo sheets up to form a long sausage. Gently coil the sausage into a spiral and place it on one of the baking trays.

Continue the process with the remaining filo sheets and filling (for the first pie), adding each new sausage to the end of the spiral to extend it until the entire pie is formed. Brush the top of the spiral with olive oil and sprinkle with sesame seeds.

Repeat the process with the remaining filo and filling to create the second pie on the other baking tray.

Bake both pies for 40–45 minutes, or until the filo is golden and crisp.

Serve one pie immediately, drizzled with lemon mayonnaise (allow it to cool slightly before slicing).

Let the second pie cool completely, then wrap it tightly in plastic wrap, place it in an airtight container and freeze for up to 2 months.

Hints Ensure the spinach is thoroughly drained to avoid a soggy filling.

While preparing the pies, keep the rest of the filo pastry sheets covered with a damp tea towel (dish towel) to prevent them from drying out.

When baking the frozen pie, allow it to thaw in the fridge overnight before reheating at 180°C (360°F) for 25–30 minutes.

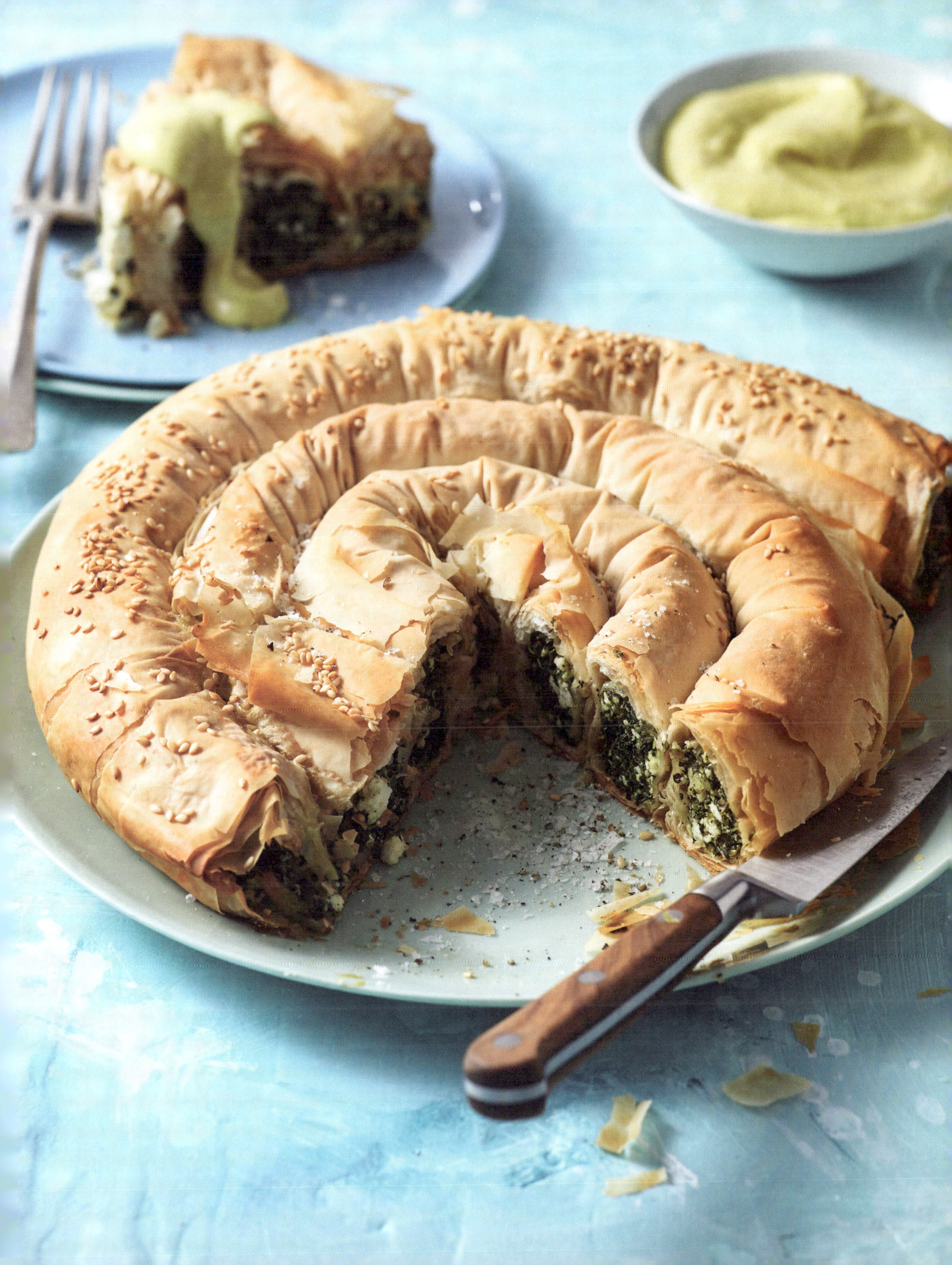

Summer tuna pasta salad

NF DF

Prep 25 minutes (plus 30 minutes marinating time)
Cook 12 minutes
Serves 4

4–5 large ripe tomatoes, grated to yield 500 ml (17 fl oz/2 cups) of pulp (the riper the better)

1 teaspoon white (granulated) sugar

½ teaspoon chilli flakes

1 garlic clove, minced

½ small red onion, finely sliced

500 g (1 lb 2 oz) rigatoni

200 g (7 oz) young green beans, tops trimmed

80 ml (2¾ oz/⅓ cup) Lemon mayonnaise (page 168)

60 ml (2 fl oz/¼ cup) extra-virgin olive oil

2 tablespoons capers, chopped

15 g (½ oz/¼ cup) flat-leaf (Italian) parsley, chopped

425 g (15 oz) tinned tuna in olive oil, drained

sea salt

basil leaves, to serve (optional)

This light and refreshing family meal requires very little cooking, making it ideal for hot nights. It can even be made a day ahead and served at room temperature.

Combine the tomato pulp, sugar, chilli flakes, garlic and red onion in a large bowl. Season with salt, mix well and let it macerate while you prepare the rest of the ingredients, allowing the flavours to meld.

Cook the rigatoni in a large pot of salted boiling water according to the packet directions until al dente, adding the trimmed beans 1 minute before finishing. Reserve 125 ml (4½ fl oz/½ cup) of the pasta cooking water before draining.

Separate the beans from the pasta, place them in a bowl and drizzle with the lemon mayonnaise (or, if you prefer, keep the mayonnaise to offer on the side).

After the tomato has macerated, add the olive oil, capers and parsley to the mixture. Stir in the drained tuna, breaking it into chunks.

Toss the cooked rigatoni directly into the bowl with the tuna mixture. Add a little reserved pasta water and toss until the sauce slightly emulsifies and coats the pasta evenly.

Season well, garnish with basil leaves (if using) and serve immediately with the lemon mayonnaise beans.

Hints If you prefer a bit more heat, add more chilli flakes or a pinch of cayenne pepper.

Pack this dish into your hamper for a summer picnic.

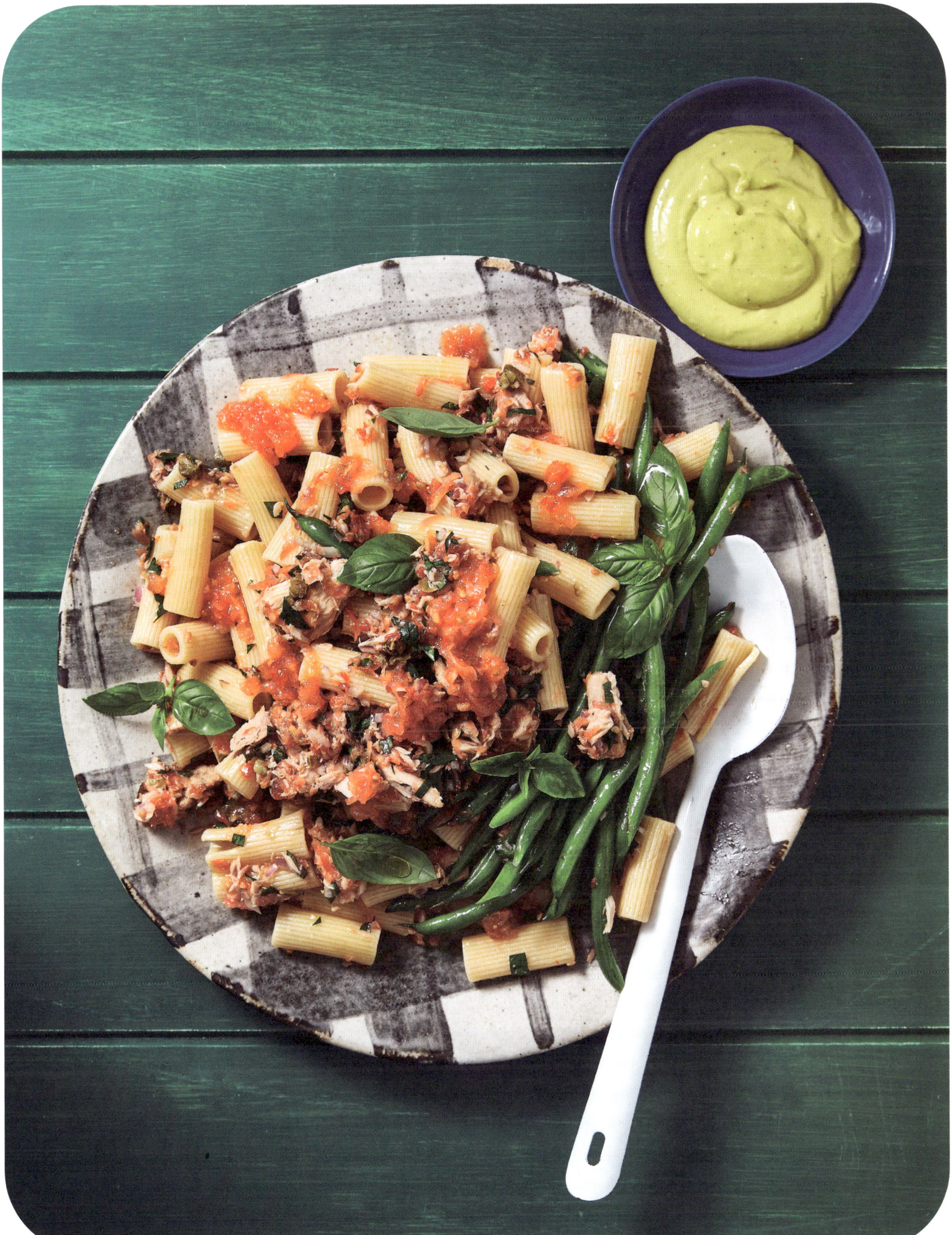

Beef koftas with grilled haloumi, zucchini and broccoli salad

NF

Prep 30 minutes
Cook 15 minutes
Serves 4

Minced beef skewers

500 g (1 lb 2 oz) Seasoned beef mince (page 169)

8 wooden skewers, soaked in water for 30 minutes

extra-virgin olive oil, for brushing

Grilled haloumi salad

190 g (6½ oz/1 cup) couscous

1 large head of broccoli, cut into florets

1 teaspoon extra-virgin olive oil, plus 1 tablespoon more

2 zucchini (courgettes), sliced lengthways into thin strips

200 g (7 oz) haloumi, sliced into 1 cm (½ in) thick pieces

60 g (2 oz/½ cup) toasted slivered almonds

20 g (¾ oz/¼ cup) mint leaves, chopped

25 g (1 oz/⅓ cup) flat-leaf (Italian) parsley, chopped

1 tablespoon lemon juice

1 tablespoon white-wine vinegar

sea salt and freshly ground black pepper

lemon wedges, to serve

Sauce

125 g (4½ oz/½ cup) Greek-style yoghurt

1 tablespoon white-wine vinegar

2 teaspoons extra-virgin olive oil

This is a great meal to cook on a barbecue if you have one. Spiced beef koftas with freshly grilled vegetables are so simple, yet so satisfying.

Preheat a barbecue or a chargrill pan to medium-high heat.

Divide the seasoned beef mince into eight portions. Shape each portion around a wooden skewer, pressing firmly to form an even kofta shape. Brush the skewers lightly with olive oil.

Cook the minced beef skewers on the barbecue for 8–10 minutes (or in the pan for 15 minutes), turning three or four times until fully cooked and slightly charred on the outside. Remove from the heat and cover with a sheet of baking paper to keep warm.

Prepare the couscous according to the package instructions. Fluff with a fork and set aside.

For the rest of the salad, toss the broccoli florets in a small bowl with 1 teaspoon of the olive oil and season with salt and pepper. Grill on the barbecue (or use the chargrill pan) for 5–7 minutes, turning occasionally, until tender and charred. Grill the zucchini slices for 2–3 minutes on each side, or until tender and charred. Grill the haloumi slices for 2 minutes on each side, until golden and slightly crispy.

Combine the grilled broccoli, zucchini and haloumi in a large bowl. Add the almonds, couscous, mint and parsley (reserving 1 teaspoon of chopped mint and 2 teaspoons of chopped parsley for the sauce), lemon juice, white-wine vinegar and remaining olive oil. Season with salt and pepper, then toss gently to combine.

For the sauce, use a fork to whisk together the yoghurt, white-wine vinegar and olive oil. Add the reserved parsley and mint, and mix until well combined.

Serve the koftas with the grilled haloumi salad, with lemon wedges and sauce on the side.

Hints For extra crunch, add some toasted pine nuts or pepitas (pumpkin seeds) to the salad.

A drizzle of honey or a sprinkle of chilli flakes can enhance the sweetness or add a bit of heat to the salad.

Serve with grilled flatbreads (page 226) or pita for a more substantial meal.

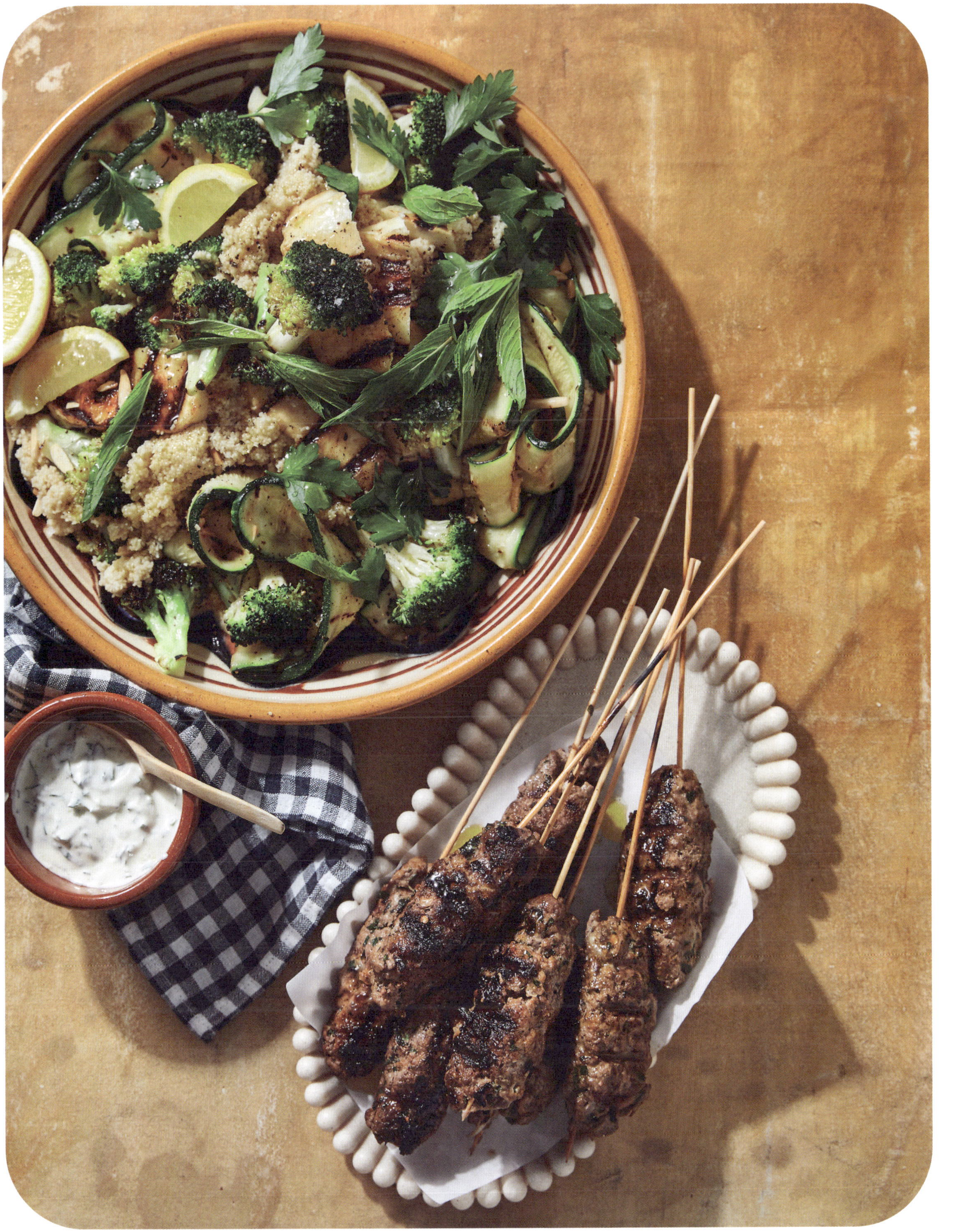

BLT omelette tray

GF NF

Prep 5 minutes
Cook 30 minutes
Serves 4

4 × large bacon rashers (slices), cut in half and rinds removed

200 g (7 oz) cherry tomatoes, cut in half

2 garlic cloves, crushed

1 tablespoon chopped oregano leaves

1 tablespoon extra-virgin olive oil

8 eggs

60 ml (2 fl oz/¼ cup) whipping cream

2 tablespoons chopped chives

125 g (4½ oz) cheddar, grated

200 g (7 oz) frozen spinach, thawed and drained

2 avocados, sliced

1 head of lettuce, leaves separated into cups

sea salt and freshly ground black pepper

lemon wedges, to serve

This protein-packed bacon–lettuce–tomato breakfast omelette is made fresh and fun with the addition of a DIY lettuce cup with creamy avocado.

Preheat the oven to 200°C (390°F). Line a 5 × 20 × 35 cm (2 × 8 ×13¾ in) baking tray with baking paper.

Arrange the bacon rashers on the tray, curling them into loose roses.

Toss the cherry tomatoes with the garlic, oregano and olive oil in a small bowl and season them with salt and pepper.

Scatter the tomatoes over the bacon and roast for 15 minutes, until the bacon starts to crisp and the tomatoes soften.

Meanwhile, whisk the eggs, cream and chives together in a large bowl with a pinch of salt. Stir in the cheese.

Remove the tray from the oven and spoon the spinach among the bacon and tomatoes. Pour the egg mixture evenly over the top, ensuring all ingredients are well coated.

Bake for an additional 15 minutes, or until the eggs are set and the cheese is golden.

While the omelette tray is baking, prepare the lettuce. Arrange the avocado slices inside the lettuce cups on a serving platter.

Once the omelette tray is cooked, slice it into eight rectangles. Serve alongside the avocado and lettuce cups and lemon wedges, allowing everyone to create their own handheld breakfast.

Hints When buying bacon, look for a preservative-free option that doesn't contain added nitrates.

For extra flavour, add a sprinkle of chilli flakes to the egg mixture.

Swap cream with milk if you prefer a lighter omelette.

Use any leftover omelette slices as a filling for sandwiches or wraps the next day.

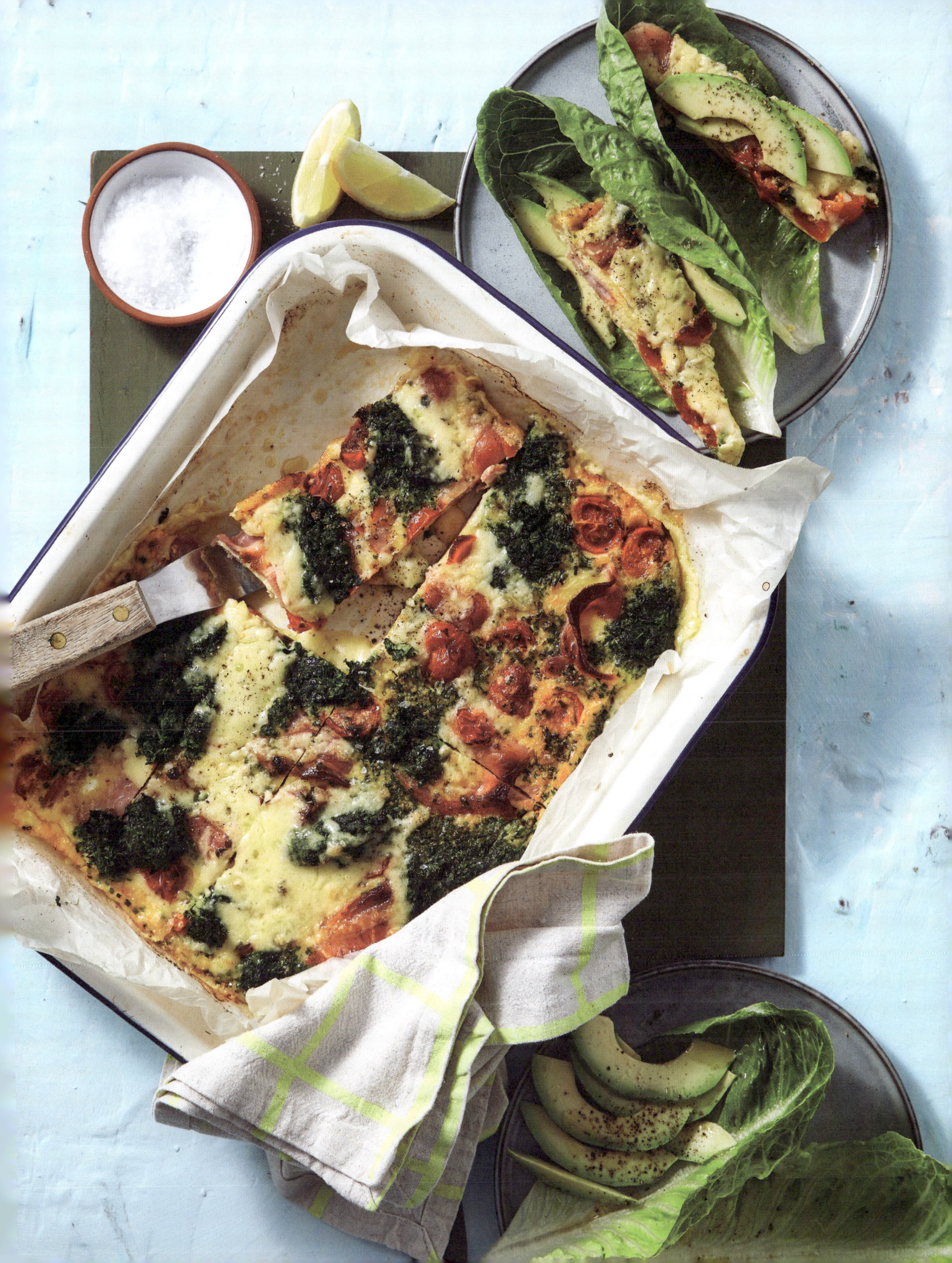

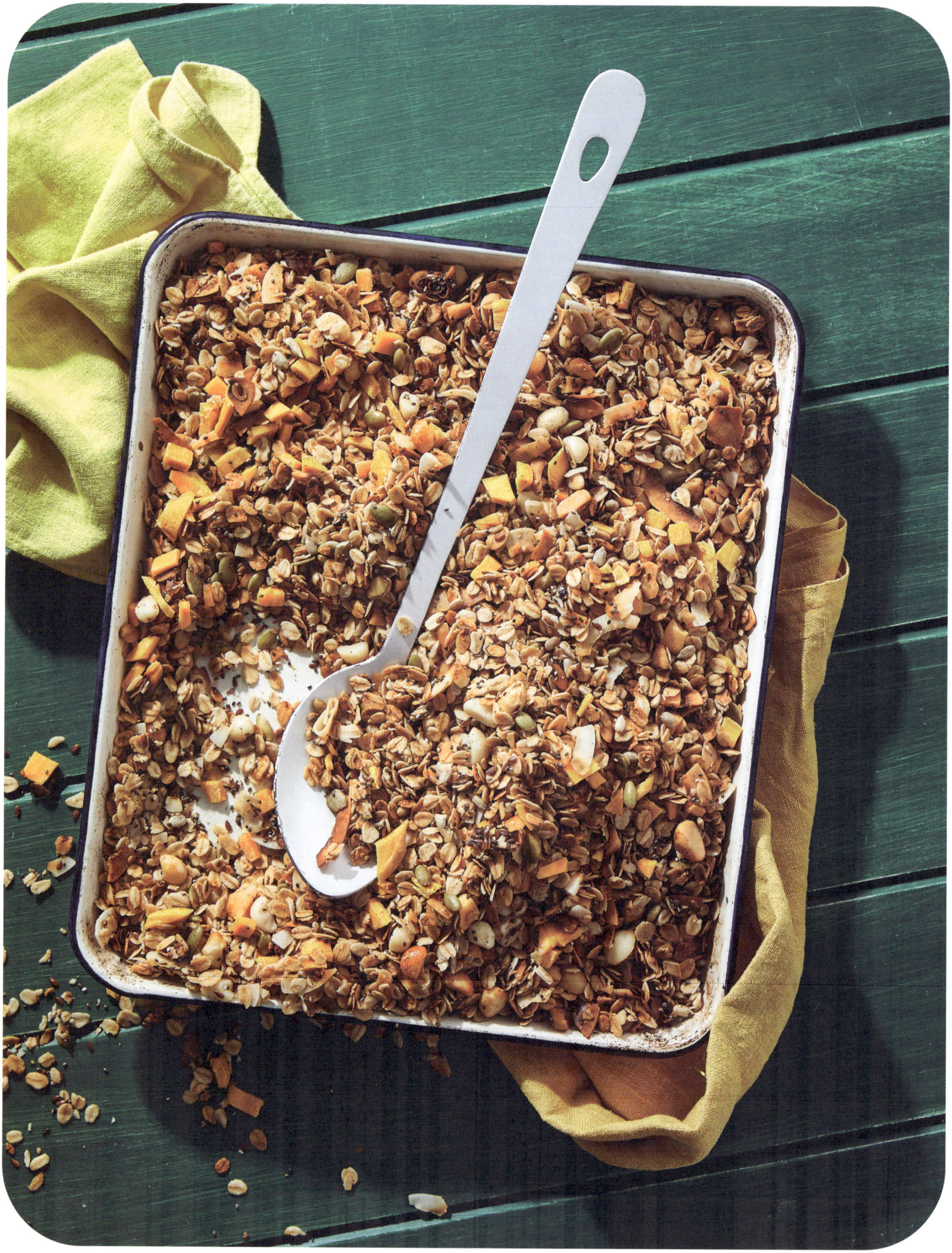

Home-made granola

DF V VG

Prep 15 minutes
Cook 30 minutes
Serves 12

300 g (10½ oz/3 cups) rolled (porridge) oats

55 g (2 oz/1 cup) coconut flakes

80 g (2¾ oz/½ cup) raw macadamia nuts, roughly chopped

40 g (1½ oz/¼ cup) pepitas (pumpkin seeds)

40 g (1½ oz/¼ cup) sunflower seeds

40 g (1½ oz/¼ cup) chia seeds

40 g (1½ oz/¼ cup) linseeds (flax seeds)

½ teaspoon ground cinnamon

60 ml (2 fl oz/¼ cup) coconut oil, melted

60 ml (2 fl oz/¼ cup) honey or pure maple syrup

1 teaspoon vanilla extract

90 g (3 oz/½ cup) dried mango, chopped

The smell of freshly baked granola will fill your soul with joy! The fact that this recipe requires only one bowl and comes together in a flash is an added bonus.

Preheat the oven to 160°C (320°F) and line a large baking tray with baking paper.

Combine the rolled oats, coconut flakes, macadamia nuts, pepitas, sunflower seeds, chia seeds, linseeds and cinnamon in a large bowl.

Add the melted coconut oil, honey and vanilla extract to the dry ingredients and stir well until everything is evenly coated.

Spread the granola mixture out evenly onto the baking tray. Press it down slightly with the back of a spoon to create clumps.

Bake for 25–30 minutes, stirring once halfway through, until the granola is golden brown and fragrant.

Remove the tray from the oven and allow the granola to cool completely on the tray. Once cooled, mix in the dried mango pieces.

Store the granola in an airtight container at room temperature for up to 2 weeks.

Hints For a gluten-free granola, use puffed rice or gluten-free rolled oats.

For a summer twist, consider adding a handful of freeze-dried berries to the cooled granola.

You can substitute the dried mango with other dried fruits, such as pineapple or apricots.

To make the granola extra crunchy, let it cool completely without stirring, which will help form larger clusters.

LIGHT & FRESH

Corn cobettes with cheese, chilli mayonnaise and lime

GF NF V

Prep 5 minutes
Cook 25 minutes
Serves 4

4 corn cobs, husked and cut in half

2 tablespoons extra-virgin olive oil

60 ml (2 fl oz/¼ cup) Lemon mayonnaise (page 168)

½ teaspoon Chilli jam marinade (page 111) or chilli powder

50 g (1¾ oz/½ cup) parmesan, grated

sea salt

2 limes, cut into wedges, to serve

Snacks don't get better than these fun and flavoursome corn cobettes, which also make a popular side dish. Make them when corn is at its best (see page 31 for how to select good cobs).

Preheat the oven to 200°C (390°F). Line a baking tray with baking paper.

Toss the corn cobs in olive oil and season with salt. Wrap the cobs in baking paper and arrange them on the baking tray.

Roast for 15 minutes, until the corn is tender, then carefully unwrap the cobs and place them on the baking tray. Switch the oven heat to the grill (broiler) setting and grill for 5–10 minutes, turning occasionally, until lightly charred.

Meanwhile, mix the lemon mayonnaise with the chilli jam marinade or chilli powder in a small bowl until well combined. Set aside.

When the corn is cooked, remove it from the oven and brush each cob generously with the chilli mayonnaise. Sprinkle the parmesan on the corn cobs while they are still hot.

Serve the corn on a platter with lime wedges on the side.

Note If you want to keep this snack vegetarian, use chilli powder rather than chilli jam marinade (or substitute the fish sauce in the chilli jam marinade).

Hints For extra smokiness, add a pinch of smoked paprika to the chilli mayonnaise.

If you prefer a milder flavour, reduce or omit the chilli jam marinade.

The corn cobettes can also be served with a drizzle of melted butter for added richness.

THE WEEKLY GROCERY SHOP

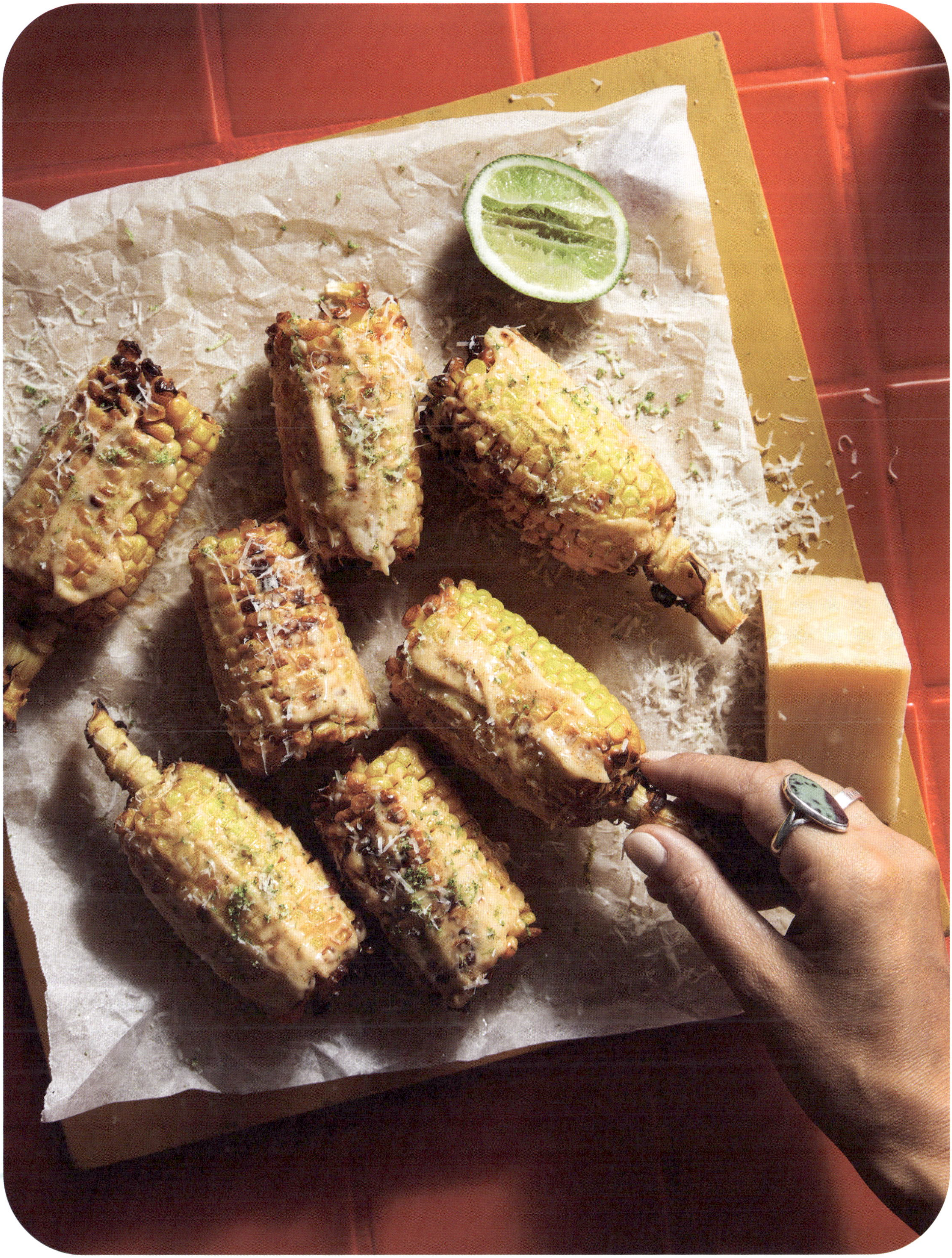

Carrot cake energy bites

GF V

Prep 40 minutes
(plus 15 minutes chilling time)
Makes 12

8 rice cakes
50 g (1¾ oz/½ cup) walnuts
1 carrot, peeled and chopped
180 g (6½ oz/1 cup) dates, pitted
1 teaspoon ground cinnamon
½ teaspoon ground cardamom
½ teaspoon ground ginger
60 g (2 oz/¼ cup) cream cheese, softened
zest of ½ orange
25 g (1 oz/¼ cup) desiccated coconut
65 g (2¼ oz) white chocolate, chopped (optional)

These no-bake bites, combining the warm spiced flavours of carrot cake with wholesome ingredients, are easy to pack for a snack on the go.

Place the rice cakes, walnuts, carrot, dates, cinnamon, cardamom and ginger in a food processor and pulse until the mixture comes together and resembles a sticky paste. If the mixture is too crumbly, add more dates or a teaspoon of melted coconut oil.

In a separate bowl, use a fork to mix the cream cheese with the orange zest until well combined.

Using your hands, form walnut-sized balls of the carrot mixture. Flatten each ball slightly, place ½ teaspoon of the cream cheese mixture in the centre, then close the carrot mixture around it, rolling it back into a ball.

Place the balls in the freezer for 15 minutes to firm up.

Place the desiccated coconut in a shallow bowl.

If using the white chocolate, place it in a microwave-safe bowl, heat for 20-seconds, then stir. Repeat until the chocolate has melted.

Take the balls out of the freezer and roll them in the desiccated coconut. (If using the white chocolate, dip each one into the melted white chocolate first, then roll them in desiccated coconut.)

Enjoy the bites right away or store them in the fridge for up to 1 week.

Hints If the mixture is too sticky to work with, slightly wet your hands when forming the balls.

For an extra flavour boost, toast the coconut before rolling the bites in it.

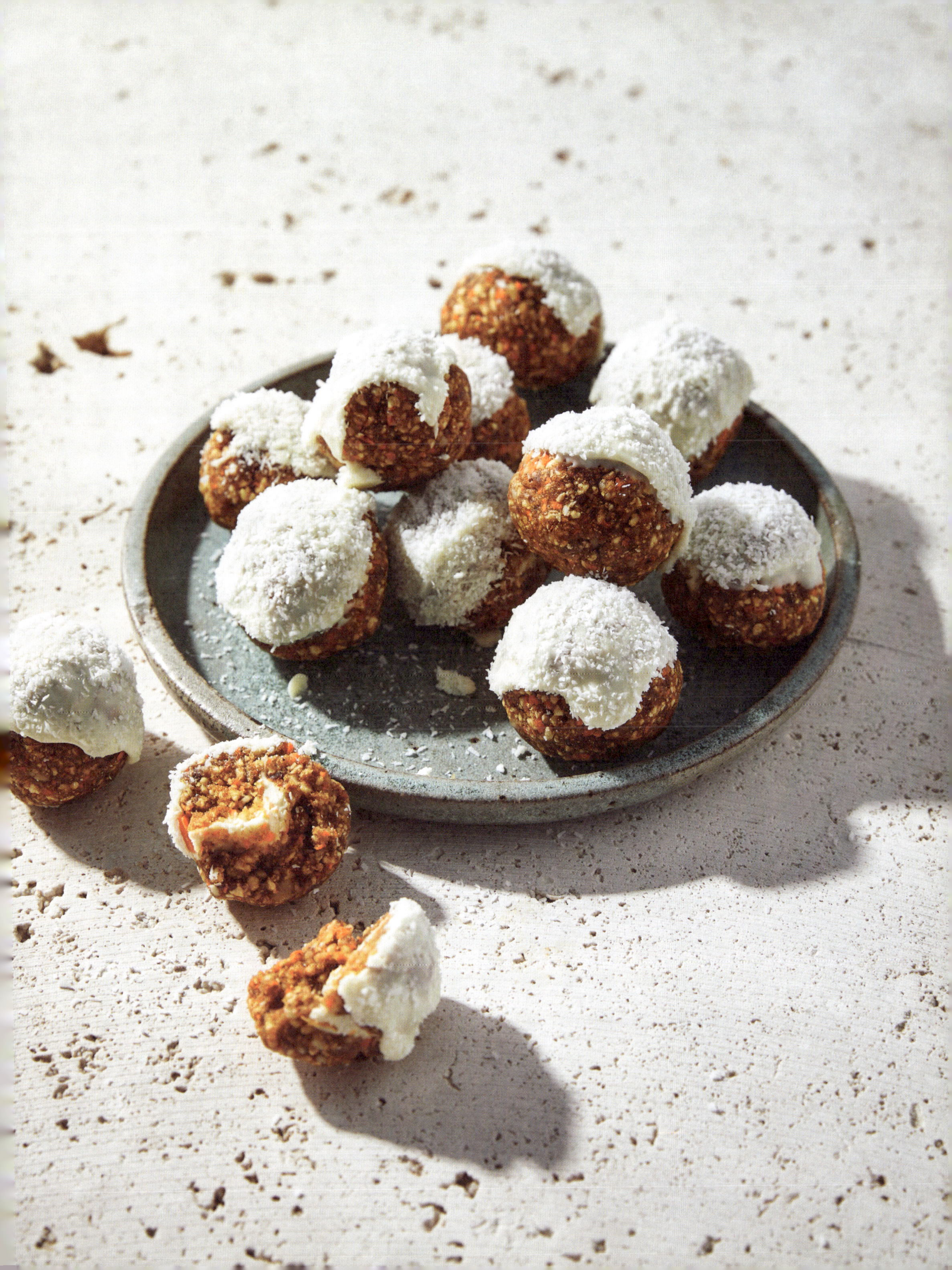

Week 2 menu

Power prep

Seasoned chicken mince
Marinated tofu
Everyday marinade
Home-made tortillas

Dinners

Beef and vegetable skewers with salsa verde
Sweet and tangy tofu noodles
Chicken chorizo paella
Mini chicken mozzarella meatballs with garlic mash
Lazy fish tacos
Lamb chops with Mediterranean salad and yoghurt tahini dressing
Prawn spaghetti

Breakfasts

Breakfast tacos
Tropical overnight chia

Snack

Puff pastry pizza pinwheels

Sweet

Coconut yoghurt and peach smoothie popsicles

Week 2 shopping list

Fruit & vegetables
- [ ] 1 bunch asparagus
- [ ] 1 avocado
- [ ] 1 bunch basil
- [ ] 1 bunch Thai basil
- [ ] 200 g (7 oz) green beans
- [ ] 250 g (9 oz) bean sprouts
- [ ] 150 g (5½ oz) cabbage or cos (romaine) lettuce
- [ ] 1 green capsicum (bell pepper)
- [ ] 1 red capsicum (bell pepper)
- [ ] 1 red chilli (optional)
- [ ] 1 bunch coriander (cilantro)
- [ ] 1 Lebanese (short) cucumber
- [ ] 2 garlic bulbs
- [ ] 8 lemons
- [ ] 3 limes
- [ ] 1 mango
- [ ] 1 bunch mint
- [ ] 200 g (7 oz) button mushrooms
- [ ] 1 large + 1 medium + 1 small onion
- [ ] 1 red onion
- [ ] 1 bunch flat-leaf (Italian) parsley
- [ ] 800 g (1 lb 12 oz) potatoes
- [ ] 600 g (1 lb 5 oz) baby (chat) potatoes
- [ ] 100 g (3½ oz) large rocket (arugula) leaves
- [ ] 1 shallot
- [ ] 200 g (7 oz) cherry tomatoes
- [ ] 1 large + 2 medium zucchini (courgettes)

Meat & poultry
- [ ] 1 kg (2 lb 3 oz) minced (ground) chicken
- [ ] 200 g (7 oz) chorizo
- [ ] 1 × 600 g skinless firm white fish fillet (e.g. snapper, cod or barramundi)
- [ ] 4 × lamb chump chops
- [ ] 500 g (1 lb 2 oz) rump steak

Pantry & baking
- [ ] 25 g (1 oz) fresh breadcrumbs
- [ ] 15 g (½ oz) Japanese breadcrumbs
- [ ] 400 g (14 oz) tinned chickpeas
- [ ] 15 g (½ oz) desiccated coconut
- [ ] 200 g (7 oz) tinned corn kernels
- [ ] 125 g (4½ oz) mayonnaise
- [ ] 280–300 g (10–10½ oz) flat rice noodles
- [ ] 700 ml (23½ fl oz) passata (pureed tomatoes)
- [ ] 100 g (3½ oz) unsalted peanuts
- [ ] 300 g (10½ oz) paella rice
- [ ] 500 g (1 lb 2 oz) spaghetti
- [ ] 40 g (1½ oz) tahini
- [ ] 400 g (14 oz) tinned diced tomatoes
- [ ] 60 ml (2 fl oz) white wine
- [ ] 8 wooden skewers

Fridge
- [ ] 65 g (2¼ oz) salted butter
- [ ] 1 egg
- [ ] 100 g (3½ oz) feta
- [ ] 200 g (7 oz) hummus
- [ ] 60 ml (2 fl oz) milk
- [ ] 100 g (3½ oz) mozzarella
- [ ] 95 g (3¼ oz) kalamata olives
- [ ] 60 g (2 oz) parmesan
- [ ] 450 g (1 lb) firm tofu
- [ ] 500 g (1 lb 2 oz) Greek-style yoghurt

Freezer
- [ ] 150 g (5½ oz) frozen peas
- [ ] 400 g (14 oz) peeled, deveined frozen prawns (shrimp)

LIGHT & FRESH

Seasoned chicken mince

Prep 15 minutes
Makes 2 meals for 4 people

1 kg (2 lb 3 oz) minced (ground) chicken
1 small onion, finely grated
2 garlic cloves, minced
7 g (¼ oz/¼ cup) flat-leaf (Italian) parsley, finely chopped
25 g (1 oz/¼ cup) fresh breadcrumbs
1 egg, lightly beaten
1 teaspoon dried oregano
1 teaspoon dried thyme
½ teaspoon smoked paprika
½ teaspoon freshly ground black pepper
1 teaspoon salt

(NF) (DF)

This recipe, which can be varied to suit your taste and the cuisine you plan to prepare, makes enough for two different dinners: Chicken chorizo paella (page 204) and Mini chicken mozzarella meatballs with garlic mash (page 206).

Combine everything in a large mixing bowl and use your hands to mix it together until well combined, being careful not to overwork the chicken mince.

Divide the seasoned mince into two portions. Place in an airtight container and refrigerate until ready to use.

Store in the fridge for up to 4 days or freeze for up to 3 months.

Hint To use this seasoned chicken mince as a filling for Asian-style dumplings, replace the parsley with coriander (cilantro) and omit the oregano and thyme. Add 2 tablespoons soy sauce, 1 teaspoon grated ginger, 1 tablespoon avocado oil, 1 finely chopped spring onion (scallion) and a pinch of white pepper. Wrap a teaspoon of mixture in dumpling wrappers and steam or pan-fry until cooked through. Avoid overfilling the wrappers to prevent them from breaking during cooking.

Marinated tofu

Prep 15 minutes
(plus 1 hour pressing)
Makes 450 g (1 lb)

450 g (1 lb) firm tofu

250 ml (8½ fl oz/1 cup) Black bean sauce (page 72), Chilli jam marinade (page 111) or another Asian-style dressing

By marinating tofu during your 'hour of power', you will have protein-packed meals and snacks at your fingertips during the week. This quantity is enough for Sweet and tangy tofu noodles (page 203), but you could also use it in Fried rice (page 236) or as a delicious vegetarian alternative to the meat in the Beef and vegetable skewers with salsa verde (page 200).

Press the tofu by draining off the water and wrapping the block in several layers of paper towel. Place the wrapped tofu on a baking tray and put another baking tray on top. Place something heavy (like a tin of tomatoes) on top and put it in the fridge for at least 1 hour, allowing liquid to be released from the tofu. (Pressing the tofu enables it to absorb more of the marinade and produces a tastier result.)

When ready, remove the tofu from the fridge, unwrap it and dice, cube or julienne it, depending on your preference.

Place the tofu in a large reusable ziplock bag and add the marinade. Gently massage the marinade into the tofu to ensure it is well covered, then place it in the fridge. Marinate for at least 1 hour before using.

Store in the fridge for up to 4 days or freeze for up to 3 months.

Note If you want to keep the tofu vegetarian or vegan, use black bean sauce or another plant-based dressing rather than chilli jam marinade (or substitute the fish sauce in the chilli jam marinade).

Hint Adjust the flavours in the marinade to suit your taste.

(GF) (NF) (DF) (VG) (V)

Everyday marinade

Prep 10 minutes
Makes 250 ml (8½ fl oz/1 cup)

60 ml (2 fl oz/¼ cup) red-wine vinegar

1 tablespoon Dijon mustard

1 tablespoon honey or pure maple syrup

1 garlic clove, finely grated

½ teaspoon dried oregano

¼ teaspoon dried thyme

½ teaspoon freshly ground black pepper

125 ml (4½ fl oz/½ cup) extra-virgin olive oil

sea salt

GF NF DF VG V

This versatile sauce can be used as a marinade or a salad dressing (as in Mini chicken mozzarella meatballs with garlic mash, page 206), or turned into a salsa verde by adding chopped herbs and capers (as in Beef and vegetable skewers with salsa verde, page 200).

Combine the red-wine vinegar, Dijon mustard, honey, garlic, oregano, thyme and pepper in a bowl or jar.

Gradually whisk in the olive oil until the dressing is emulsified and well combined. Taste and adjust the seasoning with salt as needed.

Use immediately or store in an airtight container in the fridge for up to 1 week. Shake well before use.

Hints Pour the marinade over your protein of choice, ensuring it's well coated, and marinate for at least 30 minutes – or up to 4 hours for a more intense flavour.

For a slightly sweeter salad dressing, increase the honey or maple syrup by 1–2 teaspoons.

Add a pinch of chilli flakes for a bit of heat if desired.

Home-made tortillas

Prep 30 minutes
Cook 30 minutes
Makes 16

600 g (1 lb 5 oz/4 cups) plain (all-purpose) flour
1 teaspoon baking powder
1 teaspoon salt
125 ml (4 fl oz/½ cup) extra-virgin olive oil
375 ml (12½ fl oz/1½ cups) warm water

These tortillas make great tacos, including the Lazy fish tacos (page 208) and the Breakfast tacos (page 214). Or you can serve them alongside meals such as Lamb chops with Mediterranean salad and yoghurt tahini dressing (page 210). This recipe makes a double batch; freeze any extra for later use.

Mix the flour, baking powder and salt together in a large bowl. Add the olive oil and warm water and stir until a dough forms.

Knead the dough on a lightly floured surface for about 5 minutes, until smooth and elastic.

Divide the dough into sixteen equal portions and shape them into balls. Cover with a clean tea towel (dish towel) and let them rest for 15 minutes.

On a floured surface, roll each ball into a thin circle, about 15–18 cm (6–7 in) in diameter.

Heat a dry frying pan over medium–high heat. Cook each tortilla for 1 minute on each side, or until lightly browned and puffy. Keep them warm in a clean towel if serving straight away or cool and store in an airtight container in the fridge for up to 3 days.

To freeze, place the tortillas on a baking tray lined with baking paper, layering baking paper between each one. Freeze the tray for 60–90 minutes, until the tortillas are firm, then transfer them to a reusable ziplock bag or airtight container. Store in the freezer for up to 3 months, ensuring they're well wrapped to prevent freezer burn. The tortillas can be cooked from frozen.

Hints To keep tortillas soft and pliable, stack them on a plate and cover them with a damp tea towel.

If you prefer wholemeal (whole-wheat) tortillas, substitute half the plain flour with wholemeal flour.

To make these into spinach tortillas, thaw and blend 100 g (3½ oz/½ cup) of frozen spinach with the warm water (reduce the warm water to 125 ml/4 fl oz/½ cup).

Experiment with adding spices like cumin seeds or garlic powder.

(NF) (DF) (VG) (V)

LIGHT & FRESH

Beef and vegetable skewers with salsa verde

GF NF

Prep 45 minutes (plus 30 minutes marinating time)
Cook 30 minutes
Serves 4

500 g (1 lb 2 oz) rump steak, sliced

1 × quantity Everyday marinade (page 198)

8 wooden skewers, soaked in water for 30 minutes

200 g (7 oz) button mushrooms, cut in half

2 zucchini (courgettes), sliced into thick rounds

600 g (1 lb 5 oz) baby (chat) potatoes

200 g (7 oz) green beans, trimmed

25 g (1 oz) salted butter

80 ml (2½ fl oz/⅓ cup) extra-virgin olive oil

1 tablespoon finely chopped flat-leaf (Italian) parsley, plus 15 g (½ oz/¼ cup) more

15 g (½ oz/¼ cup) basil leaves, chopped

2 tablespoons chopped mint leaves

2 tablespoons capers, rinsed, squeezed dry and finely chopped

zest of 1 lemon

sea salt

hummus, to serve

Greek-style yoghurt, to serve

Quick to prepare and easy to share, this vibrant summer meal is ideal for weeknight dinners or outdoor gatherings. You can vary the vegetables for the skewers, depending on what is in season; just make sure you cut them to about the same size so that they cook evenly.

Place the sliced steak in a shallow dish and pour in half of the Everyday marinade. Toss to coat, then cover and marinate in the fridge for at least 30 minutes.

Preheat the oven grill (broiler) or a barbecue to medium–high heat.

Thread the sliced steak onto the skewers (reserve the marinade to brush them with later), alternating with the mushrooms and zucchini slices.

Boil the baby potatoes in salted water until tender, about 15 minutes. Drain and set aside.

Meanwhile, blanch the green beans for 2–3 minutes in a saucepan of simmering water until just tender. Melt the butter in a small saucepan with the olive oil and 1 tablespoon of parsley and cook for 2 minutes. Place the blanched beans in the saucepan and toss them in the butter mixture with a little salt.

Grill the skewers on a baking tray on the top shelf of the oven (or on the barbecue) for about 2–3 minutes on each side, brushing with the leftover marinade as they cook, or until the beef is cooked to your desired doneness and the vegetables are tender.

While the skewers are grilling, mix the remaining parsley, basil, mint, capers and lemon zest into the other half of the marinade to create a salsa verde.

Serve the grilled beef skewers drizzled with the salsa verde, alongside hummus, yoghurt, boiled baby potatoes and green beans.

Hints The salsa verde can be made ahead of time and kept in the fridge for up to 3 days.

For a burst of extra flavour, add a squeeze of fresh lemon juice to the salsa verde just before serving.

If you prefer a different herb mix, try adding coriander (cilantro) or dill to the salsa verde.

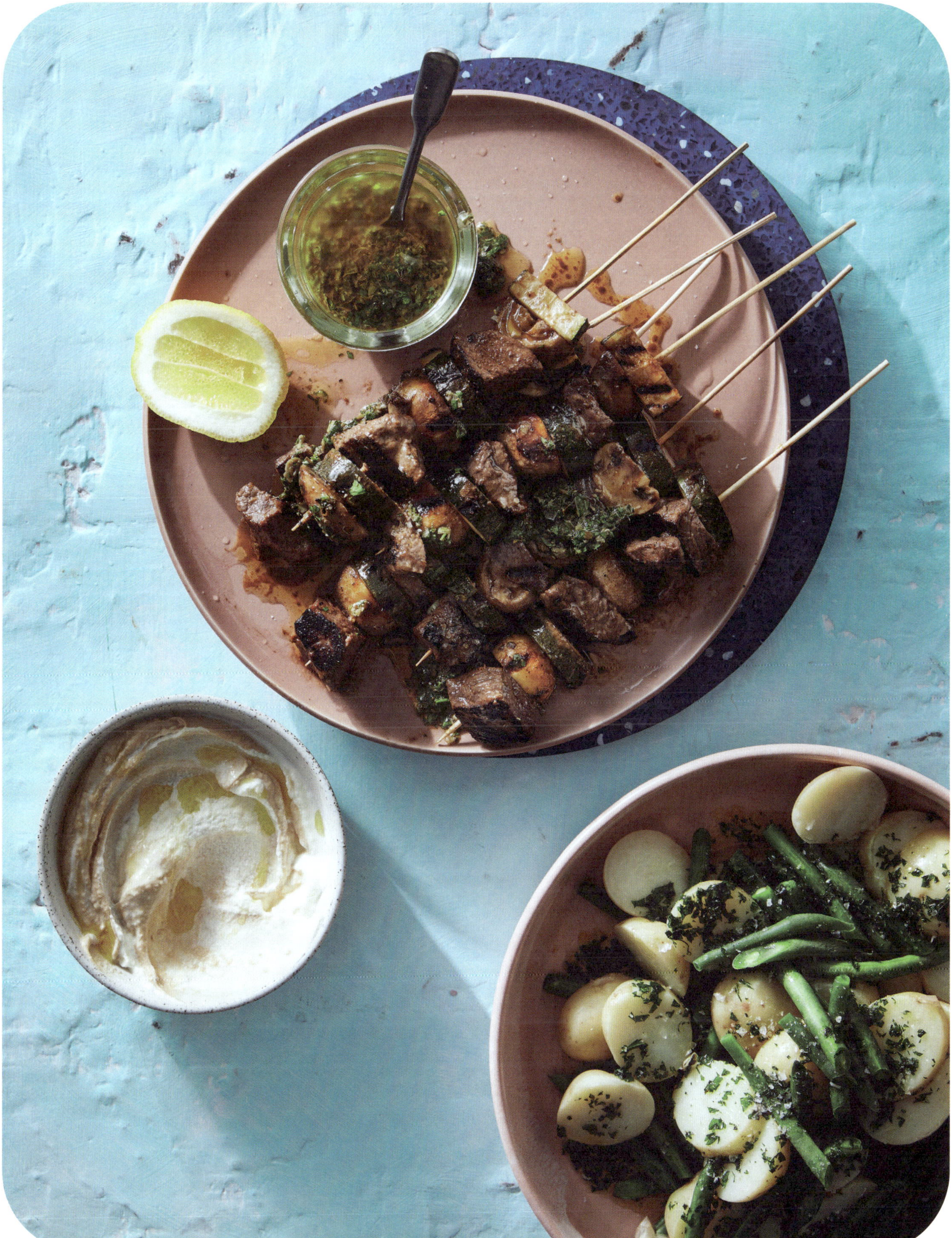

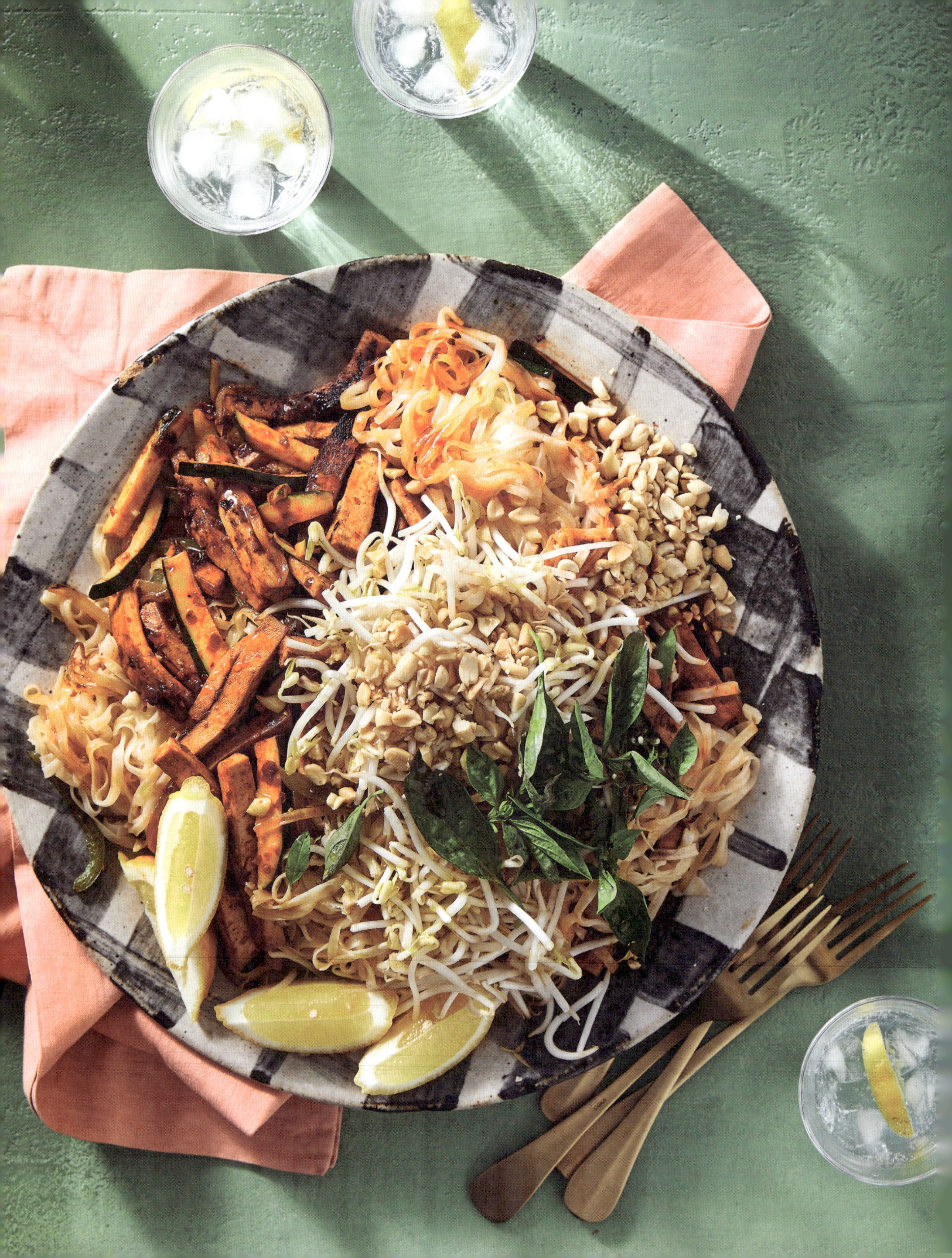

Sweet and tangy tofu noodles

GF DF VG V

Prep: 10 minutes
Cook: 40 minutes
Serves: 4

1 × quantity Marinated tofu (page 197)

1 large zucchini (courgette), cut into 1 × 5 cm (½ × 2 in) sticks

2 tablespoons extra-virgin olive oil or coconut oil

1 green capsicum (bell pepper), finely sliced

1 onion, finely sliced

280–300 g (10–10½ oz) flat rice noodles, soaked in cold water until soft, drained

sea salt

bean sprouts, to serve

unsalted peanuts, chopped, to serve

Thai basil leaves, to serve

lemon wedges, to serve

Packed with vibrant textures and aromas, this flavourful stir-fry combines crispy tofu, fresh vegetables and rice noodles for a fuss-free dinner that will please everyone.

Heat a large non-stick frying pan over medium–high heat. Remove the tofu from the marinade (reserving the marinade), then place the tofu in the hot pan and stir-fry for 10–15 minutes, or until the edges are golden and crispy. Remove from the pan and set aside.

In the same pan, add the zucchini and stir-fry for about 5 minutes, or until softened. Remove from the pan and set aside. Wipe the pan clean.

Return the pan to medium–high heat and add the oil. Add the capsicum and onion and sauté for a few minutes until the onion is golden brown.

Add the soaked rice noodles to the pan and stir-fry for 2 minutes, until softened and the edges begin to crisp.

Return the tofu, zucchini and reserved marinade to the pan. Season with salt and toss everything together with tongs until well combined.

Serve topped with bean sprouts, peanuts and Thai basil with the lemon wedges on the side.

Hints Ensure the rice noodles are well-drained before adding to the pan to avoid excess moisture.

For an added kick, sprinkle a pinch or two of chilli flakes over the finished dish.

LIGHT & FRESH

Chicken chorizo paella

GF NF DF

Prep 15 minutes
Cook 35 minutes
Serves 4

2 tablespoons extra-virgin olive oil

200 g (7 oz) chorizo, crumbled or thinly sliced

½ × quantity Seasoned chicken mince (page 196)

1 large onion, finely chopped

1 red capsicum (bell pepper), diced

3 garlic cloves, minced

1 teaspoon smoked paprika

½ teaspoon ground cumin

¼ teaspoon ground turmeric

¼ teaspoon chilli flakes (optional)

300 g (10½ oz/1½ cups) paella rice

1 litre (34 fl oz/4 cups) Chicken bone broth (page 139) or chicken stock, warm

400 g (14 oz) tinned diced tomatoes

150 g (5½ oz) frozen peas

sea salt

chopped flat-leaf (Italian) parsley, to serve

lemon wedges, to serve

The pre-seasoned chicken mince gives this colourful paella a head start in the flavour race. Serve it straight from the pan at the table.

Heat the olive oil in a large paella pan or a wide, shallow frying pan over medium heat. Add the chorizo and cook for 5 minutes, until the fat has rendered and the chorizo is crispy. Remove the chorizo with a slotted spoon and set it aside, leaving the oil in the pan.

Add the chicken mince to the pan and cook, breaking it up with a wooden spoon, until browned and cooked through. Check the seasoning and adjust if needed. Remove the chicken and set it aside with the chorizo.

In the same pan, add the onion and capsicum. Cook for 5–7 minutes, until softened. Add the garlic, smoked paprika, cumin, turmeric and chilli flakes (if using) and cook for an additional minute until fragrant. Stir in the paella rice, ensuring each grain is coated in the seasoned oil. Pour in the warm chicken stock and diced tomatoes, stirring to combine. Bring the mixture to a simmer.

Return the cooked chicken and chorizo to the pan, distributing them evenly throughout the rice. Reduce the heat to low and let the paella simmer gently for 20 minutes, stirring occasionally, until the rice is cooked and has absorbed most of the liquid.

Scatter the frozen peas over the top of the paella and cook for an additional 5 minutes until the peas are heated through.

Turn off the heat, cover the pan with a lid and let it rest for 5 minutes.

To serve, top with parsley and serve with lemon wedges on the side.

Hints For extra flavour, add a pinch of saffron threads to the warm chicken stock before adding it to the rice.

If you prefer a crispier bottom layer (*socarrat*), increase the heat slightly in the last few minutes of cooking.

This dish pairs well with a simple green salad dressed in olive oil and lemon juice.

THE WEEKLY GROCERY SHOP

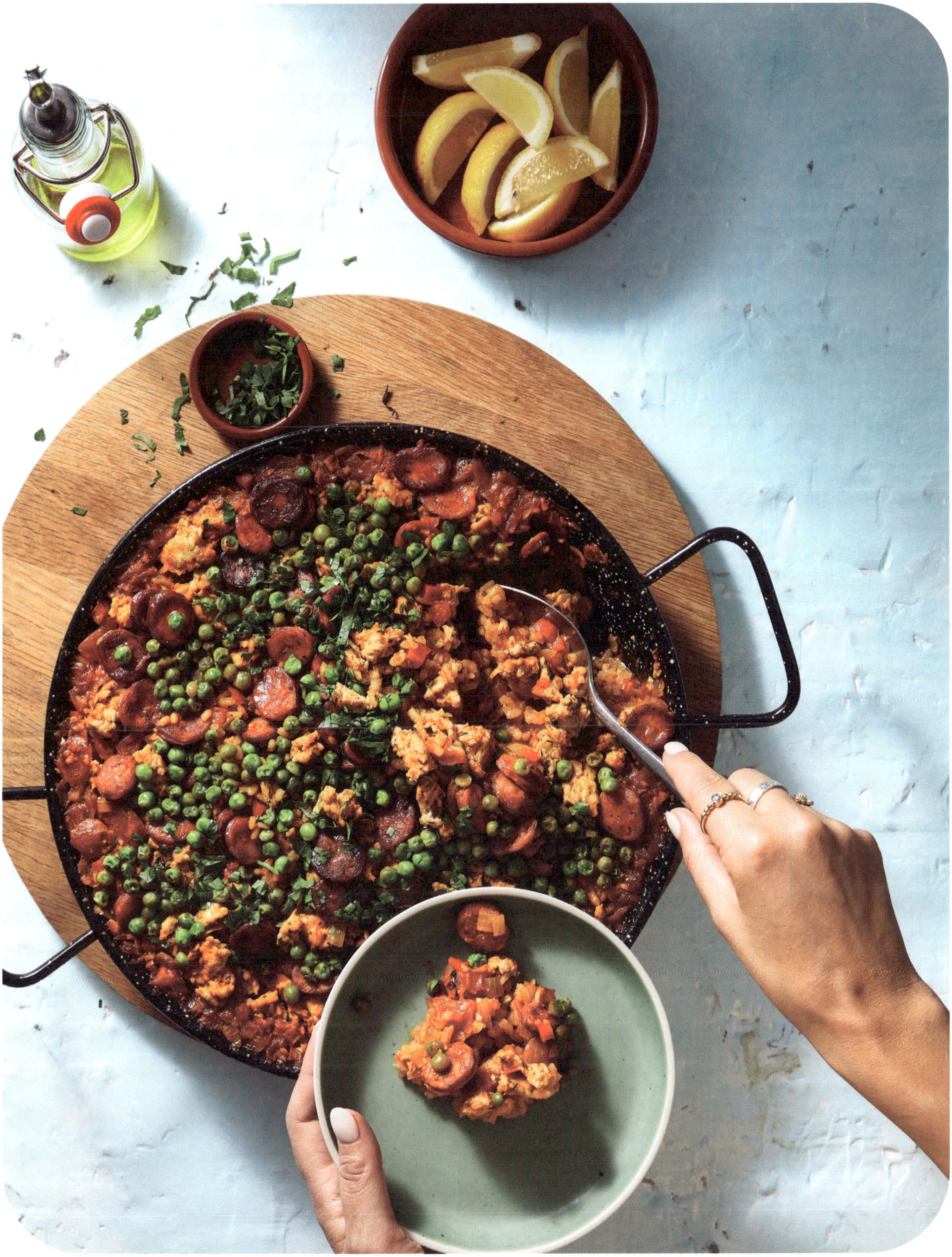

Mini chicken mozzarella meatballs with garlic mash

NF

Prep 15 minutes
Cook 30 minutes
Serves 4

½ × quantity Seasoned chicken mince (page 196)

100 g (3½ oz) mozzarella, cut into small cubes

1 garlic bulb, cut in half horizontally

800 g (1 lb 12 oz) potatoes, peeled and chopped

60 ml (2 fl oz/¼ cup) milk

2 tablespoons extra-virgin olive oil

1 × quantity Home-made tomato passata (page 110) or store-bought passata (pureed tomatoes)

100 g (3½ oz) large rocket (arugula) leaves

2 tablespoons Everyday marinade (page 198)

sea salt and freshly ground black pepper

grated parmesan, to serve

These mini meatballs will delight both adults and kids, especially served alongside garlicky mashed potatoes and a well-dressed rocket (arugula) salad.

Preheat the oven to 180°C (360°F). Line a baking tray with baking paper.

Divide the chicken mince into small portions, about the size of a walnut. Flatten each portion slightly, place a cube of mozzarella in the centre, then shape the mince around the mozzarella to form a mini meatball. Repeat with the remaining mince and mozzarella.

Place the meatballs on the baking tray and bake for 15–20 minutes, or until just cooked through and lightly golden.

Place the garlic halves on a square of baking paper and drizzle the cut sides with ½ tablespoon of olive oil. Wrap tightly in the baking paper and place in the oven with the meatballs for 15 minutes.

While the meatballs are baking, place the potato in a large pot of salted water and bring to a boil. Simmer until tender, about 15–20 minutes. Once the potato is tender, drain and return it to the pot. Squeeze the roasted garlic out of its skins onto the potato. Mash together with the milk and 1 tablespoon of olive oil until smooth. Season with salt, to taste.

In a large saucepan, heat the passata over medium heat until simmering. Add the baked meatballs to the sauce and simmer gently for 5–10 minutes, allowing the flavours to meld and the meatballs to be fully cooked.

In a large bowl, toss the rocket with the marinade and remaining ½ tablespoon of olive oil and season with pepper.

Serve the meatballs in passata alongside the garlicky potato mash, the rocket salad and a shower of grated parmesan.

Hints To intensify the tomato flavour, simmer the passata with a few basil leaves before adding the meatballs.

For a smoother mash, pass the potato through a ricer before adding the roasted garlic and milk.

The rocket salad can be complemented with thinly sliced red onion or a handful of cherry tomatoes for additional freshness.

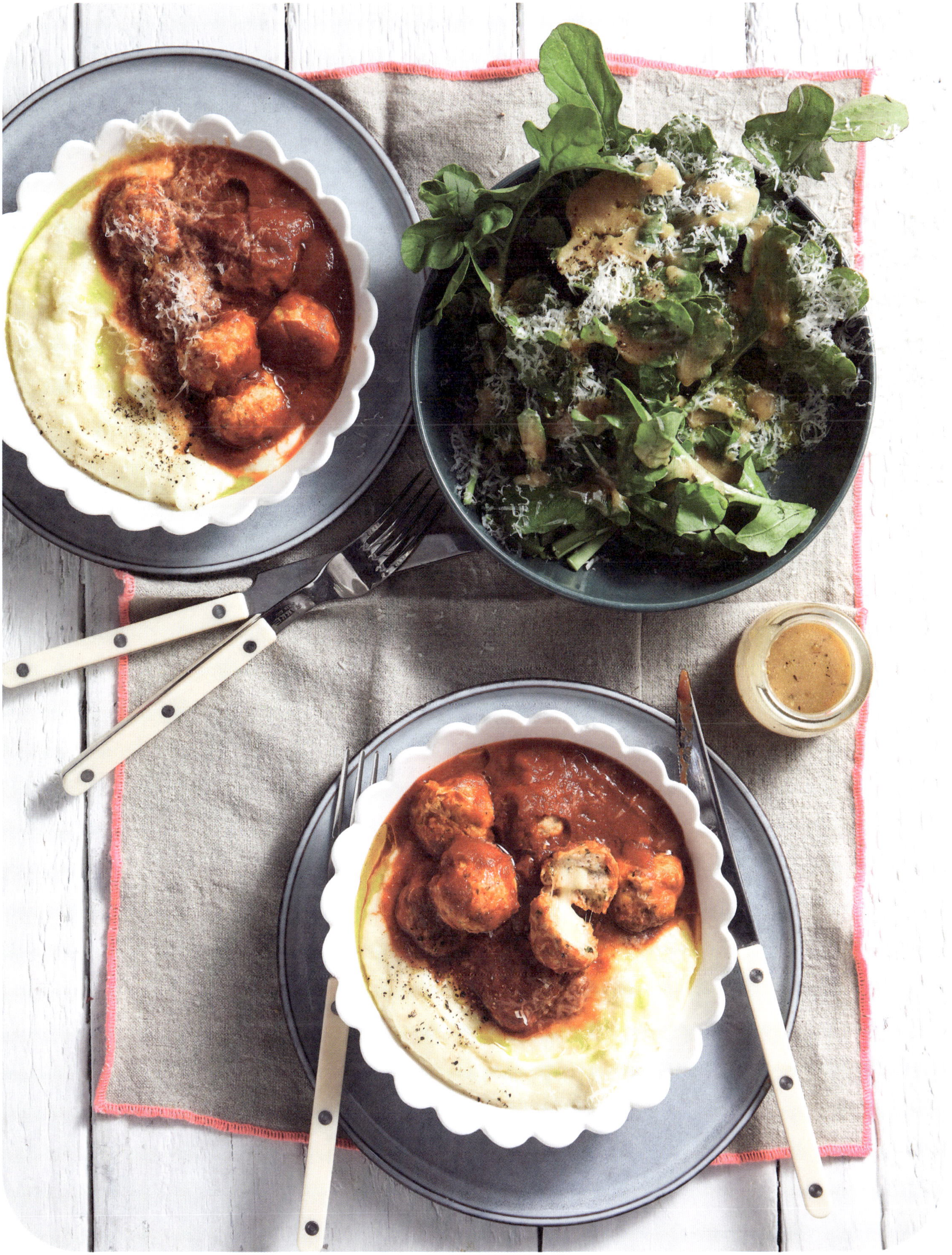

Lazy fish tacos

NF DF

Prep 45 minutes
Cook 10–15 minutes
Serves 4

1 × 600 g skinless firm white fish fillet

½ × quantity Home-made tortillas (page 199) or 8 store-bought

150 g (5½ oz/2 cups) cabbage or cos (romaine) lettuce, shredded

lime wedges, to serve

Crumb

15 g (½ oz/¼ cup) Japanese breadcrumbs

15 g (½ oz/¼ cup) desiccated coconut

1 teaspoon smoked paprika

½ teaspoon ground cumin

2 tablespoons extra-virgin olive oil

sea salt

Salsa

1 mango, diced

1 avocado, diced

200 g (7 oz/1 cup) corn kernels (fresh, tinned or thawed frozen)

1 shallot, finely diced

25 g (1 oz/½ cup) coriander (cilantro) leaves or flat-leaf (Italian) parsley, chopped

juice of 1 lime

sea salt

Lime mayonnaise

125 g (4½ oz/½ cup) mayonnaise

zest and juice of 1 lime

½ teaspoon garlic powder

sea salt

Lazy or smart? Either way, DIY fish tacos take the fuss out of meal time. A salsa of mango and avocado is a deliciously fresh, sweet addition.

Preheat the oven to 200°C (390°F). Line a baking tray with baking paper.

Pat the fish fillet dry with paper towel, then place it on the baking tray.

For the crumb, combine the breadcrumbs, desiccated coconut, paprika, cumin, olive oil and a pinch of salt in a small bowl and mix until the breadcrumbs are evenly coated.

Sprinkle the crumb mixture all over the fish, pressing it gently to adhere.

Bake for 15–20 minutes, or until the fish is cooked through and the crumb is golden and crisp.

While the fish is baking, prepare the salsa. Combine the mango, avocado, corn kernels, shallot and coriander in a bowl. Squeeze the lime juice on top and season with salt. Gently toss to combine, then set aside.

Prepare the lime mayonnaise by whisking the mayonnaise, lime zest and juice, garlic powder and a pinch of salt in a small bowl until smooth.

Once the fish is cooked, remove it from the oven and allow it to cool slightly. Use a fork to flake the fish into bite-sized pieces.

Warm the tortillas in a dry pan for a few seconds on each side before serving.

Assemble the tacos by placing some flaked fish on each tortilla, and topping with the salsa, a drizzle of lime mayonnaise and some shredded cabbage or cos lettuce. Serve two tacos per person with lime wedges on the side.

Hints For the fish fillet, snapper, cod or barramundi are all good options for this recipe.

Add some finely chopped fresh chilli to the salsa if you prefer it spicier.

For an authentic experience, try heating the tacos over an open flame until soft and slightly charred.

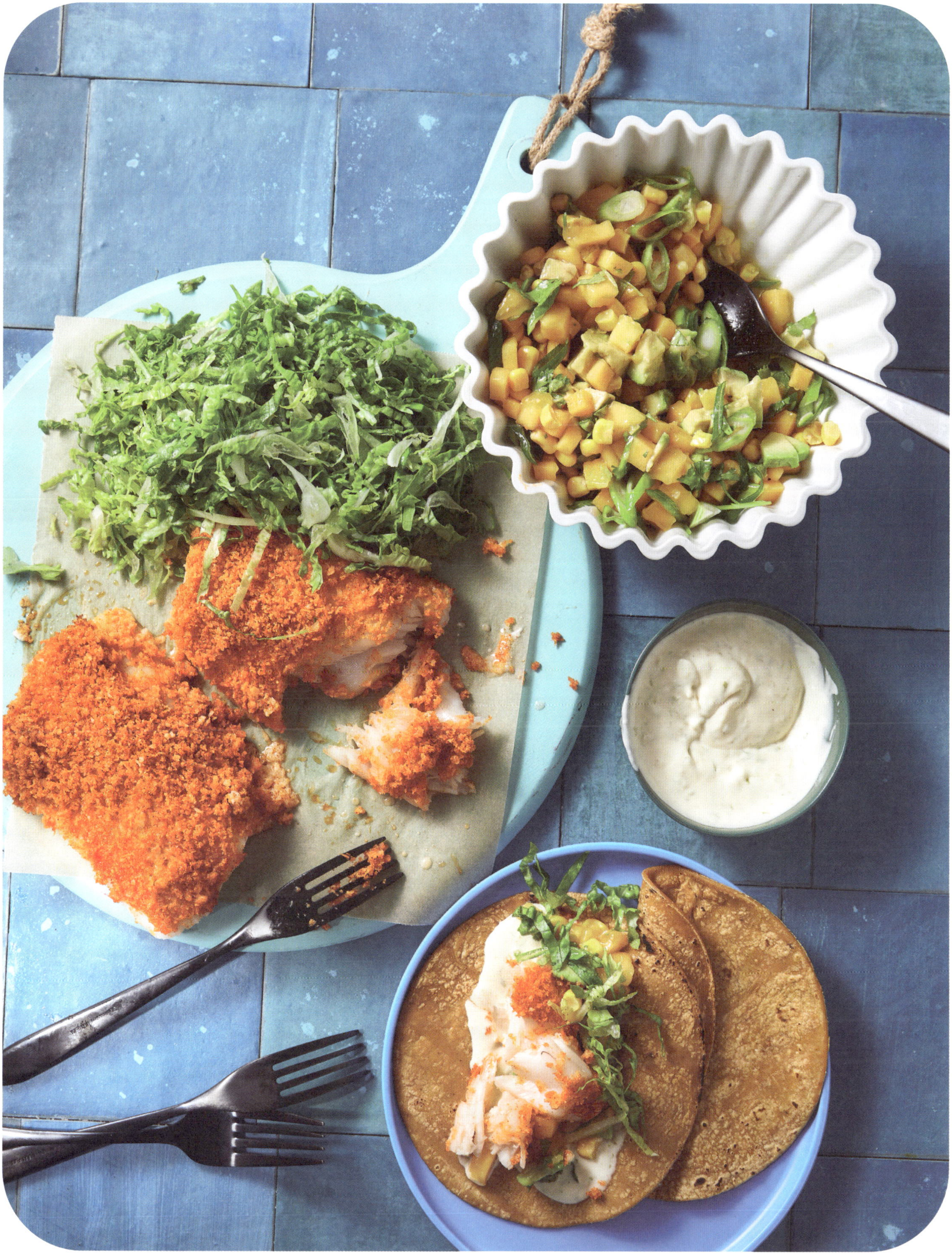

Lamb chops with Mediterranean salad and yoghurt tahini dressing

NF

Prep 30 minutes (plus 30 minutes marinating time)
Cook 10 minutes
Serves 4

4 × lamb chump chops

½ × quantity Home-made flatbreads (page 226) or 4 store-bought, warmed

Lamb seasoning

1 tablespoon extra-virgin olive oil

2 teaspoons ground cumin

1 teaspoon ground coriander

1 teaspoon smoked paprika

½ teaspoon dried oregano

½ teaspoon garlic powder

zest of 1 lemon and juice of ½ lemon

sea salt

Mediterranean salad

400 g (14 oz) tinned chickpeas, drained and rinsed

½ Lebanese (short) cucumber, diced

½ red onion, finely diced

200 g (7 oz) cherry tomatoes, cut in half

95 g (3¼ oz) kalamata olives, pitted and halved

100 g (3½ oz) feta, crumbled

15 g (½ oz/¼ cup) flat-leaf (Italian) parsley, roughly chopped

15 g (½ oz/¼ cup) mint leaves, roughly chopped

1 tablespoon red-wine vinegar

1 tablespoon extra-virgin olive oil

sea salt

This impressive-looking dinner is healthy, fresh and fast, especially if you marinate the lamb the night before.

For the lamb seasoning, combine the olive oil, cumin, ground coriander, paprika, oregano, garlic powder, lemon zest and juice in a small bowl and season with salt.

Rub this mixture all over the lamb chump chops. Cover and refrigerate for at least 30 minutes. (If time, marinate overnight for a deeper flavour.)

For the yoghurt tahini dressing, whisk the yoghurt, tahini, lemon juice, garlic and cumin together in a small bowl and season with salt.

For the salad, combine the chickpeas, cucumber, onion, cherry tomatoes, olives, feta, parsley and mint in a large bowl. Drizzle the red-wine vinegar and olive oil on top, season with salt and toss to combine.

Heat a frying pan over medium–high heat. Fry the marinated lamb chump chops for 3–4 minutes on each side, or until cooked to your liking. Let the lamb rest for a few minutes.

Slice and plate the lamb chops with the Mediterranean salad on the side. Drizzle the yoghurt tahini sauce over the lamb and serve with the warmed flatbreads.

Yoghurt tahini dressing

250 g (9 oz/1 cup) Greek-style yoghurt

1 tablespoon tahini

juice of ½ lemon

1 garlic clove, finely grated

1 teaspoon ground cumin

sea salt

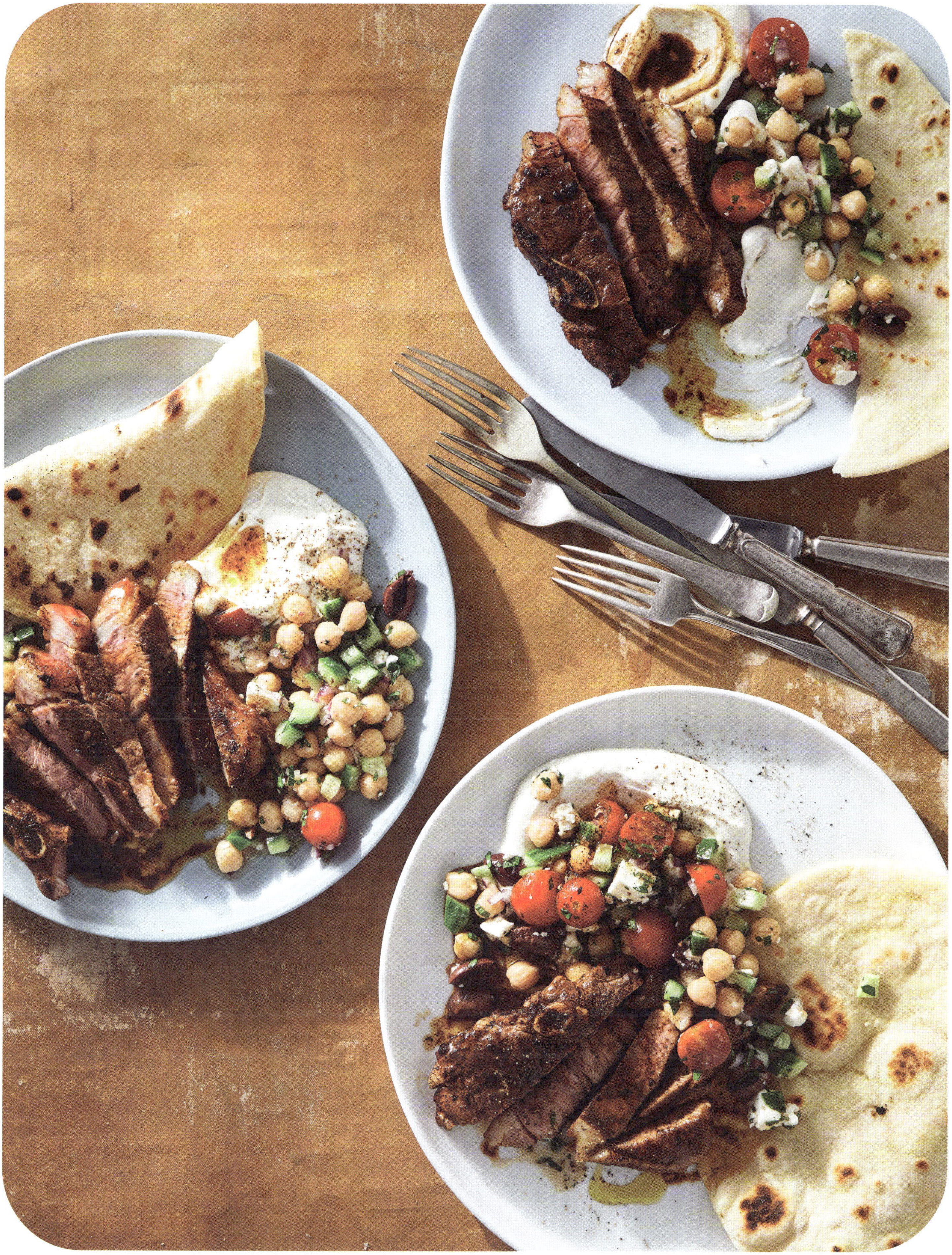

Prawn spaghetti

NF

Prep 25 minutes
Cook 25 minutes
Serves 4

500 g (1 lb 2 oz) spaghetti

400 g (14 oz) peeled, deveined frozen prawns (shrimp)

60 ml (2 fl oz/¼ cup) extra-virgin olive oil, halved

3 garlic cloves, finely sliced

1 red chilli, finely sliced (optional)

60 ml (2 fl oz/¼ cup) white wine

zest and juice of 2 lemons, halved, plus extra zest to serve

40 g (1½ oz) salted butter

1 bunch asparagus, cut diagonally into 2 cm (¾ in) pieces

7 g (¼ oz/¼ cup) flat-leaf (Italian) parsley, chopped, plus extra to serve

25 g (1 oz/¼ cup) parmesan, grated, plus extra to serve

sea salt and freshly ground black pepper

A classic for a reason: the combination of simple flavours is hard to beat. Plus, the asparagus (which is particularly good in spring) gives this dish a nutrient boost.

Cook the spaghetti in a large pot of salted boiling water according to package instructions. Drain and reserve 125 ml (4½ fl oz/½ cup) of the pasta water.

While the spaghetti cooks, thaw the frozen prawns under cold running water until fully defrosted. Pat dry with paper towel and roughly chop.

Heat half of the olive oil in a large saucepan over medium heat. Add the garlic and chilli (if using) and cook until fragrant but not browned, about 1–2 minutes.

Add the chopped prawns to the pan and cook for 3–4 minutes, stirring occasionally, until the prawns are pink and cooked through. Season with salt and pepper.

Stir in the white wine and half of the lemon juice, stirring to deglaze the pan. Then stir in the butter to emulsify. Let it simmer for 2 minutes to reduce slightly.

Add the cooked spaghetti and asparagus to the pan, tossing to coat in the sauce. Drizzle with the remaining olive oil and lemon juice, adding some of the reserved pasta water if needed to loosen the sauce.

Stir the lemon zest, parsley and parmesan through the spaghetti and season with salt and pepper, to taste.

Serve immediately, topped with extra lemon zest, parsley and a sprinkle of parmesan.

Hints For a nutty flavour, toss in a handful of toasted pine nuts or slivered almonds just before serving.

If you prefer a bit more sauce, increase the white wine or add a splash of vegetable stock.

Try adding some fresh baby spinach at the end for extra greens.

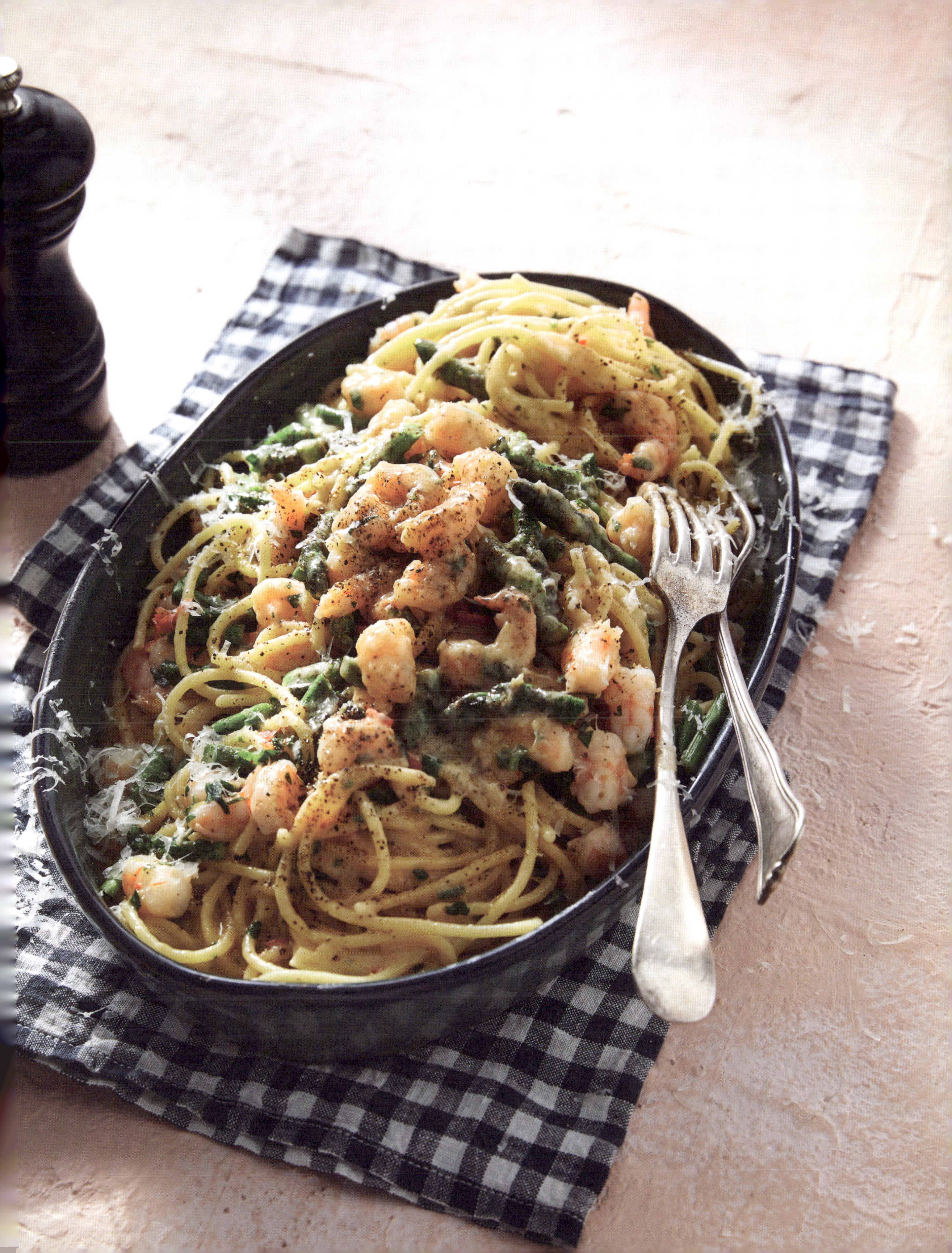

Breakfast tacos

NF

Prep 20 minutes
Cook 15 minutes
Serves 4

½ × quantity Home-made tortillas (page 199) or 8 store-bought

8 eggs

60 ml (2 fl oz/¼ cup) milk

2 teaspoons extra-virgin olive oil

4 × bacon rashers (slices) or 200 g (7 oz) hot smoked trout, flaked

2 avocados, sliced

sea salt and freshly ground black pepper

green chilli, thinly sliced into rounds, to serve (optional)

Tabasco sauce, to serve (optional)

Easy to customise with your favourite topping, these tacos are the perfect dish for a relaxed weekend brunch.

Warm the tortillas in a dry frying pan for 1 minute or until soft and slightly charred. Keep warm.

Whisk the eggs with the milk in a bowl and add a pinch of salt.

Heat a frying pan over medium heat, add a splash of olive oil, then pour in the egg mixture. Cook, stirring gently, until just set but still soft.

If using bacon, cook it in a separate frying pan over medium–high heat for 2–4 minutes on each side, until crispy.

Place a warm tortilla on each serving plate. Top each tortilla with some of the scrambled egg, bacon rashers or trout, sliced avocado and salt and pepper. For some added heat, finish with a sprinkle of green chilli and a dash of Tabasco sauce (if using) to taste.

Hints For an authentic taco experience, try heating the tacos over an open flame until soft and slightly charred.

When buying bacon, look for a preservative-free option that doesn't contain added nitrates.

If using bacon, consider cooking the egg mixture in the rendered bacon fat for added flavour.

Add herbs like coriander (cilantro) or chives for a burst of freshness.

Serve with a wedge of lime for an extra zingy finish.

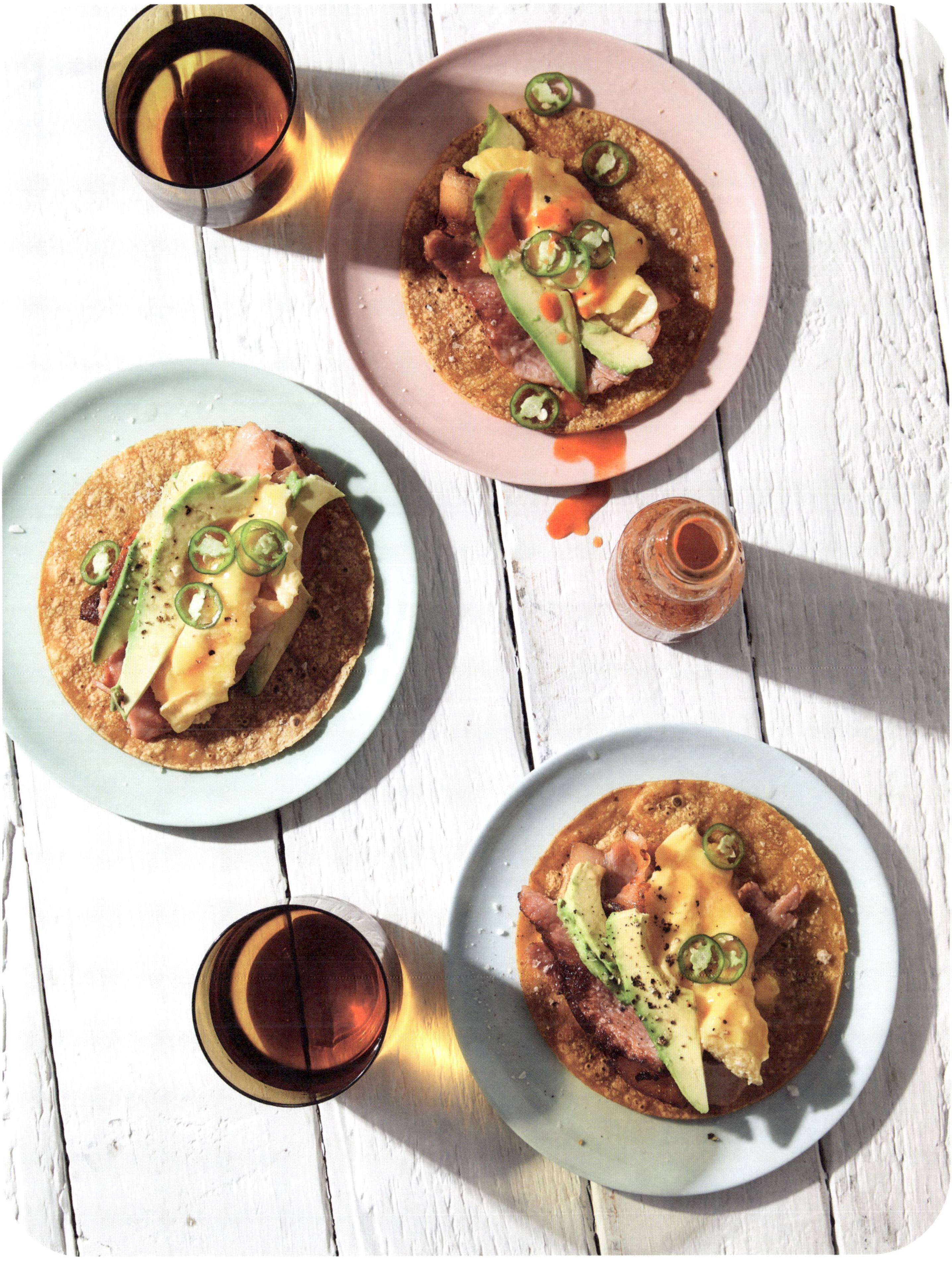

Tropical overnight chia

GF NF DF VG V

Prep 10 minutes (plus overnight soaking)
Makes 1.5 litres (51 fl oz/6 cups)

1 apple, peeled and chopped

1 banana, sliced

750 ml (25½ fl oz/3 cups) unsweetened coconut milk (from a carton)

155 g (5½ oz/1 cup) chia seeds

95 g (3¼ oz/½ cup) mango, chopped

zest and juice of 1 lime, plus extra zest to serve

sea salt

toasted coconut flakes, to serve

coconut yoghurt, to serve

Summer in a jar! This breakfast is prepared the night before so that you can get out and about sooner, whether to work, school or the beach. Vary the fruits according to the season and your taste.

Use a food processor to blend the apple, banana and coconut milk until smooth.

Pour the mixture into a large bowl, add the chia seeds, mango and lime zest and juice. Stir well to combine.

Transfer the mixture into four individual jars or a large airtight container. Cover and refrigerate overnight.

In the morning, serve the puddings topped with toasted coconut flakes, a dollop of coconut yoghurt, a little extra lime zest and a small pinch of salt.

Hints You can substitute the fresh mango with frozen mango chunks if preferred; just allow them to thaw slightly before adding to the mixture.

For extra texture, stir in some chopped nuts like almonds or macadamias before serving

If the pudding is too thick in the morning, stir in a little more coconut milk or coconut water to achieve the desired consistency.

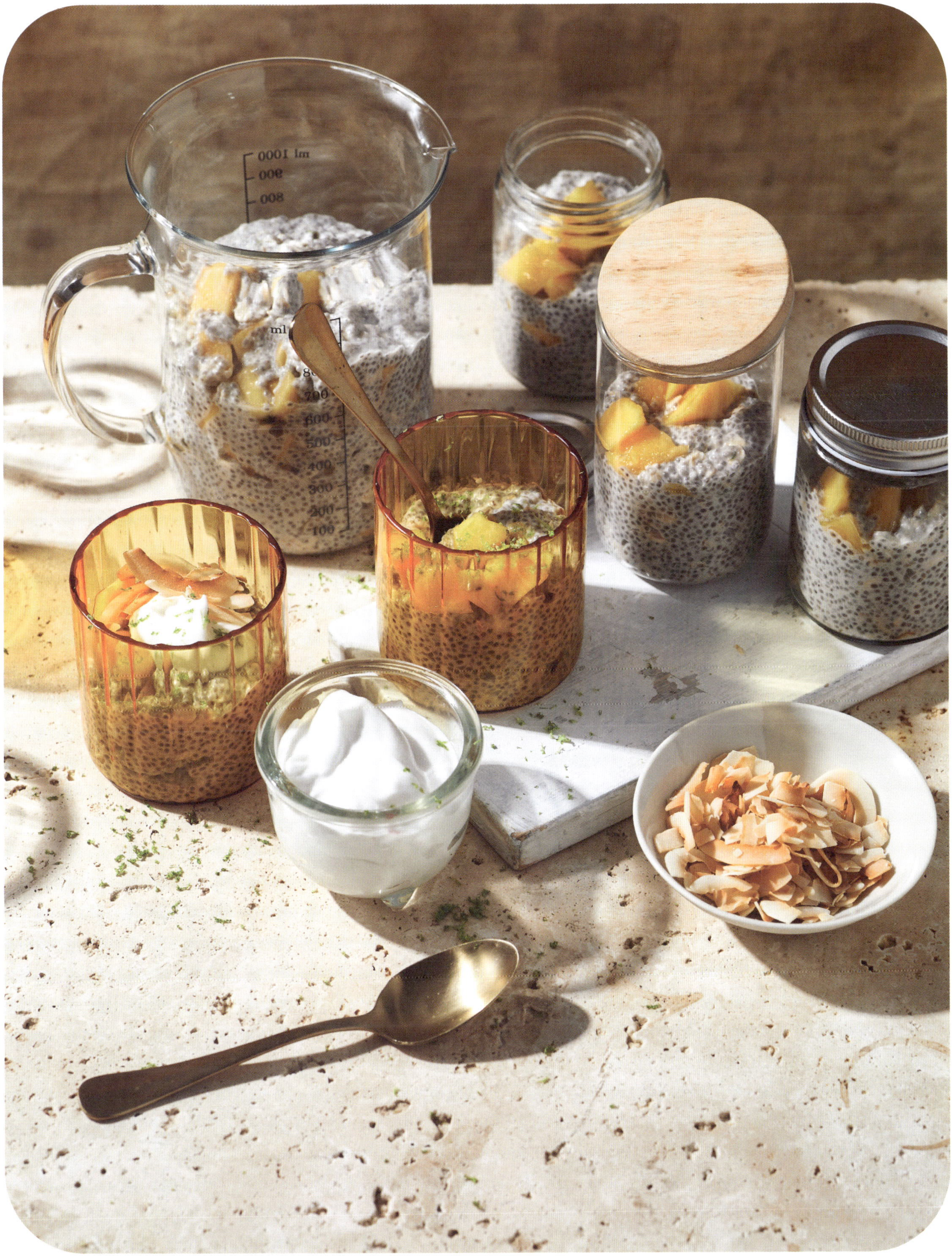
ml
700
600
500
400
300
200
100

Puff pastry pizza pinwheels

NF V

Prep 35 minutes (plus 15 minutes freezing time)
Cook 20 minutes
Serves 4

2 tablespoons tomato paste (concentrated puree)
27 × 36 cm (10¾ × 14¼ in) sheet puff pastry, thawed
1 teaspoon garlic powder
½ teaspoon dried oregano
75 g (2¾ oz/½ cup) mozzarella, grated
25 g (1 oz/¼ cup) parmesan, grated, plus extra for sprinkling
¼ red capsicum (bell pepper), diced
3 tablespoons sliced black olives
30 g (1 oz) spinach leaves, chopped
1 egg, beaten (for egg wash)
sea salt

Busy little monkeys will love this tasty, crispy snack on the run. (Just don't mention that they're packed with vegetables!)

Preheat the oven to 200°C (390°F). Line a baking tray with baking paper.

Spread the tomato paste evenly over the puff pastry, leaving a 2.5 cm (1 in) border on one long side. Sprinkle the garlic powder and dried oregano over the tomato paste, then scatter the mozzarella and parmesan on top. Add the capsicum, olives and spinach and season with salt.

Roll the puff pastry sheet up tightly from the long side into a log shape, finishing with the clean border. Place in the freezer for 15 minutes to firm up.

Slice the log into 2.5 cm (1 in) thick rounds and place them cut side up on the baking tray.

Brush the tops with the beaten egg to create a golden finish.

Bake for 15–20 minutes, or until the pinwheels are puffed and golden brown.

Serve warm or at room temperature, sprinkled with extra parmesan.

Hints For a milder flavour, replace chilli flakes with smoked paprika.

Use a sharp knife to slice the puff pastry log to ensure clean cuts.

For a kid-friendly twist, poke wooden skewers into the baked pinwheels, but be sure to cut off the sharp, pointy ends first.

These pinwheels can be made ahead and frozen; bake from frozen for an extra 5–7 minutes.

THE WEEKLY GROCERY SHOP

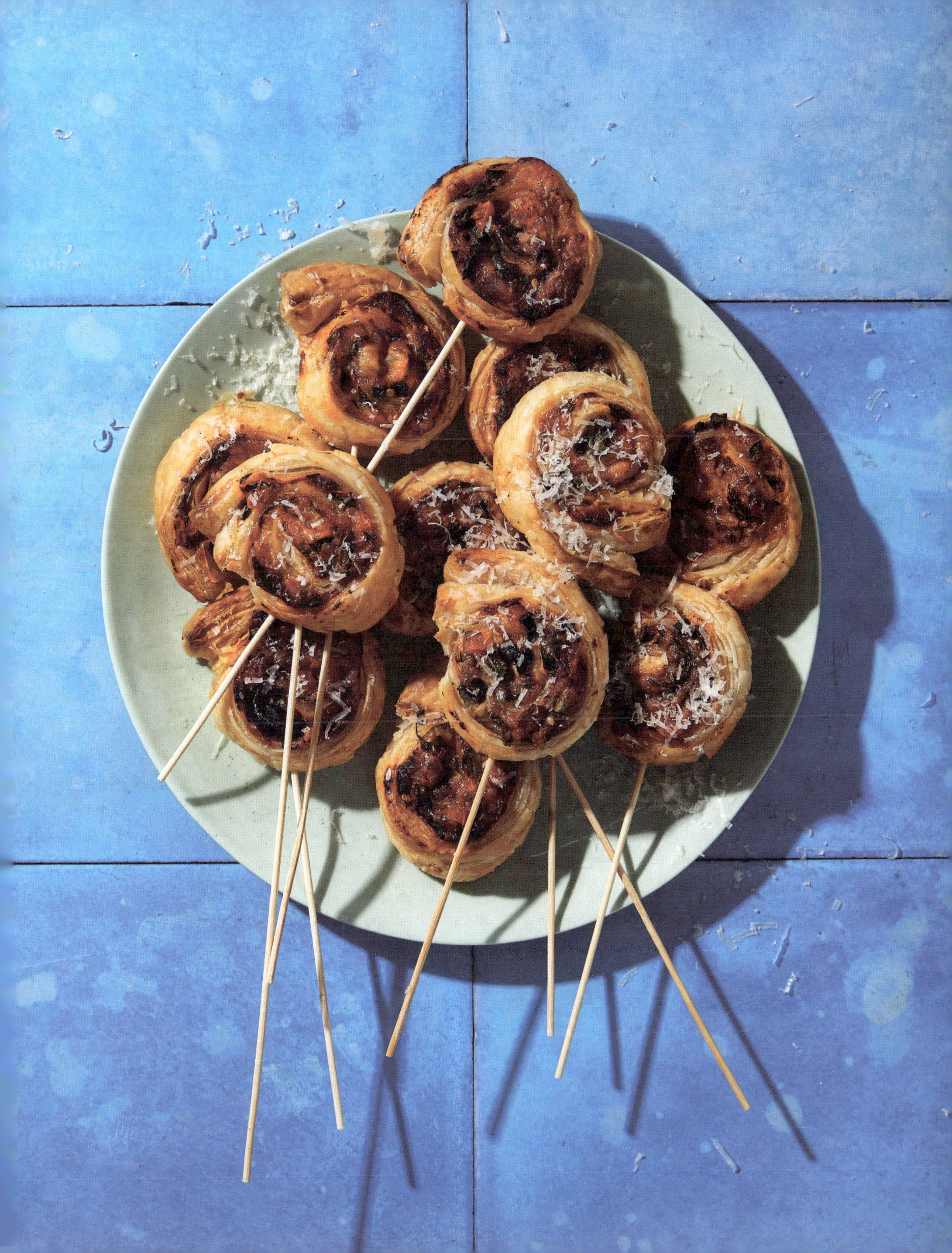

Coconut yoghurt and peach smoothie popsicles

GF NF DF VG V

Prep 20 minutes (plus 4 hours freezing time)
Makes 8

400 g (14 oz) unflavoured coconut yoghurt

1 teaspoon vanilla extract

410 g (14½ oz) tinned peach slices in juice, drained

45 g (1½ oz/¼ cup) dried apricots, chopped

80 g (2¾ oz/¼ cup) peach or apricot jam

8 wooden popsicle sticks

150 g (5½ oz) white chocolate

1 tablespoon coconut oil

Add a cool, fruity twist to your day with this refreshing and healthy snack that's so much better than the store-bought options.

Use a food processor to blend the yoghurt and vanilla extract with the drained peach slices until smooth. Fold in the dried apricot.

Spoon half of the mixture into ice popsicle moulds, filling each halfway. Add a small spoonful of jam to each mould, swirling it gently with a skewer or spoon.

Top with the remaining yoghurt and peach mixture.

Insert the sticks and freeze for at least 4 hours, or until completely solid.

Once frozen, melt the white chocolate by placing it in a microwave-safe bowl, heat for 20-seconds, then stir. Repeat until the chocolate has melted, then add the coconut oil and stir until well combined.

Unmould the popsicles and drizzle each one with the white chocolate mixture before placing them on a tray lined with baking paper.

Return to the freezer for a final 30 minutes to set the chocolate.

Once the chocolate has set, store the popsicles in reusable ziplock bags or an airtight container in the freezer for up to 2 weeks.

Hints Substitute the tinned peaches with fresh or frozen peaches if preferred.

For a slightly tangier flavour, add a squeeze of lime juice to the yoghurt mixture before blending.

Try drizzling the popsicles with dark or milk chocolate for a different flavour profile.

Unused white chocolate mixture can be stored at room temperature for up to 1 week in an airtight container in the pantry.

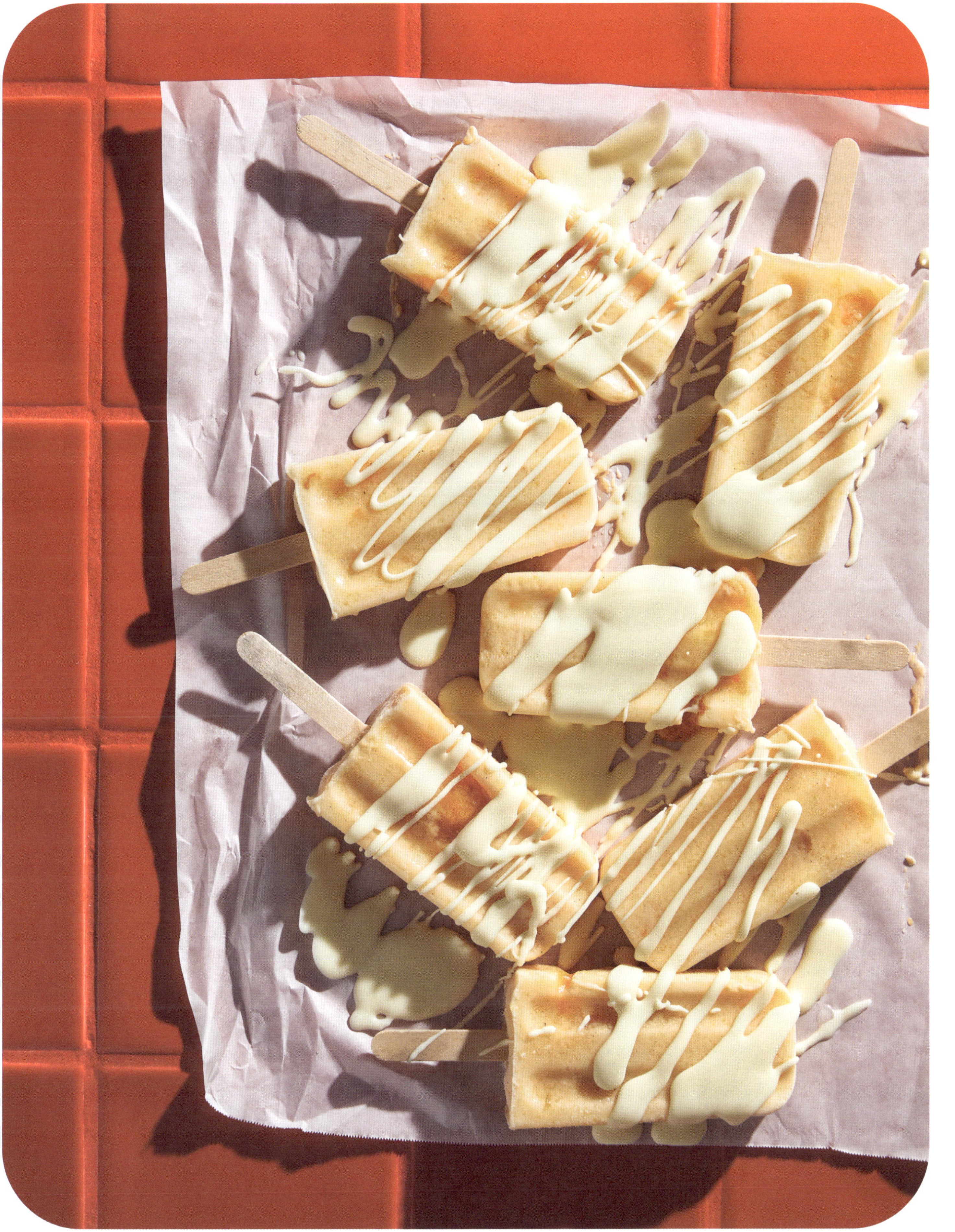

Week 3 menu

Power prep

Rose sauce
Marinated pork skewers
Home-made flatbreads
Roasted lamb rumps

Dinners

Marinated pork skewers with grilled potato salad
Roast lamb and zesty potato medley
Yiros with flatbread and crispy roasted chickpeas
Rose rigatoni
Fried rice
Prawn mango noodle salad
Chicken Caesar tray bake

Breakfasts

Fluffy trout omelette
Blueberry share pancake

Snack

Sushi sandwich

Sweet

Fruity tart

Week 3 shopping list

Fruit & vegetables

- [ ] 200 g (7 oz) asparagus
- [ ] 2 red capsicums (bell peppers)
- [ ] 1 large + 1 medium carrot
- [ ] 2 celery stalks
- [ ] 1 red chilli (optional)
- [ ] 1 bunch coriander (cilantro) (optional)
- [ ] 2 Lebanese (short) cucumbers
- [ ] 1 bunch dill
- [ ] 1 garlic bulb
- [ ] 2.5 cm (1 in) piece of fresh ginger
- [ ] 5 lemons
- [ ] 2 cos (romaine) lettuces
- [ ] 1 lime
- [ ] 1 mango
- [ ] 1 bunch mint
- [ ] 2 medium onions
- [ ] 2 small + 1 medium red onion
- [ ] 1 bunch oregano
- [ ] 1.6 kg (3½ lb) baby (chat) potatoes
- [ ] 1 bunch flat-leaf (Italian) parsley
- [ ] small bunch rosemary
- [ ] 30 g (1 oz) baby spinach leaves
- [ ] 4 spring onions (scallions)
- [ ] 250 g (9 oz) cherry tomatoes
- [ ] 6 large tomatoes
- [ ] 2 zucchini (courgettes)

Meat & poultry

- [ ] 4 anchovy fillets
- [ ] 200 g (7 oz) streaky bacon
- [ ] 8 × skin-on, bone-in chicken thighs
- [ ] 200 g (7 oz) roasted, shredded chicken, lamb or pork (optional)
- [ ] 6 × 300 g (10½ oz) lamb rumps
- [ ] 1 kg (2 lb 3 oz) deboned pork neck

Pantry & baking

- [ ] sourdough bread
- [ ] 400 g (14 oz) tinned chickpeas
- [ ] 600 g (1 lb 5 oz) wholemeal (whole-wheat) self-raising (rising) flour
- [ ] 170 g (6 oz) mayonnaise
- [ ] 2 tablespoons wholegrain mustard
- [ ] 200 g (7 oz) rice noodles
- [ ] 100 g (3½ oz) pitted green olives
- [ ] 150 g (5½ oz) crushed roasted peanuts
- [ ] 40 g (1½ oz) pine nuts
- [ ] 265 g (9½ oz) jasmine rice
- [ ] 500 g (1 lb 2 oz) rigatoni, penne or fusilli
- [ ] 3 tablespoons tomato paste (concentrated puree)
- [ ] 8 wooden skewers

Fridge

- [ ] 125 ml (4 fl oz) whipping cream
- [ ] 2 eggs
- [ ] 200 g (7 oz) smooth feta
- [ ] 120 g (4½ oz) haloumi
- [ ] 100 g (3½ oz) parmesan
- [ ] 125 g (4½ oz) ricotta
- [ ] 200 g (7 oz) tofu (optional)
- [ ] 700 g (1 lb 9 oz) Greek-style yoghurt

Freezer

- [ ] 400 g (14 oz) peeled, deveined frozen prawns (shrimp)

Rose sauce

Prep 30 minutes
Cook 30 minutes
Makes 500 ml (17 fl oz/2 cups)

2 tablespoons extra-virgin olive oil
1 onion, finely chopped
3 garlic cloves, minced
1 red capsicum (bell pepper), finely chopped
1 zucchini (courgette), grated
4 large tomatoes, chopped
1 teaspoon finely chopped oregano leaves
½ teaspoon chilli flakes (optional)

This fresh tomato sauce, which can be chunky or smooth according to your preference, is a great all-rounder. I love to make it in summer, when tomatoes are abundant. Serve it with pasta (such as Rose rigatoni, page 234), use it for home-made pizzas or make it the base of a stew.

Heat the olive oil in a large saucepan over medium heat. Add the onion and sauté for 3–4 minutes, until soft and translucent. Add the garlic and cook for another minute, until fragrant. Stir in the capsicum and zucchini and cook for 5–7 minutes more, until the vegetables soften. Add the tomato, oregano and chilli flakes (if using). Simmer for 25–35 minutes, allowing the sauce to thicken slightly.

Allow to cool. If you prefer a smooth sauce, transfer to a food processor and blend.

Store in an airtight container in the fridge for up to 1 week or freeze for up to 3 months.

(GF) (NF) (DF) (VG) (V)

Marinated pork skewers

Prep 25 minutes (plus 2 hours marinating time)
Makes 8

1 kg (2 lb 3 oz) deboned pork neck or pork scotch, cut into 3 cm (1¼ in) cubes

8 wooden skewers, soaked in water for 30 minutes

Marinade

3 tablespoons extra-virgin olive oil

3 tablespoons lemon juice

3 tablespoons tomato paste (concentrated puree)

5 garlic cloves, minced

2 tablespoons dried oregano

2 teaspoons dried thyme

1 tablespoon smoked paprika

1 tablespoon ground coriander

1 teaspoon ground cumin

½ teaspoon ground cinnamon

1 teaspoon black pepper

sea salt

By pre-preparing pork skewers, you can have Marinated pork skewers with grilled potato salad (page 228) on the table in a flash during the week. These are also delicious served with flatbreads, tzatziki, fresh salad and a sprinkle of herbs.

Combine the marinade ingredients with a generous pinch of salt in a large bowl and mix well.

Toss the pork cubes through the marinade, ensuring each piece is well coated. Cover the bowl or transfer the pork and marinade to a container or resealable bag. Refrigerate for at least 2 hours, preferably overnight.

Thread the marinated pork cubes onto the skewers, leaving a small gap between each piece. Store the skewers in an airtight container in the fridge until ready to use.

Store in the fridge for up to 2 days or freeze for up to 3 months.

(GF) (NF) (DF)

Home-made Flatbreads

Prep 30 minutes
(plus freezing time)
Cook 6 minutes
Makes 8

600 g (1 lb 5 oz/4 cups) wholemeal (whole-wheat) self-raising (rising) flour

500 g (1 lb 2 oz/2 cups) Greek-style yoghurt

½ teaspoon salt

1–2 tablespoons extra-virgin olive oil

NF V

Make these to serve for dinner with Yiros with flatbread and crispy roasted chickpeas (page 233) or Marinated pork skewers with grilled potato salad (page 228). You can also use them for a scrumptious breakfast of Spiced egg and tomato flatbreads (page 157).

Combine the flour, yoghurt and salt in a large bowl until it comes together. Turn it out onto a bench and knead the mixture until a smooth dough forms, about 5 minutes.

Divide the dough into eight equal portions and roll each portion into a ball.

Lightly flour a clean surface and roll each ball into a flat round, about 5 mm (¼ in) thick.

Place the flatbreads on a baking tray lined with baking paper, layering baking paper between each one.

Freeze the tray for 60–90 minutes, until the flatbreads are firm, then transfer them to a reusable ziplock bag or airtight container. Store the flatbreads in the freezer for up to 3 months, ensuring they're well wrapped to prevent freezer burn.

The flatbreads can be cooked from frozen. Heat a dry frying pan (or barbecue) over medium–heat. Brush each side of the flatbreads with olive oil, then place them on the hot frying pan (or barbecue). Cook for 2–3 minutes on each side, until puffed and charred in spots.

Hints If the dough is too sticky, add a little more flour, a tablespoon at a time, until it's manageable.

For a flavour boost, mix some chopped herbs like rosemary or thyme into the dough before kneading.

Roasted lamb rumps

Prep 45 minutes
Cook 40 minutes
Makes 2 meals for 4 people

2 tablespoons extra-virgin olive oil, halved

6 × 300 g (10½ oz) lamb rumps, caps trimmed

sea salt

Roast six lamb rumps at once and you'll have enough for Yiros with flatbread and crispy roasted chickpeas (page 233), as well as a delicious Roast lamb and zesty potato medley (page 230). You might even have a little left over for lunchbox sandwiches (delicious with hummus).

Preheat the oven to 180°C (360°F). Drizzle half of the olive oil in a baking tray.

Rub the remaining olive oil all over the lamb rumps and season them with salt.

Heat a large frying pan over high heat. Sear the rumps in batches in the hot pan for 2–3 minutes on each side until brown all over. Place the rumps in the baking tray once browned.

Roast the lamb for 30 minutes, or until it reaches medium doneness (internal temperature of 63°C/145°F).

Remove the tray from the oven and cover it loosely with baking paper. Allow it to rest for 10 minutes before carving the lamb into slices.

Store the cooled lamb slices in an airtight container in the fridge for up to 2 days or freeze for up to 3 months.

To reheat, wrap the lamb in baking paper and place it on a baking tray in a preheated oven at 180°C (360°C F) for 15 minutes or in an air fryer at 240°C (460°C F) for 6 minutes.

(GF) (NF) (DF)

LIGHT & FRESH

Marinated pork skewers with grilled potato salad

GF NF DF

Prep 45 minutes
Cook 25 minutes
Serves 4

600 g (1 lb 5 oz) baby (chat) potatoes, cut in half and parboiled until just cooked

1 tablespoon extra-virgin olive oil

1 × quantity Marinated pork skewers (page 225)

2 tablespoons wholegrain mustard

2 tablespoons mayonnaise

1 tablespoon red-wine vinegar

juice of 1 lemon, halved

1 small red onion, finely sliced

2 celery stalks, finely sliced

2 tablespoons capers, rinsed and squeezed dry

15 g (½ oz/¼ cup) flat-leaf (Italian) parsley, chopped, plus extra to serve (optional)

sea salt and freshly ground black pepper

An easy (especially if you pre-prepped your skewers), crowd-pleasing dish ready for your next barbecue or family dinner.

Preheat a barbecue or a chargrill pan to medium–high heat.

Toss the halved baby potatoes in 1 tablespoon of olive oil and season with salt and pepper. Grill, cut side down, for about 10–15 minutes until the potatoes are charred and cooked through. Remove from the grill and set aside.

Cook the marinated pork skewers on the barbecue for 3–4 minutes (or the chargrill pan for 4–6 minutes) on each side, until cooked through and caramelised. Remove from the grill and allow to rest.

In a large bowl, whisk together the wholegrain mustard, mayonnaise, red-wine vinegar and half of the lemon juice. Add the grilled potatoes, red onion, celery, capers and parsley. Toss everything together to coat the potatoes.

Serve the grilled pork skewers alongside the potato salad, drizzling the remaining lemon juice over the pork before serving. Garnish with additional parsley if desired.

Hints If you have leftover pork skewers, the meat can be sliced and added to sandwiches or wraps the next day.

The potato salad can be made ahead of time and stored in the fridge for up to 2 days.

For a bit of crunch, add some toasted pine nuts or pepitas (pumpkin seeds) to the salad before serving.

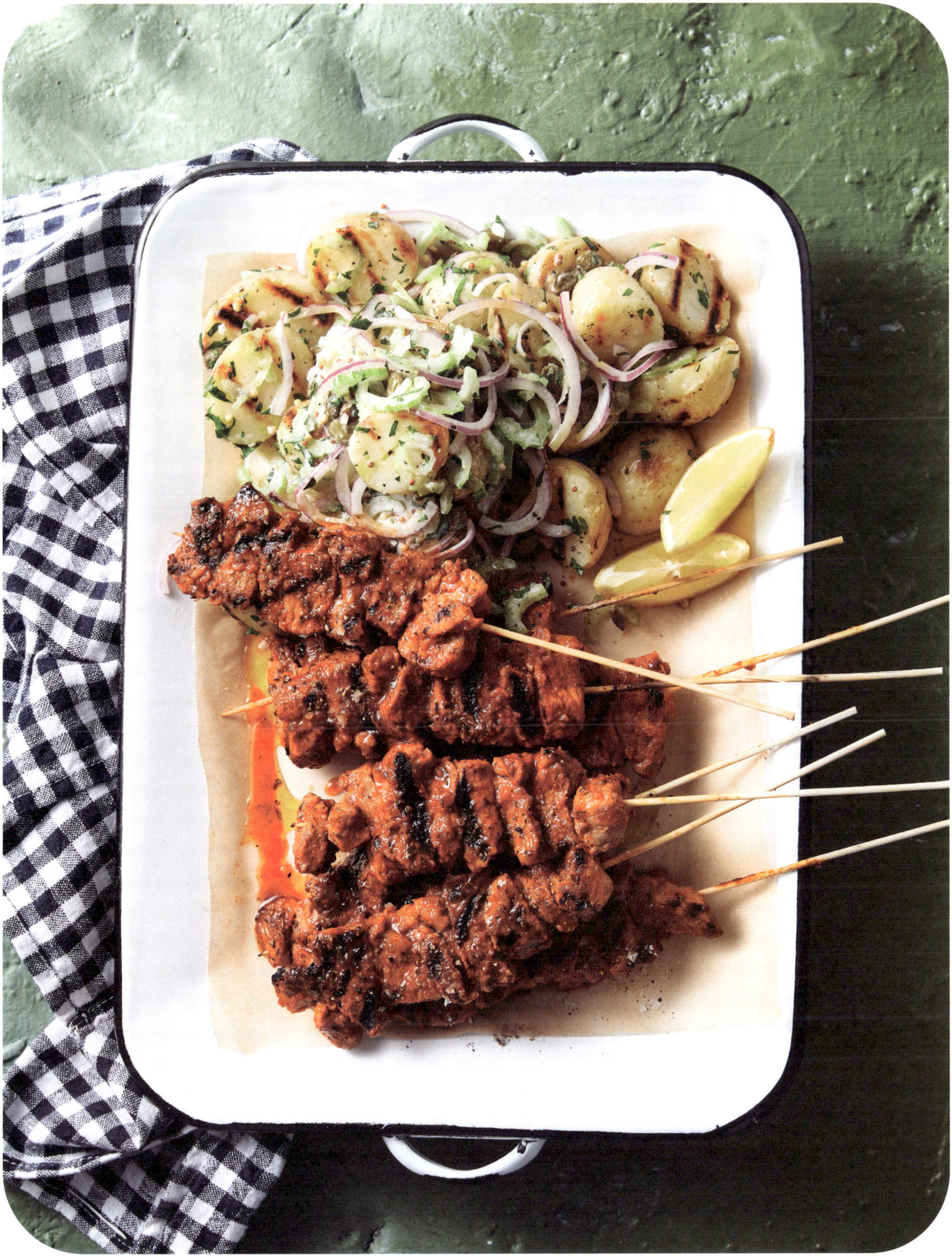

Roast lamb and zesty potato medley

GF NF

Prep 45 minutes
Cook 45 minutes
Serves 4

1 kg (2 lb 3 oz) baby (chat) potatoes, cut in half

200 ml (7 fl oz) beef stock

juice of 1 lemon

1 teaspoon paprika

100 g (3½ oz) pitted green olives

250 g (9 oz) cherry tomatoes, cut in half

2 sprigs rosemary, leaves picked

2 teaspoons extra-virgin olive oil, halved

3 × Roasted lamb rumps (page 227), sliced

1 tablespoon chopped flat-leaf (Italian) parsley

1 tablespoon grated haloumi

sea salt

Being a one-tray bake, this recipe will save you time, but it's still bursting with flavour. The grated haloumi adds a mouth-watering, salty touch to the potatoes.

Preheat the oven to 200°C (390°F).

Toss the halved baby potatoes in a roasting tin with the beef stock, lemon juice, paprika, olives, cherry tomatoes and rosemary leaves. Drizzle 1 teaspoon of the olive oil on top and season with salt. Roast for 35 minutes.

Increase the oven temperature to 220°C (430°CF). Remove the roasting tin from the oven. Place the lamb slices on top of the potato mixture and drizzle with the remaining olive oil. Scatter a large handful of parsley and haloumi over the potatoes and return the tin to the oven. Roast for another 10 minutes, or until the lamb is warmed through and the potatoes are tender.

Hints For an extra layer of flavour, add a few whole garlic cloves with the potatoes.

Serve with a fresh side salad to balance the richness of the roast.

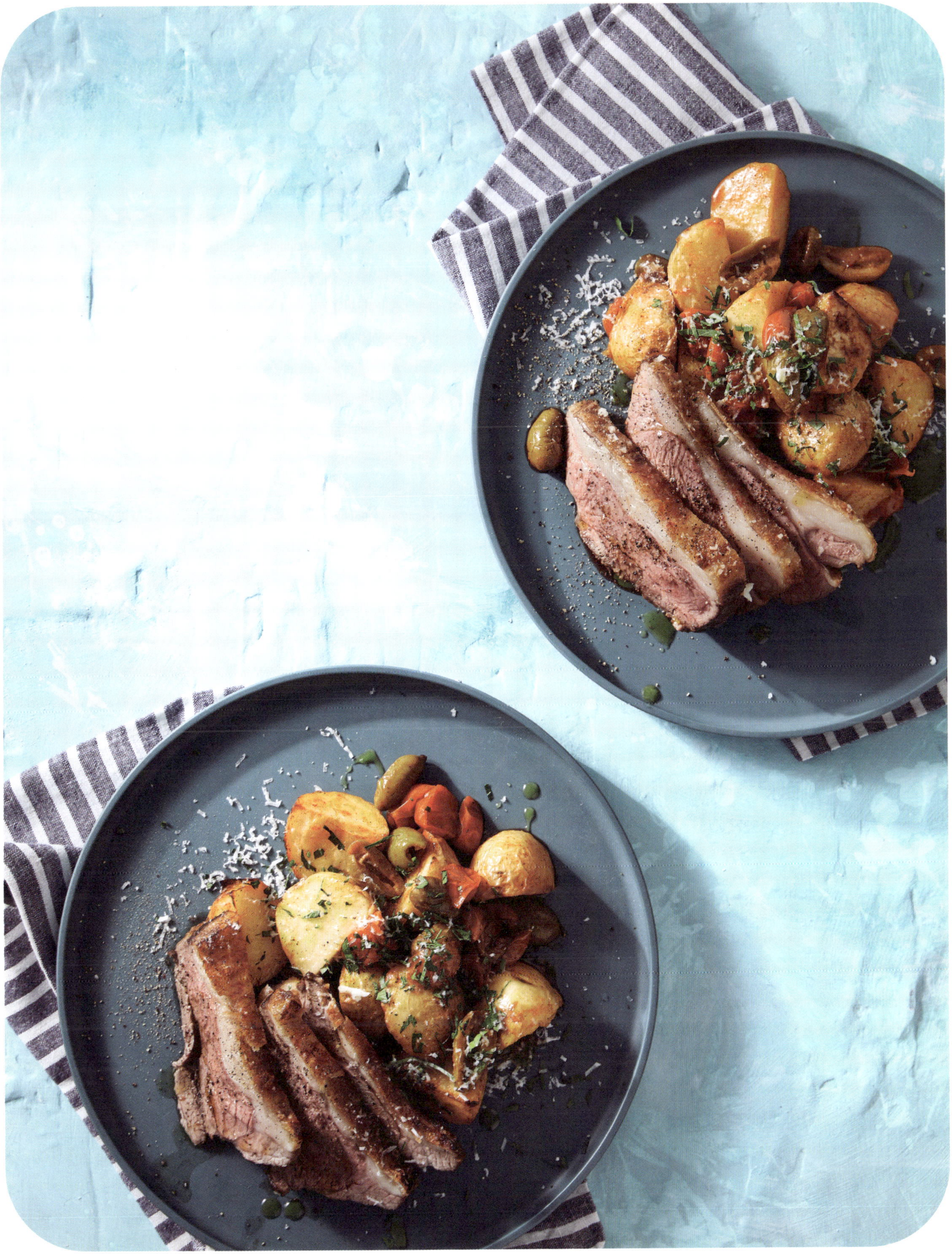

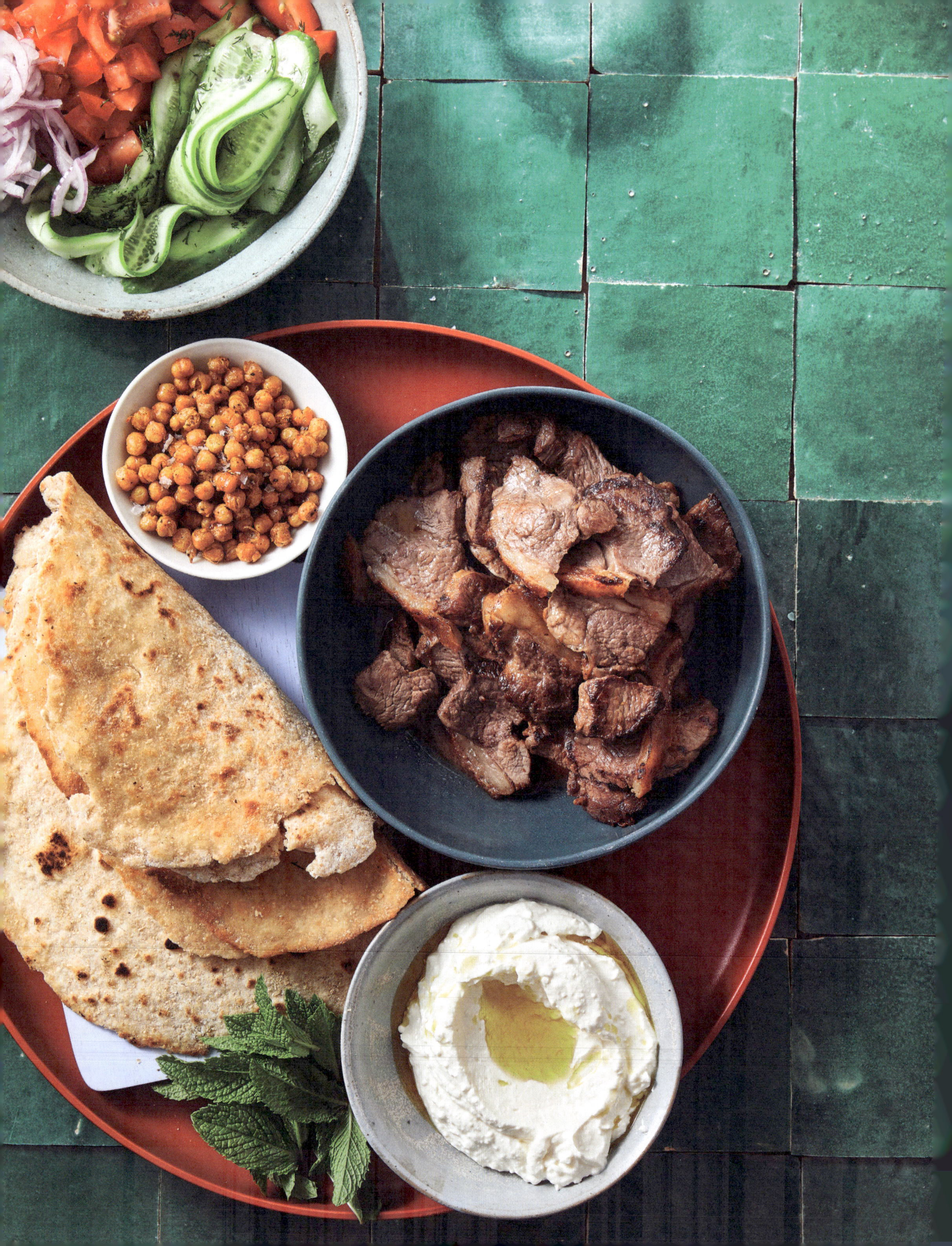

Yiros with flatbread and crispy roasted chickpeas

Prep 25 minutes
Cook 45 minutes
Serves 4

1 Lebanese (short) cucumber, cut into ribbons

1 tablespoon chopped dill

200 g (7 oz) smooth feta

60 g (2 oz/¼ cup) Greek-style yoghurt

2 tablespoons extra-virgin olive oil, halved

2 × Roasted lamb rumps (page 227), sliced

½ × quantity Home-made flatbreads (page 226) or 4 store-bought pita breads

2 large tomatoes, chopped

small handful of mint leaves, torn

1 small red onion, thinly sliced

sea salt

Crispy roasted chickpeas

400 g (14 oz) tinned chickpeas, drained and rinsed

1 tablespoon extra-virgin olive oil

½ teaspoon smoked paprika

sea salt and freshly ground black pepper

Roasted chickpeas are easy to make and add a lovely spicy crunch to this well-balanced meal.

For the roasted chickpeas, preheat the oven to 200°C (390°F). Line a baking tray with baking paper.

Pat the chickpeas dry with paper towel, removing as much moisture as possible. Toss the chickpeas with the olive oil and paprika and season with salt and pepper. Spread them out on the baking tray in a single layer and roast for 25–30 minutes, shaking the tray halfway through, until crispy and golden brown. Set aside in a serving bowl.

In a small bowl, combine the cucumber, dill and a pinch of salt. Set aside.

Blend the feta and yoghurt together in a small food processor until smooth, then top with 1 tablespoon of the olive oil. (Alternatively, use a fork to whip the feta and yoghurt together.)

Heat the remaining olive oil in a large frying pan over medium–high heat. Quickly sear the carved lamb rump slices until hot and slightly crisp on the edges, around 10 minutes. Season with salt. Place the hot seared lamb slices on the platter.

Warm the flatbreads in the oven or on a dry frying pan for 1 minute, or until soft and slightly toasted.

Place the tomato and onion in a serving bowl along with the cucumber.

Serve the lamb platter with the flatbreads, chickpeas, mint leaves and whipped feta on the side, along with the cucumber, tomato and onion, allowing everyone to build their own wraps.

Hints Store any leftover roasted chickpeas in an airtight container for up to 3 days.

Add a squeeze of lemon juice over the lamb for an extra burst of freshness.

Consider adding a few olives or pickled vegetables to the platter for additional flavour contrasts.

If you have any leftover grilled vegetables, they would be a great addition to the wraps.

Rose rigatoni

NF V

Prep 30 minutes
Cook 25 minutes
Serves 4

1 × quantity Rose sauce (page 224)

125 g (4½ oz) ricotta

125 ml (4 fl oz/½ cup) whipping cream

500 g (1 lb 2 oz) rigatoni, penne or fusilli

25 g (1 oz/¼ cup) parmesan, grated

40 g (1½ oz/¼ cup) toasted pine nuts

30 g (1 oz) baby spinach leaves

sea salt and freshly ground black pepper

When you have a quality home-made tomato sauce pre-prepared, you don't need much else to make a meal. The addition of a little ricotta and cream makes this into a deeply satisfying dish.

Gently reheat the Rose sauce until hot. Stir in the ricotta and cream, mixing until the sauce turns a smooth, pink colour. Season with salt.

Meanwhile, cook the pasta according to the packet instructions until al dente. Drain and set aside.

Serve the pasta in bowls, topped with grated parmesan, toasted pine nuts and freshly ground black pepper, with spinach leaves on the side.

Hints For a protein boost, add cooked chicken or prawns (shrimp) to the sauce before serving.

Replace baby spinach with rocket (arugula) for a slightly peppery taste.

For a dairy-free version, substitute the ricotta and cream with coconut cream and a spoonful of nutritional yeast, and omit the parmesan.

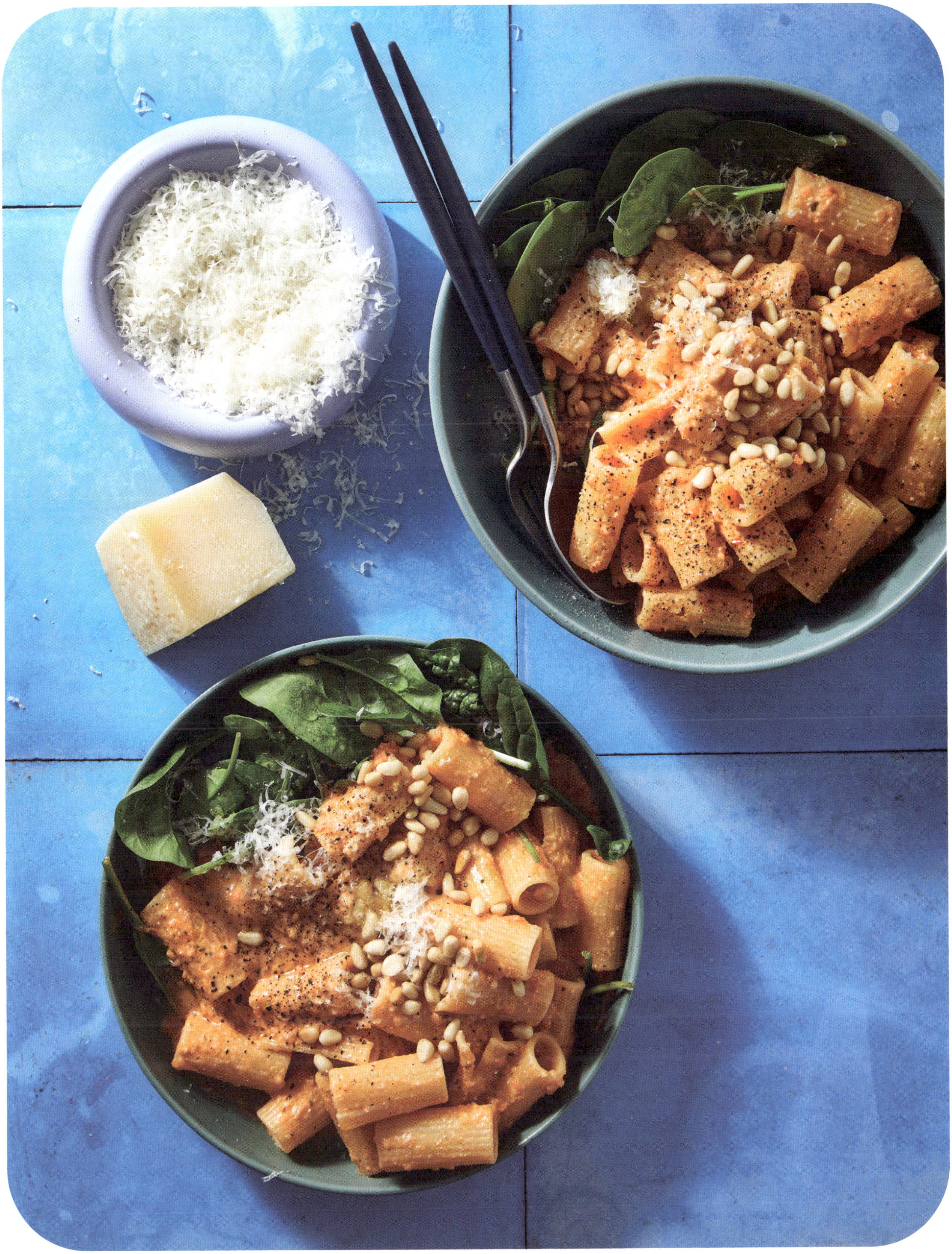

Fried rice

GF NF DF V

Prep 30 minutes
Cook 15 minutes
Serves 4

| 740 g (1 lb 10 oz/4 cups) cold leftover steamed jasmine rice |
| 2 eggs, lightly scrambled |
| 1 tablespoon extra-virgin olive oil |
| ½ onion, finely diced |
| 2 garlic cloves, minced |
| 1 tablespoon grated fresh ginger or Garlic-ginger paste (page 72) |
| 400–450 g (14–16 lb/3 cups) mixed grated vegetables, such as carrots, zucchini (courgette), cabbage and capsicum (bell pepper) |
| 1 tablespoon soy sauce |
| 1 teaspoon chicken or vegetable stock (bouillon) powder |
| 1 teaspoon rice vinegar |
| 1 teaspoon honey |
| 200 g (7 oz) roasted, shredded protein such as chicken, lamb, pork or tofu (optional) |
| sea salt |
| spring onions (scallions), finely sliced, to serve |
| toasted sesame seeds, to serve |

Cooking the rice the night before, or using leftover cooked rice, not only gives you a head start on this dish, but enables the rice to dry out and gives a better result. Vary the vegetables to suit your taste.

Massage the cold rice with the scrambled egg in a large bowl until the grains are coated and separated.

Heat the olive oil in a large frying pan or wok over medium-high heat. Add the onion, garlic and ginger and stir-fry for 2 minutes, or until fragrant. Stir in the grated vegetables and continue to stir-fry for 5–6 minutes, until softened. Add the soy sauce, stock powder, rice vinegar and honey and mix well.

Fold in the egg-coated rice and cooked protein (if using) and stir-fry until everything is well combined and heated through, about 3–4 minutes.

Season to taste with salt and top with spring onion and toasted sesame seeds.

Hints To make the rice ahead of time, cook 400 g (14 oz/2 cups) of rice according to packet instructions, allow it to cool, then store in an airtight container in the fridge for up to 3 days.

If you want a spicier kick, toss in some chilli flakes or sriracha before serving.

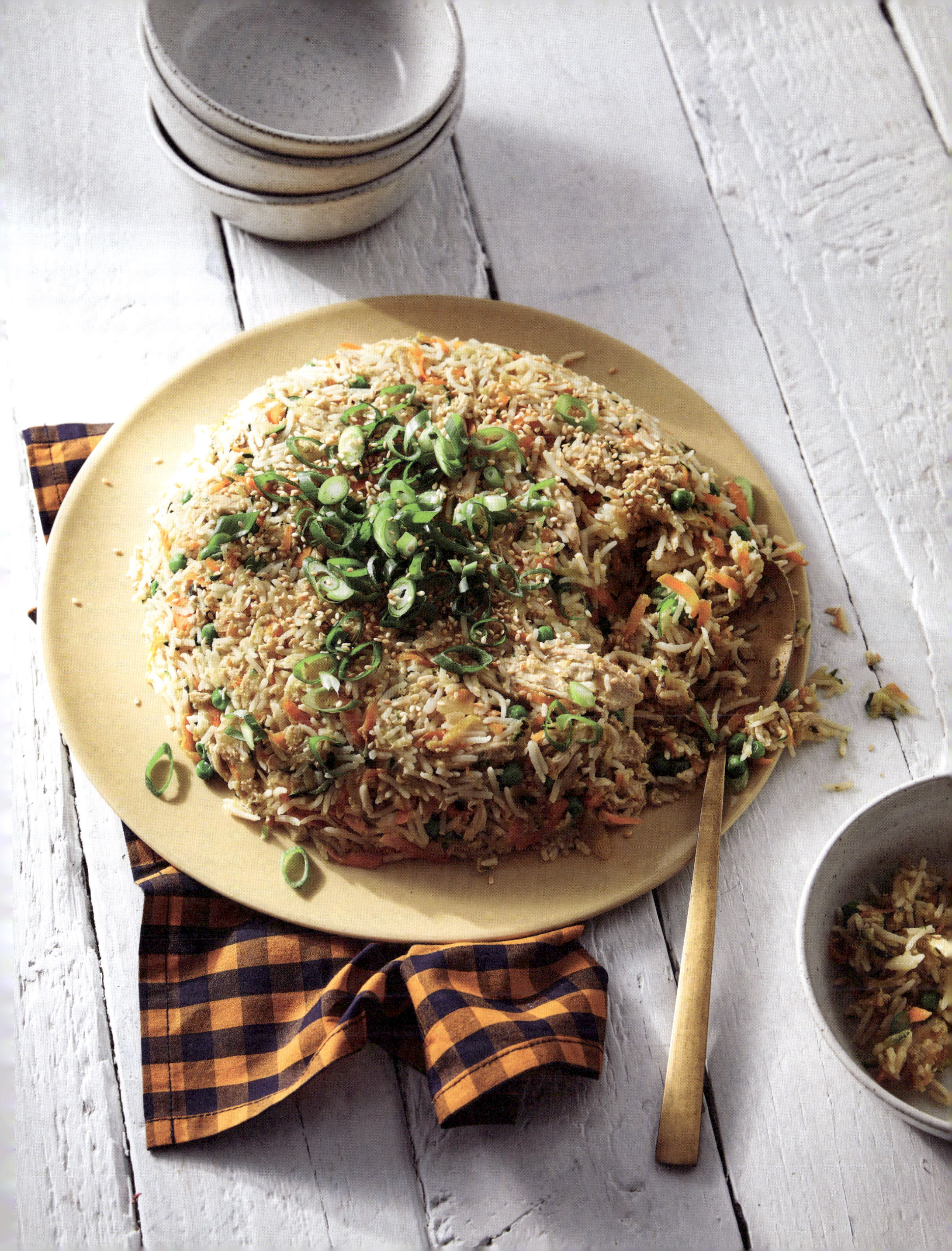

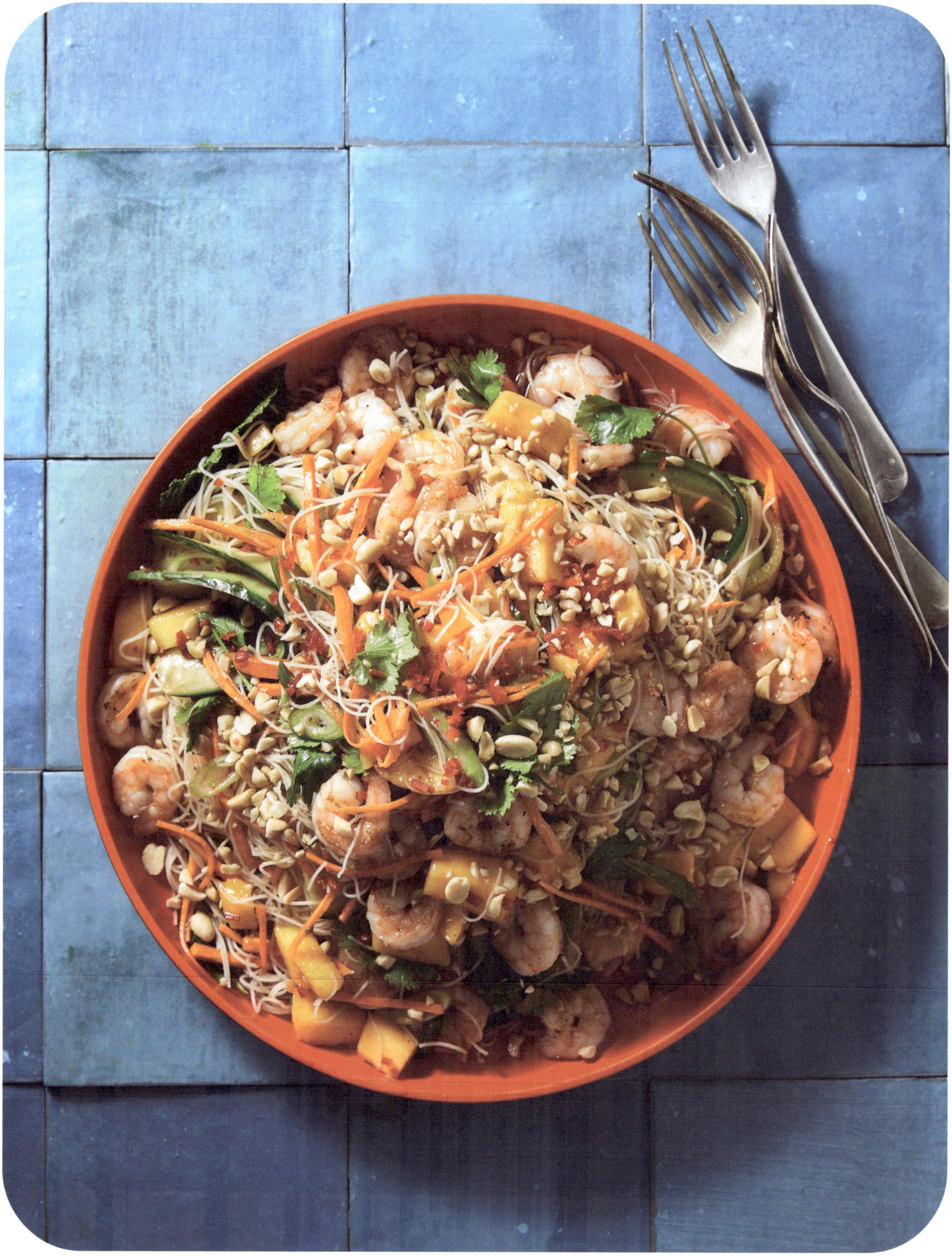

Prawn mango noodle salad

GF DF

Prep 30 minutes
Cook 10 minutes
Serves 4

200 g (7 oz) rice noodles
400 g (14 oz) peeled, deveined frozen prawns (shrimp), thawed
1 tablespoon extra-virgin olive oil
1 ripe mango, peeled and sliced
1 Lebanese (short) cucumber, cut into ribbons
1 carrot, julienned
2 spring onions (scallions), thinly sliced
sea salt
mint leaves, to serve
coriander (cilantro) leaves, to serve (optional)
red chilli, diced, to serve (optional)
crushed roasted peanuts, to serve

Dressing

2 tablespoons soy sauce
1 tablespoon fish sauce
juice of 1 lime
1 teaspoon honey
1 teaspoon coconut oil
1 garlic clove, minced
1 teaspoon minced fresh ginger

This bold, tangy summer salad, bursting with goodness, is my go-to when mangoes are in season.

Cook the rice noodles according to package instructions. Rinse under cold water, drain and set aside.

Heat a chargrill pan over medium–high heat. While the pan is heating, toss the thawed prawns with 1 tablespoon of olive oil and a pinch of salt. Grill the prawns for 2–3 minutes on each side, until they are opaque and slightly charred. Remove from the heat and set aside.

Whisk the dressing ingredients together in a small bowl and set aside.

In a large bowl, combine the cooked noodles, mango, cucumber, carrot and spring onion. Pour the dressing on top and toss well to combine.

Add the grilled prawns to the salad, gently tossing to incorporate.

Top the salad with mint, coriander (if using), chilli (if using) and peanuts before serving.

Hints For extra flavour, marinate the prawns in half of the dressing for 10 minutes before cooking.

Swap the rice noodles with soba or vermicelli noodles for a different texture.

Add avocado slices for a creamy contrast to the fresh, crisp vegetables.

LIGHT & FRESH

Chicken Caesar tray bake

(NF)

Prep 10 minutes
Cook 45 minutes
Serves 4

8 × skin-on, bone-in chicken thighs
200 g (7 oz) streaky bacon, cut into thin strips
1 red onion, sliced into thick wedges
3 tablespoons extra-virgin olive oil, plus 1 tablespoon more
4 slices of sourdough bread, crusts removed and bread cubed
200 g (7 oz) asparagus, ends trimmed and sliced in half lengthways
2 cos (romaine) lettuces, washed and separated, larger leaves cut, hearts kept whole
sea salt and freshly ground black pepper
parmesan, shaved, to serve

Caesar dressing

125 g (4½ oz/½ cup) Greek-style yoghurt
125 g (4½ oz/½ cup) mayonnaise
2 tablespoons lemon juice
2 teaspoons Dijon mustard
2 garlic cloves, minced
4 anchovy fillets, finely chopped
25 g (1 oz/¼ cup) parmesan, grated
sea salt and freshly ground black pepper

This play on a classic salad is fun, filling and all cooked in one tray to reduce washing up.

Preheat the oven to 220°C (430°F). Line a large baking tray with baking paper.

Place the chicken thighs, skin side up, on the baking tray. Arrange the bacon standing up between the chicken thighs (the thighs will help to prevent the bacon falling over). Nestle the onion between the chicken and bacon. Drizzle everything with 3 tablespoons of olive oil and season with salt and pepper. Place the baking tray in the oven and roast for 20 minutes.

Meanwhile, toss the bread cubes in the extra tablespoon of olive oil.

Remove the tray from the oven and scatter the cubes around the chicken. Place the tray back in the oven and continue cooking for another 25 minutes, until the bacon and croutons are crispy and the chicken is cooked through.

While the chicken is cooking, prepare the Caesar dressing. Whisk the dressing ingredients together in a bowl. Season with salt and pepper, to taste.

Blanch the asparagus in a bowl with boiling water for 30 seconds, then rinse under cold water.

Arrange the lettuce leaves and asparagus on a serving platter, then drizzle with the Caesar dressing and sprinkle with shaved parmesan.

Once the chicken is done, let it rest for a few minutes before serving alongside the salad.

Hints When buying bacon, look for a preservative-free option that doesn't contain added nitrates.

Add some cherry tomatoes to the baking tray for a pop of colour and extra flavour.

If you prefer a more intense Caesar flavour, increase the number of anchovy fillets in the dressing.

Consider adding a few soft-boiled eggs, cut in half, for a more traditional Caesar salad touch.

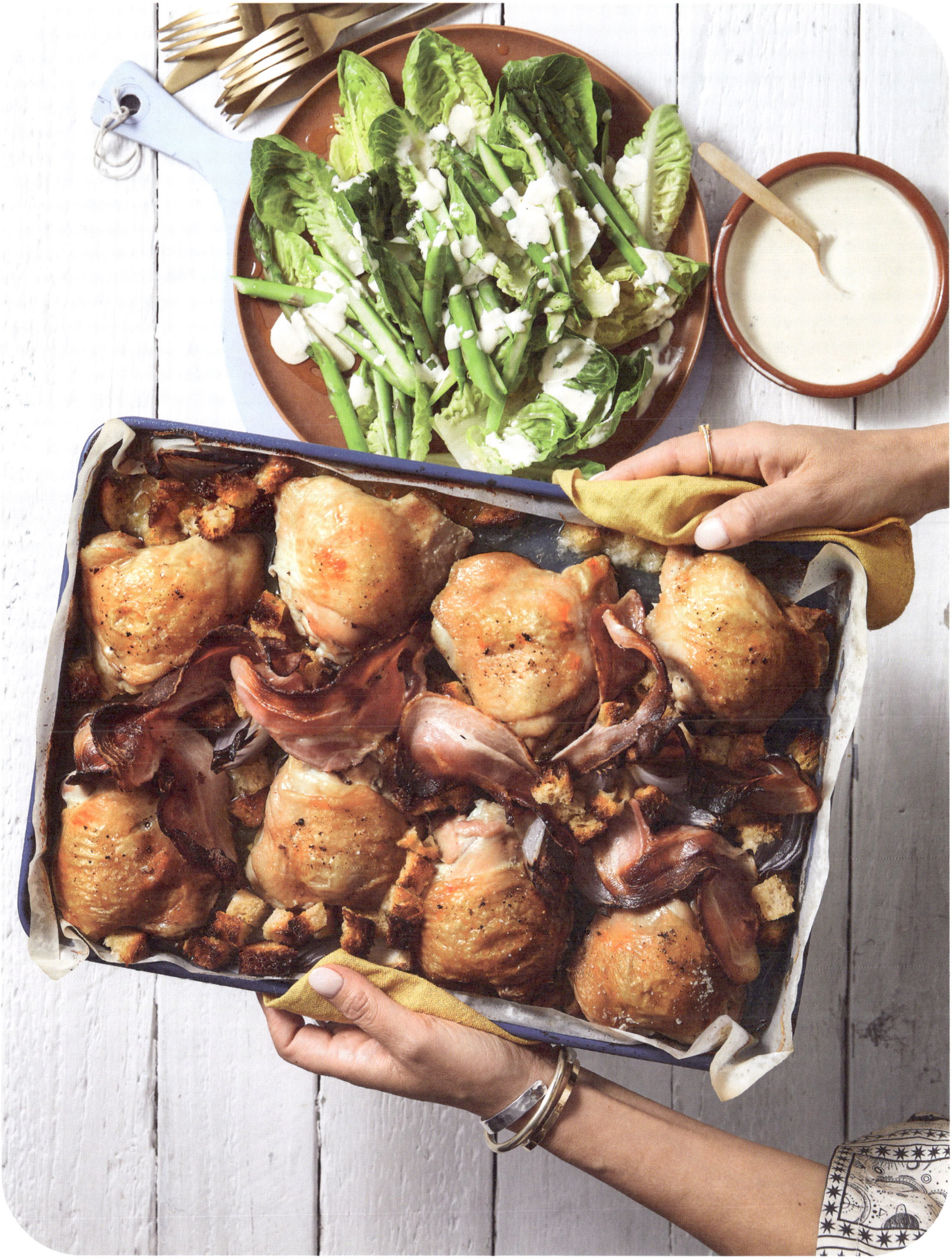

Fluffy trout omelette

GF NF

Prep 10 minutes
Cook 30 minutes
Serves 4

| 6 eggs, separated |
| 60 ml (2 fl oz/¼ cup) whipping cream |
| butter, for greasing |
| 2 tablespoons mixed chopped herbs such as chives, parsley and dill |
| 100 g (3½ oz) goat's cheese |
| 100 g (3½ oz) hot smoked trout, flaked and divided |
| sea salt and freshly ground black pepper |
| lemon wedges, to serve |

The delicate flavours of hot smoked trout, fresh herbs and creamy goat's cheese make for an elegant yet simple breakfast omelette.

Preheat the oven to 180°C (360°F).

Whisk the egg yolks with the cream until well combined. Beat the egg whites in a separate bowl until soft peaks form. Gently fold the egg whites into the egg yolk mixture.

Heat an ovenproof frying pan over medium heat and grease it with butter. Pour half of the egg mixture into the pan and allow it to cook undisturbed for 10 minutes.

Scatter half of the herbs, half of the goat's cheese and half of the hot smoked trout over the omelette.

Using a spatula, carefully fold one side of the omelette over the filling, holding it in place.

Transfer the pan to the oven and bake for 5 minutes.

Repeat the process to make a second omelette.

Serve with sea salt and freshly ground black pepper, and lemon wedges on the side.

Hint Ensure the egg whites are just at soft peak stage to keep the omelette light and airy.

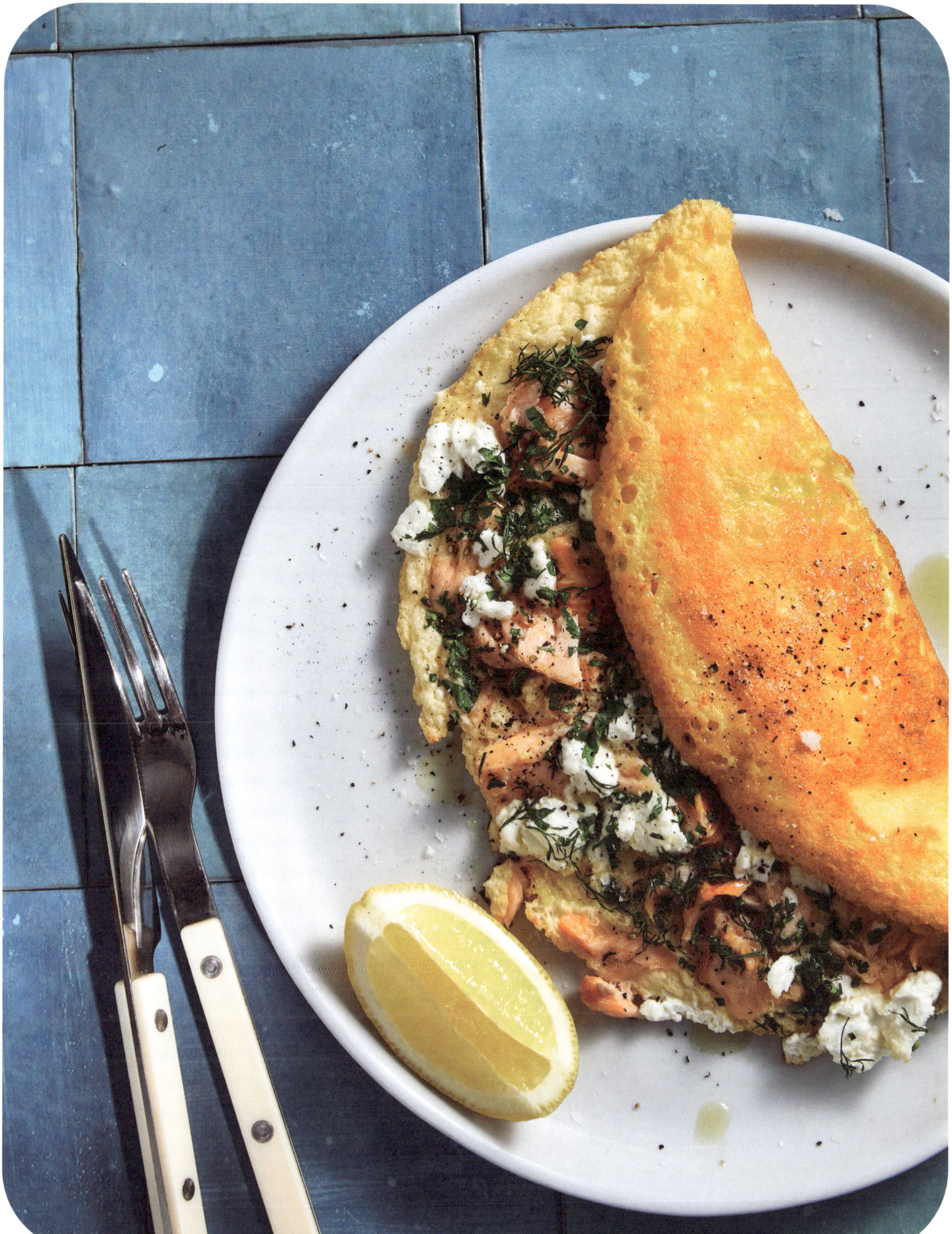

Blueberry share pancake

NF V

Prep 30 minutes
Cook 15 minutes
Serves 4

300 g (10½ oz/2 cups) self-raising (rising) flour

55 g (2 oz/¼ cup) soft brown sugar

½ teaspoon bicarbonate of soda (baking soda)

¼ teaspoon salt

2 eggs, separated

375 ml (12½ fl oz/1½ cups) milk

25 g (1 oz) unsalted butter

200 g (7 oz) fresh blueberries

pure maple syrup, to serve

salted butter, to serve

Perfect for sharing, this oven-baked, no-fuss fluffy pancake is served straight from the pan and makes the most of seasonal berries.

Combine the self-raising flour, brown sugar, bicarbonate of soda and salt in a large jar. Close the jar and shake to combine.

Preheat the oven to 180°C (360°F).

In a clean bowl, whisk the egg whites until they form soft peaks and are light and fluffy.

Add the yolks and milk to the jar with the dry ingredients. Close the jar tightly and shake well until the mixture is a smooth batter.

Gently fold the batter into the whisked egg whites until just combined, being careful not to deflate the mixture.

Preheat a large ovenproof non-stick frying pan over low-medium heat and melt the unsalted butter. Pour the pancake batter into the pan, spreading it out slightly to form a large pancake. Sprinkle the blueberries evenly on the top. Cook the pancake covered with a lid until bubbles form on the surface and the edges begin to set, around 3–4 minutes, then place it in the oven for 10–15 minutes to finish cooking all the way through.

Serve the pancake warm with a drizzle of maple syrup and a knob of salted butter.

Hints The dry mix (flour, sugar, bicarbonate of soda and salt) can be made ahead and stored in a jar, sealed, for up to 2 weeks.

For an extra flavour boost, add a teaspoon of vanilla extract to the egg yolk and milk mixture.

To make it easier to remove the pancake from the pan without breaking it, slide a large spatula under the pancake.

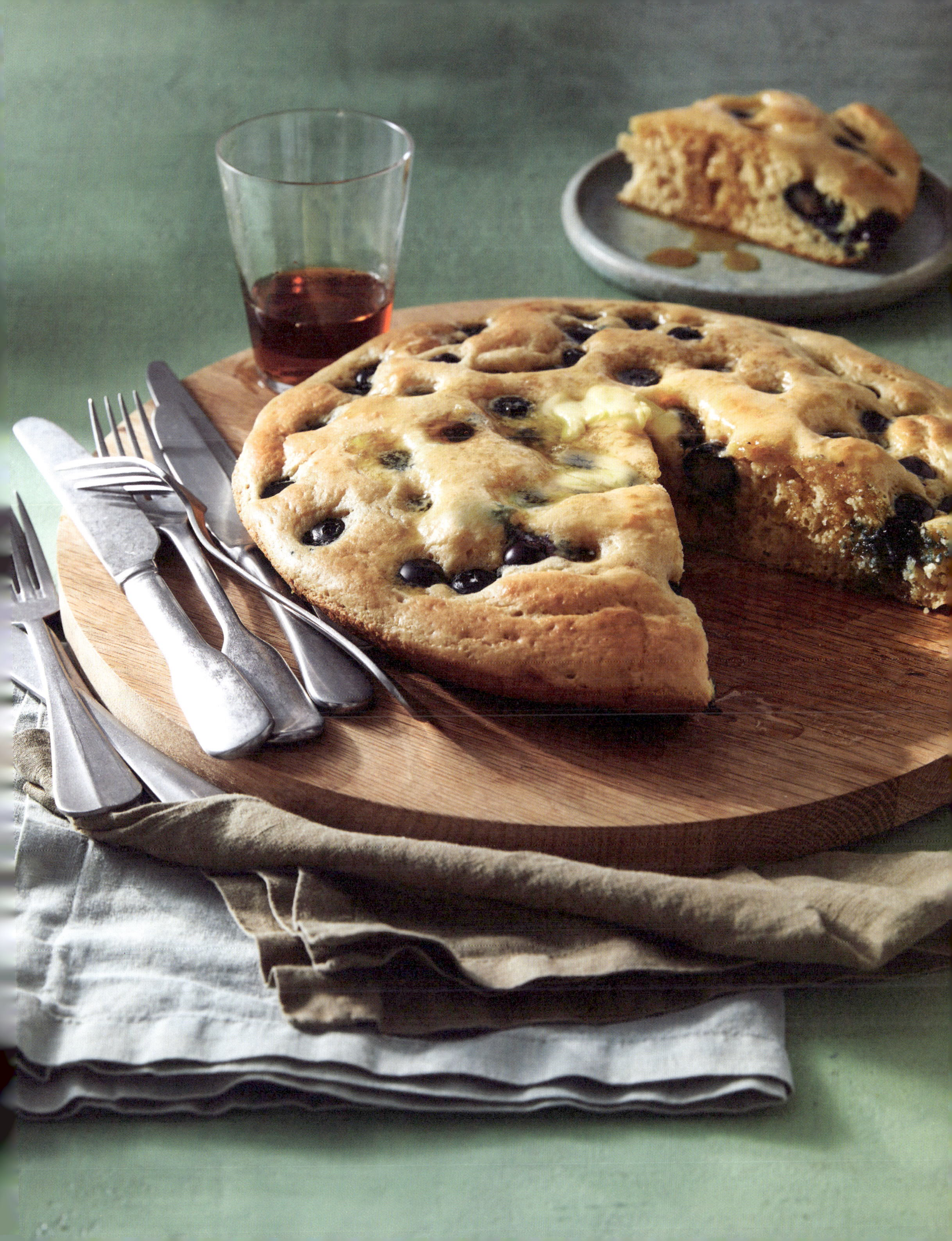

Sushi sandwich

GF NF DF

Prep 1 hour (plus overnight pressing)
Cook 15 minutes
Serves 4–6

440 g (15½ oz/2 cups) sushi rice

200 g (7 oz) hot smoked trout, flaked, or smoked salmon

1 small Lebanese (short) cucumber, thinly sliced

1 large carrot, peeled and cut into ribbons

185 g (6½ oz) tinned tuna in spring water, drained and mixed with 2 tablespoons mayonnaise

4–5 sheets nori, cut into strips

Home-made sushi wasn't for me, until I discovered the sushi sandwich. If I can do it, you can! Get a head start on this one the night before.

Rinse the sushi rice under cold water until the water runs clear. Drain well.

In a saucepan, combine the rice and 625 ml (1 lb 6 fl oz/2½ cups) of water. Bring to a boil over medium heat, then reduce to low, cover and simmer for 15 minutes. Remove from the heat and let stand, covered, for 10 minutes.

Line baking tray (approximately 35 × 25 cm/13¾ × 10 in) with baking paper, making sure you leave enough paper hanging over the edges of the tray to use later to pull the sushi out.

Spread half of the cooked rice on the bottom of the baking tray, pressing down firmly to form a 1 cm (½ in) thick layer. Arrange the smoked trout, cucumber, carrot and tuna mayonnaise mixture evenly over the rice layer. Spread the remaining rice over the fillings, pressing down firmly and evenly. Cover the top with another sheet of baking paper and place another tray or a flat object on top. Weigh it down with heavy objects to press the sushi sandwich evenly. Refrigerate overnight.

The next day, carefully lift the sushi sandwich out using the baking paper. Cut the sandwich into fingers or triangles using a sharp knife, wiping the knife with a wet cloth between each slice.

Wrap each sushi piece in nori, dampening the edges slightly to seal.

Store in an airtight container in the fridge for 4 days for snacking.

Hints You can use a bamboo rolling mat to help press the rice.

Add a touch of wasabi or pickled ginger between the layers for an extra flavour kick.

For extra crunch, press one edge of the sushi sandwich into a shallow bowl filled with sesame seeds.

Experiment with fillings like avocado, pickled radish or omelette.

You can use brown sushi rice in this recipe, but be sure to follow the packet instructions.

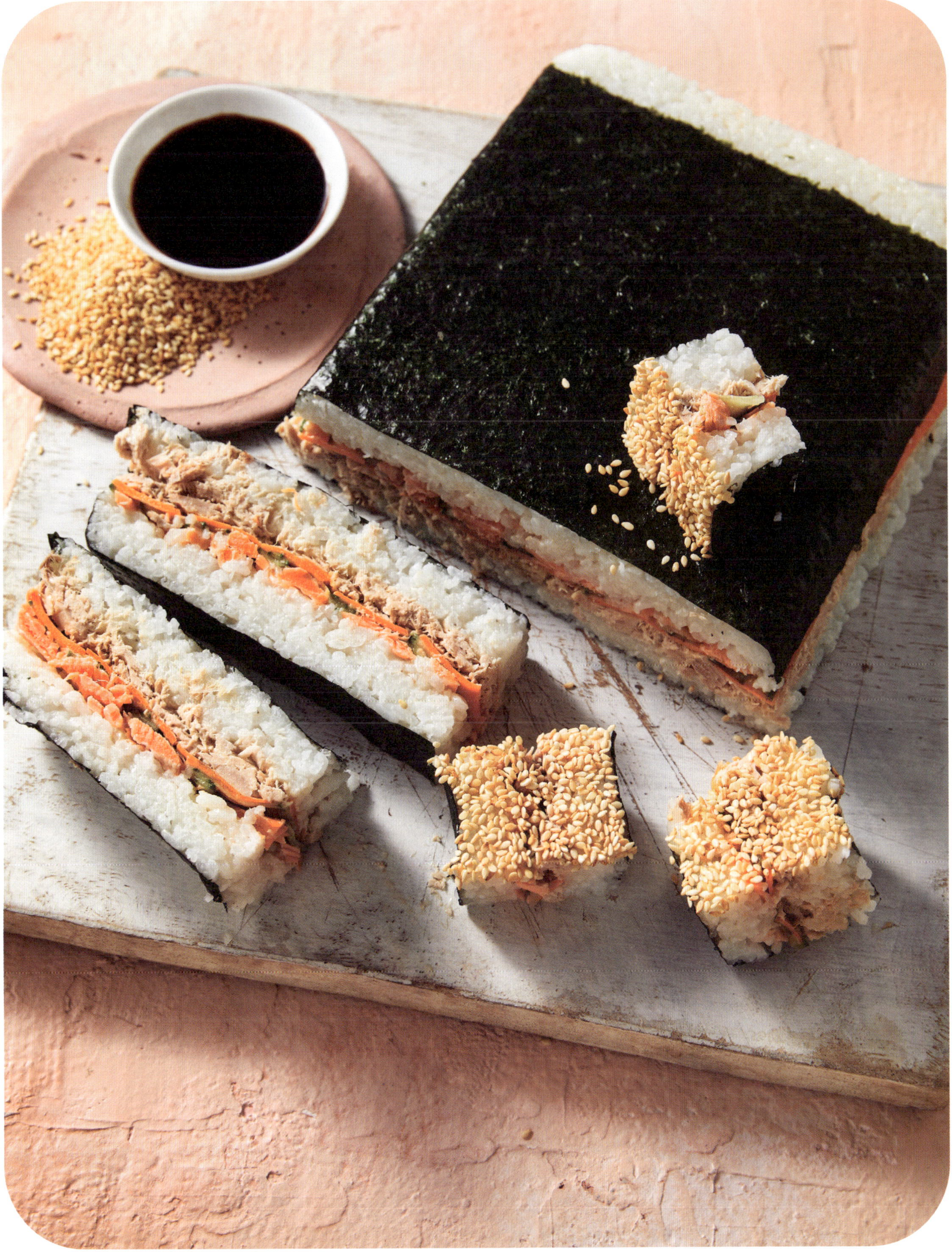

Fruity tart

(V)

Prep 15 minutes
Cook 25 minutes
Serves 4

4–5 mixed stone fruit such as peaches, nectarines and plums
2 tablespoons almond meal
2 tablespoons soft brown sugar
1 teaspoon vanilla extract
1 egg, beaten (for egg wash)
27 × 36 cm (10¾ × 14¼ in) sheet puff pastry or shortcrust (pie) pastry, thawed
natural yoghurt, to serve
passionfruit pulp, to serve

This vibrant dessert is an easy way to brighten up your table. Make it when stone fruits are at their best for a delicious sweet treat.

Preheat the oven to 240°C (460°F) and line a baking tray with baking paper.

Thinly slice or cut the fruit into bite-sized pieces, discarding the stones.

Toss the fruit with the almond meal, brown sugar and vanilla extract in a bowl until well coated. Arrange the fruit mixture on the baking tray in a square slightly smaller than your pastry sheet. Brush the baking paper around the fruit with the beaten egg. Lay the pastry on top of the fruit and press down around the edges to seal.

Use a knife to create a few small vents in the pastry. Brush the pastry with more egg wash.

Bake for 20–25 minutes, or until the pastry is golden and the fruit is nicely caramelised.

To serve, place a board over the tart and carefully flip it upside down. Peel the baking paper off to reveal the tart.

Serve with yoghurt topped with a drizzle of passionfruit pulp.

Hints Choose a mix of stone fruits for a variety of textures and flavours.

If using puff pastry, work quickly so the pastry stays cold for a better rise.

You can substitute the almond meal with finely ground hazelnuts or desiccated coconut for a different flavour.

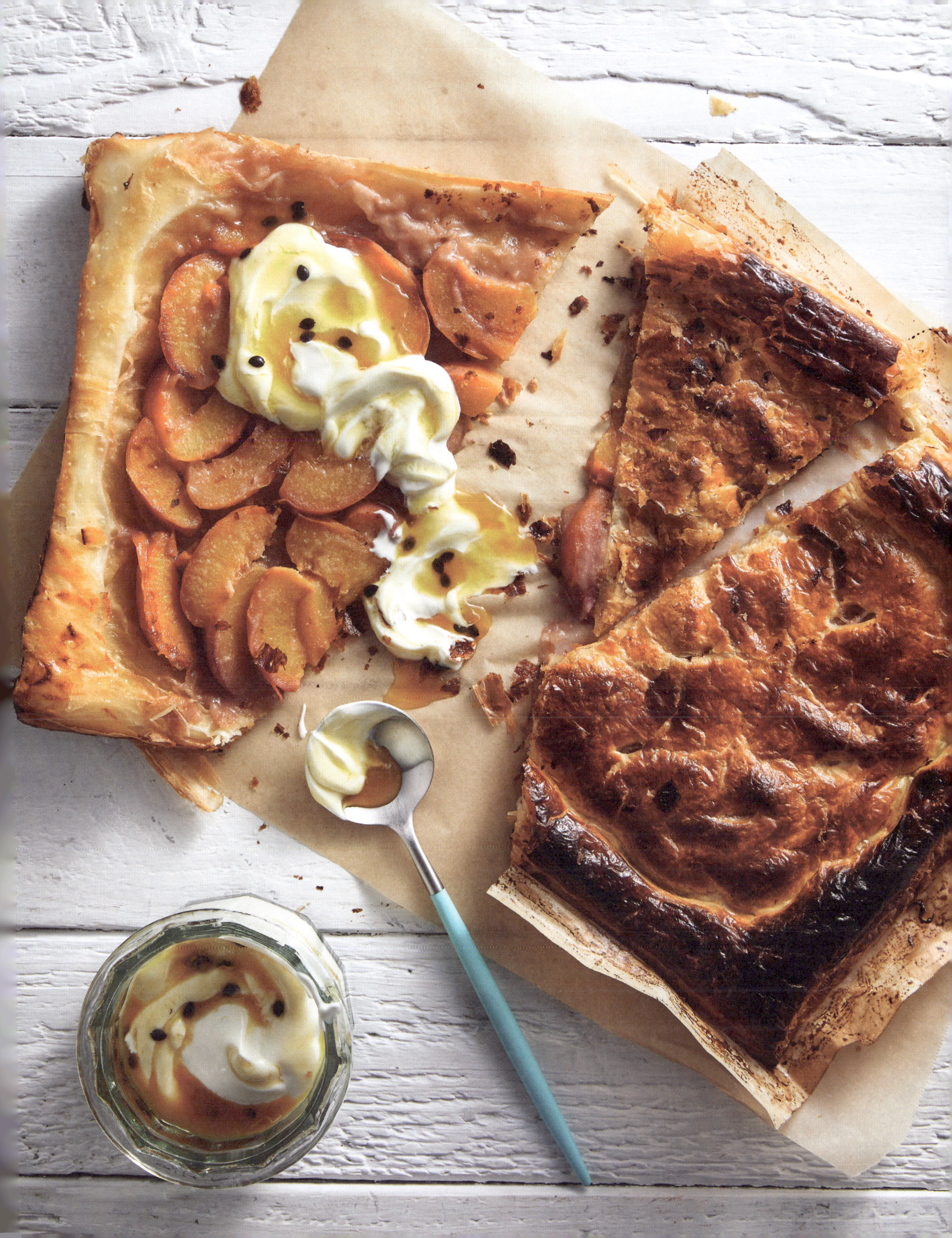

Index

A
additives 45, 46–7
artificial food colours 46
artificial sweeteners 46
asparagus
    Chicken Caesar tray bake 240
    Prawn spaghetti 212
As-you-like-it popcorn seasoning 160
avocado oil 21
avocados 31, 56
    BLT omelette tray 186
    Breakfast tacos 214
    Choc, oat and raspberry muffins 100
    Guacamole 90
    Lazy fish tacos 208

B
bacon
    BLT omelette tray 186
    Breakfast tacos 214
    Chicken Caesar tray bake 240
    Hoisin meatloaf with potato gratin 154
Baked chicken parmigiana with
    cauli-potato mash 95
bananas 30
    Choc peanut porridge 158
    Tahini maple caramel and
        choc coconut banana splits 104
    Tropical overnight chia 216
Barbecue chicken seasoning 160
batch-cooking 64, 66
beans, green
    Beef and vegetable skewers with salsa
        verde 200
    Hoisin meatloaf with potato gratin 154
    Summer tuna pasta salad 182
beans, tinned
    Nachos 90
    Roast chicken with garlic, spinach
        and dill rice 118
beef
    Beef and vegetable skewers with
        salsa verde 200
    Beef brisket 83
    Beef brisket with vegetable gratin 88
    Beef koftas with grilled haloumi,
        zucchini and broccoli salad 184
    Caprese smash burgers 176
    Chilli jam minced beef with rice and
        dressed vegetable pickles 124
    Grilled steak with stroganoff sauce 150
    Seasoned beef mince 169
    Veggie-loaded bolognese sauce 108
    see also veal
benzoates 46
berries 30, 56
    Blueberry share pancake 244
    Choc, oat and raspberry muffins 100
    Ricotta berry tart 134
Black bean sauce 72
BLT omelette tray 186
Blueberry share pancake 244
bok choy 31
bolognese sauce 66
bolognese sauce, Veggie-loaded 108
bone broth, Chicken 139
bread 29, 37
    see also flatbread, pizza, tortillas
breakfasts
    BLT omelette tray 186
    Blueberry share pancake 244
    Breakfast tacos 214
    Choc, oat and raspberry muffins 100
    Choc peanut porridge 158
    Classic French toast with
        cinnamon and maple butter 130
    Fluffy trout omelette 242
    Home-made granola 189
    One-pan wonder 98
    Spiced egg and tomato flatbreads 157
    Toasted cheese soldiers with
        dippy eggs 128
    Tropical overnight chia 216
broccoli 31
    Beef brisket with
        vegetable gratin 88
    Grilled haloumi salad 184
    Vegetable pizzas 87
    Vegetable satay noodles 96
broth, Chicken bone 139
Brown sugar whipped cream 162
bulk buying 34
burgers 66
    Burger sauce 132
    Caprese smash burgers 176
butter 21, 26, 37
Butter chicken 80
Butter chicken pizzas 86
Butter chicken with flavoured
    rice and raita 84
Butterflied roast chicken 171
Butterflied roast chicken
    with lemon potatoes 172

C
cabbage
    Chicken, noodle and cabbage salad 175
    Fried rice 236
    Lazy fish tacos 208
Caesar dressing 240
caged animals 26
cakes, Sticky date mini 162
caponata, Marinated lamb with 122
Caprese smash burgers 176
capsicums
    Chicken chorizo paella 204
    Fried rice 236
    Home-made tomato passata 110
    Marinated lamb with caponata 122
    Nachos 90
    Puff pastry pizza pinwheels 218
    Rose sauce 224
    Sweet and tangy tofu noodles 203
    Vegetable satay noodles 96
    Vegetable sauce 82
    Veggie-loaded bolognese sauce 108
caramel sauce, Easy 162
carbohydrates 15, 18
carrots
    Carrot cake energy bites 192
    Chicken, noodle and cabbage salad 175
    Chilli jam minced beef with rice and
        dressed vegetable pickles 124
    Fried rice 236
    Prawn mango noodle salad 239
    Sushi sandwich 246
    Vegetable satay noodles 96
    Veggie-loaded bolognese sauce 108
cauliflower
    Baked chicken parmigiana
        with cauli-potato mash 95
    Cauliflower cheese bites 103
    Vegetable sauce 82
cereal 29, 37
cheddar *see* cheese
cheese 26
    Beef brisket with vegetable gratin 88
    BLT omelette tray 186
    Cauliflower cheese bites 103
    Cheeseburger triangles 132
    Mexi-spice tray bake 114
    Nachos 90
    Potato gratin 154
    Pumpkin and sage mac 'n' cheese 142
    Sweet potato shepherd's pies 117
    Toasted cheese soldiers with
        dippy eggs 128
    see also feta, goat's cheese, haloumi,
        mozzarella, parmesan, ricotta
chia, Tropical overnight 216
chicken
    Baked chicken parmigiana
        with cauli-potato mash 95
    Butter chicken 80
    Butter chicken pizzas 86
    Butter chicken with flavoured
        rice and raita 84
    Butterflied roast chicken 171
    Butterflied roast chicken with
        lemon potatoes 172
    Chicken, noodle and
        cabbage salad 175
    Chicken bone broth 139
    Chicken Caesar tray bake 240
    Chicken chorizo paella 204
    Chicken pie with artichokes
        and olives 120
    Chicken rice mountains and
        Greek salad 127
    Fried rice 236
    Mini chicken mozzarella meatballs
        with garlic mash 206
    Roast chicken with garlic, spinach
        and dill rice 118
    Seasoned chicken mince 196
    Whole roast chicken 109
chickpeas
    Crispy roasted chickpeas 233
    Mediterranean salad 211
    Roasted tomato, kale and
        sausage penne 92
Chilli jam marinade 111
Chilli jam minced beef with rice and
    dressed vegetable pickles 124
chips 29, 37

THE WEEKLY GROCERY SHOP

chocolate
    Carrot cake energy bites 192
    Choc, oat and raspberry muffins 100
    Choc peanut porridge 158
    Coconut yoghurt and peach smoothie popsicles 220
    Tahini maple caramel and choc coconut banana splits 104
Chopped salad 176
chorizo paella, Chicken 204
Citrus yoghurt dressing 149
Classic French toast with cinnamon and maple butter 130
'Clean Fifteen' 51
coconut oil, extra-virgin 21
Coconut yoghurt and peach smoothie popsicles 220
corn 31
    Beef brisket with vegetable gratin 88
    Corn cobettes with cheese, chilli mayonnaise and lime 190
    Lazy fish tacos 208
couscous
    Grilled haloumi salad 184
    Lamb tagine with couscous 149
crackers 29, 37
cream 26
cream, Brown sugar whipped 162
Crispy roasted chickpeas 233
croquettes, Fish 138
Crusted pork fillet with juicy roast tomatoes 178
cucumbers
    Chilli jam minced beef with rice and dressed vegetable pickles 124
    Greek salad 127
    Mediterranean salad 211
    Prawn mango noodle salad 239
    Raita 84
    Sushi sandwich 246
    Yiros with flatbread and crispy roasted chickpeas 233
curries 66
    Butter chicken 80
    Butter chicken with flavoured rice and raita 84
    Curry paste 73
    Tomato coconut dal 141
    Tomato coconut dal with baked fish 152

D

dairy products 26, 37
dal, Tomato coconut 141
dates
    Carrot cake energy bites 192
    Sticky date mini cakes 162
desserts
    Coconut yoghurt and peach smoothie popsicles 220
    Fruity tart 248
    Ricotta berry tart 134
    Sticky date mini cakes 162
    Tahini maple caramel and choc coconut banana splits 104
'Dirty Dozen' 51
Dressed vegetable pickles 124

dressings
    Caesar dressing 240
    Citrus yoghurt dressing 149
    Everyday marinade 198
    Herb dressing 170
    Honey soy dressing 175
    Lemon mayonnaise 168
    Lime mayonnaise 208
    salsa verde 200
    Yoghurt tahini dressing 210
dried fruit 29

E

Easy caramel sauce 162
eggplants
    Marinated lamb with caponata 122
    No-fuss vegetable lasagne 112
eggs 26, 37
    Breakfast tacos 214
    Chilli jam minced beef with rice and dressed vegetable pickles 124
    Classic French toast with cinnamon and maple butter 130
    Fried rice 236
    One-pan wonder 98
    Spiced egg and tomato flatbreads 157
    Toasted cheese soldiers with dippy eggs 128
    see also omelettes
energy bites, Carrot cake 192
Everyday marinade 198

F

farming practices 49
fats 15, 20–1
    monounsaturated 20
    oils 21, 37
    polyunsaturated 20
    saturated 20
    trans 20
feta
    Greek salad 127
    Mediterranean salad 211
    Yiros with flatbread and crispy roasted chickpeas 233
fibre 19
    insoluble 19
    resistant starch 19
    soluble 19
fish
    Fish croquettes 138
    Fish croquettes with yoghurt tartare sauce 144
    Lazy fish tacos 208
    Tomato coconut dal with baked fish 152
    see also trout, tuna
flatbread
    Home-made flatbreads 226
    Lamb chops with Mediterranean salad and yoghurt tahini dressing 210
    Spiced egg and tomato flatbreads 157
    Yiros with flatbread and crispy roasted chickpeas 233
    see also tortillas
flavour enhancers 46

Flavoured rice 84
flavourings 45
flaxseed oil 21
flour 29
Fluffy trout omelette 242
food additives 45, 46–7
food colours, artificial 46
food labelling 39–51
    additives cheat sheet 46–7
    ingredient lists 43
    laws 48
    marketing buzzwords 50
    nutrition information panels 42
    percentage labelling 48
    place of origin 49
food processing 41
food waste 22
free-range animals 26
freezing food 58–9
French toast, Classic, with cinnamon and maple butter 130
fridge cleanliness 54
fridge storage 55–6
Fried rice 236
fruit 30
    buying seasonal produce 24–5
    'Clean Fifteen' 51
    'Dirty Dozen' 51
    fridge storage 56
    loose vs pre-packaged produce 35
    washing 61
    see also individual fruits
Fruity tart 248

G

garlic 31, 63
garlic mash, Mini chicken mozzarella meatballs with 206
Garlic-ginger paste 72
genetically modified organisms (GMOs) 49
ghee 21
ginger paste, Garlic– 72
glucose 18
glycaemic index (GI) 18
goat's cheese
    Fluffy trout omelette 242
    One-pan wonder 98
    Vegetable pizzas 87
granola, Home-made 189
grass-fed meat 26
gratin, Potato 154
gratin, vegetable 88
Greek lamb with orzo 146
Greek salad 127
Grilled haloumi salad 184
groceries
    brands 36
    bulk buying 34
    cost 14
    specials 35, 36
    ultra-processed foods (UPFs) 18, 20, 40, 41
    unit price 33, 34
    see also food labelling, fruit, vegetables
Guacamole 90

INDEX 251

H

haloumi
- Grilled haloumi salad 184
- Roast lamb and zesty potato medley 230
- Spinach spiral pie with lemon mayonnaise 180

ham: Cheeseburger triangles 132
Herb dressing 170
herbs 31
- dried 75
- freezing 59
- fridge storage 56
- prepping 63

Hoisin meatloaf with potato gratin 154
Hoisin sauce 73
Home-made flatbreads 226
Home-made granola 189
Home-made tomato passata 110
Home-made tortillas 199
Honey soy dressing 175

I

ingredient lists 43
insoluble fibre 19

K

kale
- Baked chicken parmigiana with cauli-potato mash 95
- Roasted tomato, kale and sausage penne 92

koftas 66
koftas, Beef, with grilled haloumi, zucchini and broccoli salad 184

L

labelling *see* food labelling
lamb
- Fried rice 236
- Greek lamb with orzo 146
- Lamb chops with Mediterranean salad and yoghurt tahini dressing 210
- Lamb seasoning 210
- Lamb tagine with couscous 149
- Marinated lamb with caponata 122
- Roast lamb and zesty potato medley 230
- Roasted lamb rumps 227
- Slow-cooked lamb shoulder 140
- Yiros with flatbread and crispy roasted chickpeas 233

lasagne, No-fuss vegetable 112
Lazy fish tacos 208
legumes 29
Lemon mayonnaise 168
lentils
- Mexi-spice tray bake 114
- Roasted tomato, kale and sausage penne 92
- Tomato coconut dal 141

lettuce
- BLT omelette tray 186
- Chicken Caesar tray bake 240
- Chopped salad 176
- Lazy fish tacos 208
- storage 56

Lime mayonnaise 208
linseed oil 21

M

mac 'n' cheese, Pumpkin and sage 142
macronutrients 15
mandarins 30
mangoes 30
- Lazy fish tacos 208
- Prawn mango noodle salad 239
- Tropical overnight chia 216

Maple butter 130
marinade, Chilli jam 111
marinade, Everyday 198
Marinated lamb with caponata 122
Marinated pork skewers 225
Marinated pork skewers with grilled potato salad 228
Marinated tofu 197
mayonnaise, Lemon 168
mayonnaise, Lime 208
meal planning 22, 35
meal prepping 60–3
meat 26
- minced 66
- nitrate-free smallgoods 37
- slow-cooked 66
- *see also* beef, chicken, lamb, pork

meatballs 66
- meatballs, Mini chicken mozzarella, with garlic mash 206
- meatloaf, Hoisin, with potato gratin 154

Mediterranean salad 211
Mexi-spice tray bake 114
micronutrients 15
milk 26
minerals 15
Mini chicken mozzarella meatballs with garlic mash 206
money 14, 22, 33–6
monounsaturated fats 20
mozzarella
- Baked chicken parmigiana with cauli-potato mash 95
- Butter chicken pizzas 86
- Butterflied roast chicken with lemon potatoes 172
- Caprese smash burgers 176
- Mini chicken mozzarella meatballs with garlic mash 206
- No-fuss vegetable lasagne 112
- Puff pastry pizza pinwheels 218
- Vegetable pizzas 87

MSG 47
muffins, Choc, oat and raspberry 100
mushrooms 56, 62
- Beef and vegetable skewers with salsa verde 200
- Grilled steak with stroganoff sauce 150
- One-pan wonder 98
- Veggie-loaded bolognese sauce 108

Mustard cheese sauce 142

N

Nachos 90
nitrates and nitrites 46
No-fuss vegetable lasagne 112
noodles
- Chicken, noodle and cabbage salad 175
- Prawn mango noodle salad 239
- Sweet and tangy tofu noodles 203
- Vegetable satay noodles 96

nutrition 15–21
- macronutrients 15
- micronutrients 15
- *see also* carbohydrates, fats, fibre, food labelling, proteins,

nuts 29

O

oats
- Choc, oat and raspberry muffins 100
- Choc peanut porridge 158
- Home-made granola 189

oils 21, 37, 75
olive oil, extra-virgin 21, 29
olives
- Chicken pie with artichokes and olives 120
- Greek salad 127
- Marinated lamb with caponata 122
- Mediterranean salad 211
- Puff pastry pizza pinwheels 218
- Roast lamb and zesty potato medley 230

omega-3 and -6 fats 20
omelettes
- BLT omelette tray 186
- Fluffy trout omelette 242

Grilled steak with stroganoff sauce 150
One-pan wonder 98
onions 31
oranges 30
organic farming 49
organic meat 26
orzo, Greek lamb with 146

P

paella, Chicken chorizo 204
pancake, Blueberry share 244
pantry 29, 54, 75
parmesan
- Caesar dressing 240
- Cauliflower cheese bites 103
- Corn cobettes with cheese, chilli mayonnaise and lime 190
- Crusted pork fillet with juicy roast tomatoes 178
- No-fuss vegetable lasagne 112
- Prawn spaghetti 212
- Puff pastry pizza pinwheels 218
- Pumpkin and sage mac 'n' cheese 142
- Roasted tomato, kale and sausage penne 92
- Rose rigatoni 234
- Seasoned beef mince 169

passata, Home-made tomato 66, 110

THE WEEKLY GROCERY SHOP

pasta 29, 37
    Greek lamb with orzo 146
    No-fuss vegetable lasagne 112
    Prawn spaghetti 212
    Pumpkin and sage mac 'n' cheese 142
    Roasted tomato, kale and
        sausage penne 92
    Rose rigatoni 234
    Summer tuna pasta salad 182

pastry
    Cheeseburger triangles 132
    Chicken pie with artichokes and olives 120
    Fruity tart 248
    Puff pastry pizza pinwheels 218
    Ricotta berry tart 134
    Spinach spiral pie with lemon
        mayonnaise 180

pasture-raised animals 26
peach smoothie popsicles, Coconut
    yoghurt and 220

peas
    Chicken chorizo paella 204
    Fish croquettes 138
    Greek lamb with orzo 146

penne, Roasted tomato, kale and sausage 92
percentage labelling 48

pies
    Chicken pie with artichokes and olives 120
    Spinach spiral pie with lemon
        mayonnaise 180
    Sweet potato shepherd's pies 117

pineapple 30
pinwheels, Puff pastry pizza 218

pizza
    Butter chicken pizzas 86
    Pizza bases 81
    Puff pastry pizza pinwheels 218
    Vegetable pizzas 87

polyunsaturated fats 20
popcorn seasoning, As-you-like-it 160
popsicles, Coconut yoghurt and
    peach smoothie 220

pork
    Crusted pork fillet with juicy
        roast tomatoes 178
    Fried rice 236
    Hoisin meatloaf with potato gratin 154
    Marinated pork skewers 225
    Marinated pork skewers with grilled
        potato salad 228

porridge, Choc peanut 158

potatoes 31
    Baked chicken parmigiana with
        cauli-potato mash 95
    Beef and vegetable skewers
        with salsa verde 200
    Beef brisket with vegetable gratin 88
    Butterflied roast chicken with
        lemon potatoes 172
    Fish croquettes 138
    Marinated pork skewers with
        grilled potato salad 228
    Mini chicken mozzarella meatballs
        with garlic mash 206
    Potato gratin 154
    Roast lamb and zesty potato medley 230
    Sweet potato shepherd's pies 117

prawns
    Prawn mango noodle salad 239
    Prawn spaghetti 212

processed foods 40, 41
propionates 46

proteins 15, 17
    animal sources 17
    plant sources 17

Puff pastry pizza pinwheels 218

pumpkin
    No-fuss vegetable lasagne 112
    Pumpkin and sage mac 'n' cheese 142
    storage 56
    Vegetable sauce 82

R

Raita 84
raspberry muffins, Choc, oat and 100
refrigerator *see* fridge
resistant starch 19

rice 29
    Butter chicken with flavoured
        rice and raita 84
    Chicken chorizo paella 204
    Chicken rice mountains and
        Greek salad 127
    Chilli jam minced beef with rice and
        dressed vegetable pickles 124
    Fried rice 236
    Roast chicken with garlic, spinach
        and dill rice 118
    Sushi sandwich 246

ricotta
    No-fuss vegetable lasagne 112
    Ricotta berry tart 134
    Rose rigatoni 234
    Spinach spiral pie with lemon
        mayonnaise 180

rigatoni, Rose 234
rocket: Mini chicken mozzarella meatballs
    with garlic mash 206
Roast chicken with garlic, spinach
    and dill rice 118
Roast lamb and zesty potato medley 230
Roasted lamb rumps 227
Roasted tomato, kale and sausage penne 92
Rose rigatoni 234
Rose sauce 224

S

salads
    Chicken, noodle and cabbage salad 175
    Chopped salad 176
    Dressed vegetable pickles 124
    Greek salad 127
    Grilled haloumi salad 184
    grilled potato salad 228
    Mediterranean salad 211
    Prawn mango noodle salad 239
    Summer tuna pasta salad 182

salsa verde, Beef and vegetable skewers
    with 200
salt 29
sandwich, Sushi 246
Satay sauce 96

saturated fats 20

sauces 29, 75
    Black bean sauce 72
    Burger sauce 132
    Chilli jam marinade 111
    Easy caramel sauce 162
    Hoisin sauce 73
    Home-made tomato passata 110
    Mustard cheese sauce 142
    Rose sauce 224
    Satay sauce 96
    Stir-fry sauce 72
    stroganoff sauce 150
    Vegetable sauce 82
    Veggie-loaded bolognese sauce 108
    Yoghurt sauce 86, 157
    Yoghurt tartare sauce 144
    see also dressings

sausages
    One-pan wonder 98
    Roasted tomato, kale and sausage penne 92

schnitzel 66
seafood 26
seasonal produce 24–5
Seasoned beef mince 169
Seasoned chicken mince 196

seasonings
    Barbecue chicken seasoning 160
    Lamb seasoning 210
    Sour cream and chives seasoning 160
    Sweet and tangy seasoning 160

seed oils 21, 37
shepherd's pies, Sweet potato 117

shopping 13, 14, 22, 24, 33–7, 39
    see also food labelling, fruit,
        groceries, vegetables

slow cookers 64, 66
Slow-cooked lamb shoulder 140

snacks
    As-you-like-it popcorn seasoning 160
    Carrot cake energy bites 192
    Cauliflower cheese bites 103
    Cheeseburger triangles 132
    Corn cobettes with cheese, chilli
        mayonnaise and lime 190
    Puff pastry pizza pinwheels 218
    Sushi sandwich 246

soluble fibre 19
sorbates 46
soup 66
Sour cream and chives seasoning 160
spaghetti, Prawn 212
Spiced egg and tomato flatbreads 157
spices 75

spinach
    BLT omelette tray 186
    Butter chicken 80
    Butter chicken with flavoured
        rice and raita 84
    Chicken pie with artichokes and olives 120
    No-fuss vegetable lasagne 112
    Puff pastry pizza pinwheels 218
    Roast chicken with garlic, spinach
        and dill rice 118
    Rose rigatoni 234
    Spinach spiral pie with lemon
        mayonnaise 180

starch, resistant 19
steak with stroganoff sauce, Grilled 150
Sticky date mini cakes 162
Stir-fry sauce 72
stock 29
stone fruit 30
storing food 54–9
stroganoff sauce, Grilled steak with 150
sugar 44
sugar-snap peas: Vegetable satay noodles 96
sulphites 29, 46
Summer tuna pasta salad 182
supermarket shopping *see* shopping
Sushi sandwich 246
Sweet and tangy seasoning 160
Sweet and tangy tofu noodles 203
sweet potatoes
    Sweet potato shepherd's pies 117
    Tomato coconut dal 141
sweeteners, artificial 46

T

tacos
    Breakfast tacos 214
    Lazy fish tacos 208
tagine, Lamb, with couscous 149
tahini
    Tahini maple caramel and choc coconut banana splits 104
    Yoghurt tahini dressing 210
tartare sauce, Yoghurt 144
tarts
    Fruity tart 248
    Ricotta berry tart 134
Toasted cheese soldiers with dippy eggs 128
tofu
    Fried rice 236
    Marinated tofu 197
    Sweet and tangy tofu noodles 203
    Vegetable satay noodles 96
tomatoes
    BLT omelette tray 186
    Butterflied roast chicken with lemon potatoes 172
    Caprese smash burgers 176
    Crusted pork fillet with juicy roast tomatoes 178
    Greek salad 127
    Guacamole 90
    Home-made tomato passata 110
    Mediterranean salad 211
    One-pan wonder 98
    Roast lamb and zesty potato medley 230
    Roasted tomato, kale and sausage penne 92
    Rose sauce 224
    Spiced egg and tomato flatbreads 157
    Summer tuna pasta salad 182
    Tomato coconut dal 141
    Tomato coconut dal with baked fish 152
    Vegetable sauce 82
    Yiros with flatbread and crispy roasted chickpeas 233
tortillas
    Home-made tortillas 199
    Mexi-spice tray bake 114
    see also tacos

trans fats 20
Tropical overnight chia 216
trout, hot smoked
    Breakfast tacos 214
    Fish croquettes 138
    Fluffy trout omelette 242
    Sushi sandwich 246
tuna, tinned 29
    Fish croquettes 138
    Summer tuna pasta salad 182
    Sushi sandwich 246
Two-way bolognese 114

U

ultra-processed foods (UPFs) 18, 20, 40, 41
unit price of groceries 33

V

veal
    Hoisin meatloaf with potato gratin 154
    Veggie-loaded bolognese sauce 108
vegetable gratin 88
Vegetable pizzas 87
Vegetable satay noodles 96
Vegetable sauce 82
vegetables 31
    buying seasonal produce 24–5
    'Clean Fifteen' 51
    'Dirty Dozen' 51
    fridge storage 56, 63
    loose vs pre-packaged produce 35
    prepping 62
    washing 61
    see also individual vegetables
Veggie-loaded bolognese sauce 108
vinegars 29, 75
vitamins 15

W

watermelon 30
Whole roast chicken 109

Y

Yiros with flatbread and crispy roasted chickpeas 233
yoghurt 26, 37
    Beef koftas with grilled haloumi, zucchini and broccoli salad 184
    Butter chicken 80
    Butter chicken pizzas 86
    Caesar dressing 240
    Choc, oat and raspberry muffins 100
    Citrus yoghurt dressing 149
    Coconut yoghurt and peach smoothie popsicles 220
    Home-made flatbreads 226
    Raita 84
    Spiced egg and tomato flatbreads 157
    Yiros with flatbread and crispy roasted chickpeas 233
    Yoghurt sauce 86, 157
    Yoghurt tahini dressing 210
    Yoghurt tartare sauce 144

Z

zucchini
    Beef and vegetable skewers with salsa verde 200
    Fried rice 236
    Grilled haloumi salad 184
    Marinated lamb with caponata 122
    No-fuss vegetable lasagne 112
    Rose sauce 224
    Sweet and tangy tofu noodles 203
    Vegetable sauce 82
    Veggie-loaded bolognese sauce 108

Thank you

To my son, Beau. You are the most beautiful soul; thank you for inspiring me every day. If it wasn't for my determination to help you be your happiest, calmest and healthiest self, I would never have deep dived into what is in our food. So many children are eating better because of you.

To my daughter, Ella. You are pure sunshine; thank you for always encouraging me to do my best and follow my dreams. You are the cutest mini foodie, and I cherish our adventures in the kitchen and aisle. My little ones, you are my reason for everything.

To the Supermarket Swap community. I find it hard to put into words my gratitude for you. In the early years of motherhood, when I felt isolated, I never imagined that I would one day be surrounded by the most kick-ass, supportive people online. I truly thank you for your support over the years; it means more than you will ever know.

Rebel, together we built Supermarket Swap. You have never given up on our mission to help families, even when we have been drowning in the mum–work juggle. Thank you for being there every step of the way.

Marina, thank you for losing sleep over the best way to choose a banana or store herbs. Not only are you one of my best friends, but you are also a priceless part of our team.

Emma Landorf (Accredited Practising Dietitian), you have inspired me since our first meeting. It is an honour to work with you and have your research in this book. Thank you for being an incredible advocate.

Anna Ritan (Accredited Practising Dietitian), your knowledge is extensive and your relatability is invaluable. I admire how you share the juggle, alongside realistic ways to provide children with a real food diet. Thank you for your contribution.

Big thanks to my mum and the other incredible women in my life (you know who you are) who have never stopped believing in me, especially in moments I doubted myself. Your loyalty, love and laughs mean more to me than you will ever know. I love my sister wives so much.

To Jacinta and the Hardie Grant team, thank you for your belief in Supermarket Swap and incredible support in helping me write my first book. To everyone that helped bring this book to life, I have learnt so much from each of you: Simon, Tahlia, Nicci, Martine, Lucy, Brendan and Rob – what an incredible team.

And huge thanks to YOU, for wanting to do a good a job in the aisle and the kitchen. Go you.

About the author

Nabula El Mourid launched Supermarket Swap in 2020 to share the simple 'real food' swaps and cost-saving tips she found in the supermarket. It quickly garnered a cult following online, which resulted in the launch of the first Australian independent 'real food' supermarket app, Supermarket Swap.

Nabula lives in Adelaide, Australia, with her two young children.

Published in 2025 by Hardie Grant Books, an imprint of Hardie Grant Publishing

Hardie Grant Books (Melbourne)
Wurundjeri Country
Level 11, 36 Wellington Street
Collingwood, Victoria 3066

Hardie Grant North America
2912 Telegraph Ave
Berkeley, California 94705

hardiegrant.com/books

Hardie Grant acknowledges the Traditional Owners of the Country on which we work, the Wurundjeri People of the Kulin Nation and the Gadigal People of the Eora Nation, and recognises their continuing connection to the land, waters and culture. We pay our respects to their Elders past and present.

All rights reserved. No part of this publication may be reproduced, stored in a retrieval system or transmitted in any form by any means, electronic, mechanical, photocopying, recording or otherwise, without the prior written permission of the publishers and copyright holders.

The moral rights of the author have been asserted.

Copyright text © Nabula El Mourid 2025
Copyright photography © Rob Palmer 2025
Copyright design © Hardie Grant Publishing 2025
Copyright illustrations © Evi O Studio 2025

A catalogue record for this book is available from the National Library of Australia

The Weekly Grocery Shop
ISBN 978 1 76145 152 2
ISBN 978 1 76145 153 9 (ebook)

10 9 8 7 6 5 4 3 2 1

Publishers: Tahlia Anderson and Simon Davis
Head of Editorial: Jasmin Chua
Project Editor: Nicci Dodanwela
Editor: Martine Lleonart
Creative Director: Kristin Thomas
Designer and illustrator: Evi O.Studio | Katherine Zhang
Photographer: Rob Palmer
Stylist and recipe tester: Lucy Tweed
Home Economist: Brendan Garlick
Head of Production: Todd Rechner
Production Controller: Jessica Harvie

Colour reproduction by Splitting Image Colour Studio

Printed in China by Leo Paper Products LTD.

The paper this book is printed on is from FSC®-certified forests and other sources. FSC® promotes environmentally responsible, socially beneficial and economically viable management of the world's forests.